# ENVIRONMENTAL DISCLOSURE

This book provides a description of the state of the art on environmental disclosure, illustrating the key theoretical issues, the regulatory frameworks, and the main standards developed and reporting the results of an empirical analysis on the environmental disclosure released by listed firms.

Luigi Lepore and Sabrina Pisano begin by analysing the origin and evolution of environmental disclosure. They go on to provide a description of the main theoretical frameworks used by scholars, explaining the conceptual basis of each theory and describing how the specific theory has been used to explain the company's decision to release environmental disclosure. The second part of the book highlights the role and evolution of the European regulatory frameworks, emphasising the transition from voluntary to mandatory disclosure, and the major standards and guidance developed. The book ends by providing a picture of the evolution of sustainability reporting practices in European Union nations over the past two decades.

This book investigates the critical issues and new directions in environmental disclosure, which are currently under examination by regulators and standard setters. It will therefore be of great interest to academics and students working in the areas of business and sustainability.

**Luigi Lepore** is Full Professor of Business Administration at Parthenope University. He has been visiting researcher at IE Business School and Institute for Court Management. His research interests focus on corporate governance, accounting, and public management. He has participated in several conferences and has published numerous articles in international journals.

**Sabrina Pisano** is Associate Professor of Business Administration at Parthenope University. She has been visiting researcher at Stern School of Business of New York University. Her research interests focus on voluntary disclosure, corporate social responsibility, and corporate governance. She has participated in several conferences and published numerous articles in international journals.

## Routledge Research in Sustainability and Business

**Corporate Social Responsibility in the Arctic**
The New Frontiers of Business, Management, and Enterprise
*Gisele M. Arruda and Lara Johannsdottir*

**The New Corporate Climate Leadership**
*Edward Cameron and Emilie Prattico*

**Supply Chain Sustainability in Small and Medium Sized Enterprises**
*Edited by Prasanta Kumar Dey, Soumyadeb Chowdhury, and Chrisovalantis Malesios*

**Corporate Regulation for Climate Change Mitigation in Africa**
A Case for Dilute Interventionism
*Kikelomo O. Kila*

**The Role of Business in Global Sustainability Transformations**
*Edited by Dalia D'Amato, Anne Toppinen and Robert Kozak*

**Understanding Sustainability Performance *in* Business Organizations**
Implications for the Sustainability Service Industry
*Jean-Pierre Imbrogiano*

**Comparative CSR and Sustainability**
New Accounting for Social Consequences
*Edited by Gabriel Donleavy and Carlos Noronha*

**Environmental Disclosure**
Critical Issues and New Trends
*Luigi Lepore and Sabrina Pisano*

For more information about this series, please visit: www.routledge.com/Routledge-Research-in-Sustainability-and-Business/book-series/RRSB

# ENVIRONMENTAL DISCLOSURE

## Critical Issues and New Trends

*Luigi Lepore and Sabrina Pisano*

Routledge
Taylor & Francis Group
LONDON AND NEW YORK

earthscan
from Routledge

First published 2023
by Routledge
4 Park Square, Milton Park, Abingdon, Oxon OX14 4RN

and by Routledge
605 Third Avenue, New York, NY 10158

*Routledge is an imprint of the Taylor & Francis Group, an informa business*



*British Library Cataloguing-in-Publication Data*
A catalogue record for this book is available from the British Library

ISBN: 978-1-032-15848-8 (hbk)
ISBN: 978-1-032-15850-1 (pbk)
ISBN: 978-1-003-24593-3 (ebk)

DOI: 10.4324/9781003245933

Typeset in Bembo
by codeMantra

# CONTENTS

# INTRODUCTION

This book discusses environmental disclosure and aims to describe both the current state of the field and emerging trends. Over the last decade, increasing focus has been placed on environmental issues, such as climate change, greenhouse gas emissions, deforestation, and global warming. Policymakers around the world have developed different rules and programs covering, among others, the matters of pollution, waste management, and environmental protection, the objectives of which are the preservation of natural capital, the fight against climate change, and the creation of a low-carbon, green economy. Regarding European Union (EU) member states, the European Commission released the *European Green Deal* in December 2019 with the goal of making Europe the first continent in the world to be climate-neutral. This statement outlined specific steps to increase resource efficiency and achieve net-zero greenhouse gas emissions by 2050. For this reason, it represents the reference point for other EU policies successively issued to encourage the transition to clean energy and the development of green technologies.

To respond to growing institutional pressure, companies have begun integrating environmental issues into their business model and operations and increasing the environmental disclosure released to external stakeholders. According to the 2020 KPMG survey, in recent years, the number of companies that prepared sustainability reports and disclosed environmental information has increased considerably.

Because of the growing demand for sustainability responsibility and disclosure from investors, policymakers, the media, people, and overall society, the majority of companies have chosen to share environmental information on a voluntary basis. In reality, the disclosure of information regarding a company's environmental operations and related performance provides a valuable way to

DOI: 10.4324/9781003245933-1

evaluate the company and is helpful in responding to the increased demand for sustainability information from the investment community. Today, investors are becoming increasingly aware of the ability of sustainability issues to influence the performance of a company and are more prone to allocate their private funds to sustainability-related investments. In this sense, by fostering the allocation of private capital flows into green investments, the issuance of both EU regulation 2019/2088 and EU Taxonomy regulation 2020/852 will further boost the corporate disclosure of sustainability information.

Companies also release environmental information to demonstrate their responsibility regarding sustainability to external stakeholders (e.g. media, citizens, and society) and to improve their image and reputation. In this sense, companies disclose environmental information to increase consensus among stakeholders and achieve legitimacy.

Companies that release environmental information on a voluntary basis primarily refer to different standards and guidance issued by international organisations, such as the Global Reporting Initiative (GRI) standards, the Eco-Management and Audit Scheme (EMAS), the International Integrated Reporting Framework (IIFR), and the Climate Disclosure Standards Board, in drawing up their sustainability reports. According to the 2020 KPMG survey, the Global Reporting Initiative is the most widely used worldwide standard.

The increasing attention towards environmental issues and the enhanced provision of environmental information by companies leads scholars to deepen the understanding of this phenomenon. Over the years, various studies have been conducted on environmental disclosures voluntarily released by companies. Researchers have referred to various theories, such as agency theory, stakeholder theory, legitimacy theory, signalling theory, and institutional theory. All of these previous theories have been used to strengthen the decision of companies to release environmental information as well as to investigate the quantity and quality of the information disclosed. In addition, some scholars have referred to previous theories to investigate the factors influencing a company's decision to release environmental information or its effects on external stakeholders.

According to the results of earlier studies, several factors, including corporate governance features, institutional concerns, and firm characteristics, can affect a company's decision to release environmental information. At the same time, the company's performance and the judgment of financial market operators may be impacted by that environmental disclosure.

In addition to the decision to disclose environmental information on a voluntary basis, the increasing number of companies releasing sustainability information is also motivated by enhanced legal requirements, which shift the disclosure of environmental information from voluntary to mandatory. To encourage the release of environmental information and achieve an acceptable degree of harmonisation among the rules regarding sustainability disclosure in member states, the EU has issued different directives. The first was issued in 2003 and concerned sustainability information to be disclosed in the management report

(Directive 2003/51/EC). The Modernisation Directive 2003/51/EC amended both the Fourth and Seventh Council Directives by introducing the requirement for companies to provide, where appropriate, both environmental and social information in their management reports that is useful in comprehending the company's development, performance, or position. Directive 2003/51/EC was the first attempt to introduce mandatory environmental information and required companies to release environmental information when it is relevant to stakeholders. However, the Modernisation Directive did not specify the information that should be disclosed or the format for its presentation, giving companies significant discretion in defining the data they would release. Therefore, although the requirement to report environmental information was introduced, it was not unusual to find incomparable information released by different companies.

To further strengthen the rules on sustainability disclosure and reduce the flexibility given to companies, the EU issued Directive 2014/95/EU. The Non-Financial Reporting Directive 2014/95/EU requires larger companies to release environmental information pertaining to the business model adopted, the policies pursued, the outcome of those policies, the principal risks, and non-financial key performance indicators in a specific document termed a non-financial statement.

Compared to the Modernisation Directive, Directive 2014/95/EU identifies five reporting areas that companies must discuss in the non-financial statement for the release of environmental information to be considered. However, it still does not specify the format for the presentation of the disclosed information. In addition, it identifies the reporting areas in a generic way and does not provide additional suggestions or explanations regarding the information that should be disclosed, revealing that substantial discretion in reporting environmental information continues to exist.

Although the European Commission issued two guidelines to support firms in releasing environmental disclosures, companies continue to draw up sustainability reports that are not fully comparable. Consequently, in December 2019, the European Commission committed to reviewing the Non-Financial Reporting Directive, and in February 2020, it initiated a public consultation to collect the views of stakeholders with regard to possible revisions to Directive 2014/95/EU. The consultation ended in June 2020, and the main issues concern, among others, the deficiency of the information released in terms of comparability and reliability, the necessity to disclose the materiality assessment process, the digitalisation of environmental disclosure, and the expansion of the scope. In April 2021, the European Commission issued a proposal for a Corporate Sustainability Reporting Directive, which would modify the existing requirements regarding environmental information to be released. The proposal objectives are to extend the requirement to prepare the non-financial statement to other companies and to boost the comparability, reliability, and ease of stakeholder access of the sustainability information released with the aim of overcoming the critical issues that emerged following the implementation of Directive 2014/95/EU. In coherence with the objective of increasing the comparability of information released, in May 2021, the European Commission asked EFRAG to develop draft sustainability reporting standards, which are to be used by all companies as required in the proposal.

The state of the art in environmental disclosure is described in this book, which also illustrates the main theoretical issues, legislative frameworks, and major standards created and reports the findings of an empirical investigation of the environmental disclosure released by listed European firms. The book also delves deeper into the crucial issues pertaining to the actual state of the art as well as new trends in environmental disclosure, which are currently the focus of attention of regulators and standard setters.

The book is structured as two parts. The first part illustrates key issues related to environmental disclosure. Chapter 1 clarifies the origin and evolution of both corporate social responsibility and environmental disclosure to clarify both the boundaries of environmental disclosure in the more abundant field of sustainability disclosure and the content of that disclosure. The chapter then describes the usefulness of environmental disclosure in terms of affecting stakeholders' decisions, highlighting its critical role as a governance mechanism as well as its role in stakeholder management and engagement.

Chapter 2 describes the main theoretical frameworks used by scholars in studying environmental disclosure: agency theory, stakeholder theory, legitimacy theory, signalling theory, and institutional theory. For each theory, the chapter explains both the conceptual basis and how the theory has been used to justify a company's decision to release environmental disclosures. Finally, it reports the most relevant studies that referred to the respective theory in the development of their research and critically compares their results.

Chapter 3 illustrates the main factors affecting environmental disclosure and its effects on external stakeholders. In this chapter, the determinants of environmental disclosure are categorised into two groups: (1) internal or firm-specific, including company characteristics and corporate governance features, and (2) external or institutional, consisting of the level of media exposure and other country-level determinants (i.e. normative, mimetic, and coercive factors). Similarly, research on the effects of environmental disclosure is categorised into two groups: (1) usefulness of disclosure for stakeholders and (2) impact on firm performance and financial markets.

The second part of the book illustrates practices, critical issues, and new trends in regard to environmental disclosure. More specifically, Chapter 4 illustrates the evolution of regulatory frameworks related to environmental disclosure, emphasising the transition from voluntary to mandatory disclosure. The focus is European contexts, and the analysis is comparative, investigating the main rules issued by the European legislator and how member states transposed them into national law. This chapter conducts an in-depth analysis of Non-Financial Reporting Directive 2014/95/EU, which is currently in force, illustrating the critical issues that emerged after the EU public consultation. The chapter concludes with a description of the proposed Corporate Sustainability Reporting Directive that will be issued to overcome some critical issues of Directive 2014/95/EU, deepening understanding of the new trends in environmental disclosure that are currently the subject of attention and that are under examination by regulators and standard setters.

Chapter 5 illustrates the evolution of the main standards and guidance for environmental disclosure. More specifically, it describes the main aspects of each standard, highlighting the motivation for its issuance, critical related issues, and the companies that referred to it. Comparative analysis is presented. The chapter concludes with an analysis of the similarities and differences among the main standards used to release environmental disclosures.

Chapter 6 concludes the book by reporting the results of an empirical analysis of the environmental disclosures released by listed European companies, which is useful for understanding the evolution of sustainability reporting practices among EU member states over the past two decades. More specifically, this chapter illustrates the environmental disclosure released by 5,588 non-financial listed European companies (111,760 firm-year observations) for the 2002–2021 period to examine the evolution of sustainability reporting during the transition from voluntary to mandatory environmental disclosure. To deepen the influence of different factors on environmental disclosure, this chapter also reports the findings of an analysis of the relationship between both firm-specific and institutional factors and environmental disclosure. Referring to different theoretical frameworks to develop the hypotheses, this study first investigates the direct relationship between both board characteristics (i.e. board independence, gender diversity, and the presence of a CSR committee) and institutional factors (i.e. external assurance and the adoption of GRI standards) and environmental information. As a result, the study deepens understanding of the moderating role of institutional factors on the association between board characteristics and environmental disclosure.

# 1

# THE ROLE OF ENVIRONMENTAL DISCLOSURE IN THE RELATIONSHIP WITH STAKEHOLDERS

## 1.1 Origin and evolution of environmental disclosure

The explosion of pollution and its consequences worldwide, as well as the exasperated consumption of natural resources by people and companies have highlighted the relevance of ethics in companies' activities, calling for equilibrium between economic issues and social values. Consequently, business risks are not only associated with financial outcomes, but also with other dimensions of corporate performance. Hence, stakeholders demand accurate information regarding the social and environmental impacts of companies' activities (Fonseca et al., 2014), while the media's focus on environmental issues such as climate change, deforestation, and global warming continues to grow. In addition, world leaders have devoted attention to environmental issues, signing treaties and protocols, and holding conferences on the subject, while politicians and international organisations have published various regulations, standards, and guidelines relevant to environmental issues. Consequently, companies' managers no longer merely focus on higher productivity, but also address various ethical and social issues (Alipour et al., 2019; Aerts et al., 2006), particularly those linked to environmental degeneration.

The current state of the ecosystem is alarming, despite the efforts undertaken to date. According to the Global Footprint Network (GFN), an international research institute, the overshoot day for earth in 2021 occurred on 29 July. Earth overshoot day is the day on which humanity's demand for ecological resources and services exceeds what the planet can renew in a given year. Currently, humans consume 74% more than what the planet's ecosystems can renew, which is equivalent to 1.7 earths. From earth overshoot day to the end of the year, humanity operates on ecological deficit spending. GFN confirmed that humanity maintains a deficit by depleting ecological resource reserves and generating trash,

DOI: 10.4324/9781003245933-2

primarily carbon dioxide, in the atmosphere. This means that on 29 July, with roughly half a year remaining, humanity will have exhausted the biological resources of the world for 2021. According to the National Footprint & Biocapacity Accounts (NFA) based on UN datasets, the present deficit spending is among the highest since the globe entered ecological overshoot in the early 1970s.

In 2019, earth overshoot occurred on 29 July, and in 2020, on 22 August. This slight gain recorded for 2020 as a result of pandemic-induced cutbacks in resource consumption was short-lived, underlining the need to foster an economic recovery in which all can flourish within the limits of the planet. The date for 2021 was identical to that of 2019, and temporarily pushed back in 2020 due to lockdowns caused by the coronavirus epidemic. Notable causes include the 6.6% rise in carbon footprint over the previous year and 0.5% decline in global forest biocapacity largely attributable to the increase in Amazon deforestation: Brazil alone lost 1.1 million hectares in 2020.

According to GFN, global coal use will increase in 2022. The carbon footprint of transportation will increase to pre-pandemic levels, as will global energy-related $CO_2$ emissions, as the economy recovers and demand for fossil fuels increases.

Thus, social and environmental innovation to accelerate progress towards a sustainable future is necessary for companies worldwide.

To respond to growing institutional pressures on environmental concerns, companies worldwide are increasingly engaged in corporate social responsibility (CSR) disclosure to enhance their image, consensus, trust, and social legitimacy. Corporate environmental disclosure (CED) has gained increasing importance since the 1980s as a mechanism that facilitates interrelations between parties involved in companies' businesses and enables synergies that increase firm value. Companies integrate environmental issues into their business model and operations and increase the environmental disclosure released to stakeholders. For many years, this disclosure was mainly provided voluntarily with reference to different guidelines. Among these, the Global Reporting Initiative (GRI) is the most widely used worldwide. However, today, a high degree of disharmonisation in environmental reporting practices and the necessity for further standardisation remain. In addition to the guidance, to stimulate environmental disclosure and achieve an acceptable degree of harmonisation among the rules concerning environmental disclosure in different countries, the European Union (EU) has issued directives. The most recent is the Non-Financial Reporting Directive 2014/95/EU (NFRD), which requires companies to release environmental information about the business model adopted, policies pursued and outcomes of these policies, principal risks, and non-financial key performance indicators in a document named a non-financial statement. This document should include information on environmental preservation, social responsibility and treatment of employees, respect for human rights, anti-corruption and bribery, and board diversity. This directive applies to public-interest enterprises with more than 500 employees in the EU, roughly 6,000 companies and groups (listed companies, banks, insurance companies, and other public-interest entities). It suggests using international standards such as the UN Global Compact, OECD Guidelines, ISO 2600, and GRI. This regulation modifies directive 2013/34/EU on accounting. Thus, in recent years, environmental disclosure is progressively becoming mandatory for an increasing number of companies.

In 2017, the European Commission (EC) issued guidelines to assist organisations in sharing their environmental and social information more consistently and comparably. However, these guidelines are not mandatory, and businesses are free to employ guidelines other than those listed above. As a supplement to these 2017 guidelines, which remain applicable, the EC announced in June 2019 the Guidelines on Reporting Climate-related Information, which incorporates the recommendations of the Financial Stability Board's Task Force on Climate-related Financial Disclosures (TCFD). In its 11 December 2019 message on the European Green Deal, the Commission pledged to conduct a 2020 review of the NFRD as part of its objective to enhance the foundations for sustainable investment. In accordance with this commitment, the Commission opened a public consultation on the review of the NFRD on 20 February 2020 to collect stakeholders' opinions.

The consultation ended in June 2020. Among others, the main issues concern the deficiency of the information released in terms of comparability and reliability, necessity to disclose the materiality assessment process, digitalisation of environmental disclosure, and expansion of the scope thereof. Regulators and standards setters are working on possible solutions to these problems, such as the development of a common standard or assurance of the environmental report. For example, in June 2020, the EC tasked the European Financial Reporting Advisory Group (EFRAG) with conducting preparatory work for potential EU sustainability reporting standards. In April 2021, it issued a proposal for a new directive on corporate sustainability reporting, which will amend the NFRD. The new Corporate Sustainability Reporting Directive (CSRD) expands the scope of the NFRD to include all listed companies including small and medium enterprises (SMEs) and introduces mandatory EU sustainability reporting standards for environmental, social, and governance aspects to be further developed by EFRAG. The proposed CSRD also clarifies the obligation to report in accordance with the double materiality perspective, requiring companies to report (i) information necessary to understand how sustainability issues affect them, and (ii) information necessary to understand their impact on people and the environment.

Interest in the theme of environmental reporting has developed over the past decades thanks to the attention of the media, stakeholders, national and international regulators, and standard setters, and because of progressively developing research activity regarding the issues of CSR, sustainability, sustainable development, social and environmental disclosure, etc.

The studies conducted, which started in the thirties of the last century and have progressively increased to date, have focused on the definition of the concepts of CSR, sustainability, and environmental and social disclosure; identification of their boundaries, interrelationships, and overlaps; and on the relationships between these concepts and other phenomena. An example is the relationship between corporate governance and sustainability disclosure, and between sustainability disclosure and financial performance.

An analysis of the literature developed on the subject can provide a definition of environmental disclosure to clarify the boundaries of environmental disclosure in the ample field of sustainability disclosure and the content of that disclosure.

Despite the intense research activity, there is no univocal and shared definition of CSR or environmental disclosure. The term 'Corporate Social Responsibility' still constitutes an indefinite concept into which many other concepts converge. To highlight the breadth of the concept, Blowfield and Frynas (2005) refer to CSR as an 'umbrella term for a variety of theories and practices' with some common cornerstones: companies have a responsibility for their impact on society and the natural environment, which extends beyond legal compliance and the responsibility of individuals, as well as the behaviour of those with whom they do business. Consequently, companies must manage the relationship with the society for profitability reasons and to add value to society itself.

According to Latapí Agudelo et al. (2019), while the modern concept of CSR was formalised in the 1950s, interest in the subject probably emerged in the early 1920s. On deeper study, the beginnings of the social aspect of corporate behaviour can be traced to the ancient Roman Laws and observed in institutions such as homes for the poor and elderly, asylums, hospitals, and orphanages (Chaffee, 2017). The English Law of the Middle Ages and Crown's influence in the sixteenth and seventeenth centuries, which viewed companies as a tool for social advancement, perpetuated and expanded the idea of corporations as social enterprises (Chaffee, 2017).

With the advent of industrialisation and resulting degradation of working conditions, some corporate executives in the United States began establishing groups to promote values and enhance working conditions. However, it was not until the 1920s and 1930s that corporate managers assumed responsibility for balancing profit maximisation with the needs of their consumers, staff, and the community (Carroll, 2008; Carroll, 1999; Kreps, 1940; Clark, 1939; Barnard, 1938). Later, as a result of the expansion of business during World War II, corporations were viewed as entities with social duties, and a fuller discussion of such responsibilities began (Heald, 1970).

Organised literature on this concept did not emerge until the 1950s (Carroll, 1979). The earliest scientific definition of social responsibility dates back to 1953, when Bowen published 'Social Responsibilities of Businessmen'.[1] Questioning the responsibilities of entrepreneurs towards society, Bowen (1953) offers the first definition of social responsibility, emphasising businessmen's obligations to pursue these policies, make these decisions, and follow desirable courses of action for the goals and values of our society. The 1950s marked the beginning of the contemporary definition of CSR, and a time of change and adaptation in this regard. According to Bowen (1953), the activities of huge businesses greatly impact society, and as a result, their decision-making processes need to be modified to include considerations of this effect. In other words, the decisions and actions of businessmen affected their stakeholders, employees, and consumers, and thus society's quality of life. Selekman (1959) examined the emergence of corporations' moral responsibility during the same period as a response to the labour expectations of the time.

In the 1960s, the amount of scientific writing on the subject increased, and the notion of CSR was developed. Growing societal awareness of respect for the environment and human and labour rights encouraged interest in CSR (Carroll, 1999). This awareness also encompassed a rapid population increase, pollution, and resource depletion, prompting questions about the limitations of economic expansion and impact of society and corporations on the environment (Latapí Agudelo et al., 2019).

During these years, academics turned to CSR as a response to these issues and the needs of an emerging contemporary society. For instance, Davis (1960) noted that significant social, economic, and political upheavals at the time compelled businessmen to reconsider their role in society and social responsibilities. He (1960) stated that businesspeople have a relevant commitment towards society in terms of economic and human values, and that social responsibility might be related to economic benefits for the enterprise (Carroll, 1999; Davis, 1960).

This realisation meant that the debate on the problem emphasised the conflict between the economic and social realms. In 1962, Friedman underlined the pre-eminence of the economic sphere, asserting that the sole obligation of a corporation is to maximise profits while adhering to the laws of the game and free competition. Reaffirming this view, Friedman (1970) states that enterprises have only one social obligation, namely to use resources and engage in profit-generating activities.

Interesting is also the research of Davis (1960) and Davis and Blomstrom (1966), who consider the responsibility of the firm to examine the effects of actions on the entire society, and the needs and interests of people who may be affected by the business's actions. Davis also emphasises that CSR actions might result in increased earnings over the medium term. Davis can be considered a predecessor of studies that later linked CSR to companies' financial performance.

Eells and Walton (1961) and McGuire (1963) also attempt to define social responsibility by pointing to the assumption of responsibilities that extend beyond economic and legal obligations.

Scholars' interest in social and environmental reporting is partly tied to the emergence of the political and social youth movements that marked the 1960s and 1970s (Gray, 2004, 2003; Gray et al., 1996; Parker, 1986; Puxty, 1986). Those years were distinguished by heated disputes regarding the state of environmental degradation and business ethics (Gray, 2002). Furthermore, in Anglo-Saxon nations, the discussion around CSR evolved mostly around the contributions of the middle class (Gray et al., 1996). Beginning in the 1960s, middle-class Americans and Europeans grew increasingly dissatisfied with CSR (Drucker, 1965). Consequently, expectations regarding politics and large companies grew in that time.

In response to these pressures, debates and experiments in the fields of social responsibility, social accounting, and auditing are being developed in the academic and professional fields. Moreover, some countries made significant advances in social and environmental regulations. This time was thus defined as an era of 'managing corporate social responsibility' (Carroll, 2015, p. 88), and the first unified definition of CSR was formulated during this period. Carroll (1979, p. 500) affirmed that 'the social responsibility of business encompasses the economic, legal, ethical, and discretionary expectations that society has of organizations at a given point in time'. In accordance with this definition, which rapidly became very well-known and widespread, Carroll (1979 and 1991) asserts that social responsibility can be separated into four groups of sub-responsibilities: economic, legal, ethical, and discretionary.

In the 1980s, scholarly interest continued on the topic, which focused on the development of new related disciplines of study such as business ethics, corporate social responsiveness, corporate social performance, stakeholder theory, and management (Carroll, 2008). Drucker (1984) emphasises the compatibility between profit and responsibility, and possibility of transforming socially responsible orientation into new business opportunities, thereby laying the groundwork for strategic CSR studies. Jones (1980) viewed CSR as a decision-making process that influences corporate behaviour. Dalton and Cosier (1982) emphasise the relationship between legality and responsibility of corporate behaviour, demonstrating how a company can be socially irresponsible while remaining legally compliant. Despite that Reagan and Thatcher's deregulation strategies may be exerting a countervailing force to promote economic growth, during the 1980s, an increasing number of legislations attended to social concerns and gave a broader set of responsibilities to corporations.

In the 1990s, globalisation and increased political-international attention to environmental and social issues culminated in the institutionalisation of CSR-oriented corporate activities. From a scientific standpoint, the issue is becoming increasingly global; the integration of CSR and stakeholder theory is being strengthened; and research lines on business ethics, corporate citizenship, and corporate social performance continue to emerge. In those years, Carroll (1991) presented the 'Pyramid of Corporate Social Responsibility' providing a useful approach to CSR for executives that needed to balance their commitments to shareholders with their obligations to a wider set of stakeholders. The new model defines the four main responsibilities of any company: economic, legal, ethical, and philanthropic.

The number of research publications on CSR has significantly increased in the new millennium. Scholars continue to attempt to define the notion of CSR while researching other linked phenomena such as the role of CSR in its interaction with corporate reputation or necessity for a strategic vision for social responsibility that can provide organisations with a competitive edge. For instance, Aguinis (2011, p. 855) defines organisational responsibility as 'context-specific organizational actions and policies that take into account stakeholders' expectations and the triple bottom line of economic, social, and environmental performance'. Aguinis (2011) prefers the noun 'organisational' over 'corporate' to give a broader meaning, clarify the reference to all types of organisations, and inextricably link organisations' responsibility to the Triple Bottom Line logic—developed by Elkington in 1994—and thus to the concept of sustainability.

Not only has scholars' interest in the issue increased in the new millennium, but the attention of international institutions has also grown. The definition in the EC Green Paper is still one of the most used and complete. According to the commission, CSR is a concept in which businesses voluntarily integrate social and environmental issues into their business operations and interactions with stakeholders. For a business, being socially responsible entails not just meeting all applicable legal requirements but also investing more in human capital, the environment, and relationships with stakeholders. In this manner, businesses boost their competitiveness, which can directly impact their productivity.

Using this definition, the EC identifies several crucial aspects of CSR: its voluntary nature; emphasis on economic, social, and environmental spheres; integration into a company's core business; strategic vision and link to profit; and stakeholder approach.

Based on its emphasis and pragmatic language, the definition constitutes a milestone not only for the principles set out but also because it is provided by the EC. In this way, institutional and formal recognition is offered to CSR, and the EU implicitly undertakes to promote this approach.

### *1.1.1 Corporate social responsibility, sustainability, and environmental disclosure*

Sustainability is a more modern idea than CSR; however, the relationship between the two is readily apparent to both scholars and institutions that have studied the topic. In 1987, the World Commission on Environment and Development (WCED) published the study 'Our Common Future' or 'Brundtland Report', which introduced the notion of sustainability as it is known today. The study defines sustainable development as development that meets the requirements of the present without compromising the ability of future generations to meet their own needs. In 1983, the UN General Assembly convened the WCED, an international group of environmental experts, politicians, and civil servants, in response to numerous environmental issues associated with the rising standard of living of the world's population, including ozone depletion and global warming. Through international cooperation, the WCED (also known as the Brundtland Commission) was tasked with recommending long-term solutions to achieve sustainable development in the 21st century. The commission made efforts to understand the interrelationships between social equity, economic growth, and environmental problems by examining the causes of environmental degradation and developing policy solutions that integrated all three areas. However, the focus of the report was primarily on environmental issues and consequently, the need to use natural resources to ensure greater intra- and inter-generational equity in all countries worldwide.

However, in the same year, Barbier (1987) emphasised the three spheres, defining sustainable development as the simultaneous maximisation of the objectives of biological, economic, and social systems. Furthermore, Viederman (1994) defines sustainability by highlighting all its dimensions and the necessity of a participatory process that forms and pursues a community vision that respects and wisely uses all of its resources: natural, human, material, social, cultural, scientific, etc.

The link between the two concepts became more evident when scholars began discussing corporate sustainability (CS). Bansal (2005) and Szekely and Knirsch (2005) describe sustainability at the corporate level as a multidimensional concept combining the principles of economic integrity, social equality, and environmental integrity. According to their studies, CS implies expanding economic growth and shareholder value, prestige, corporate reputation, customer relationships, and the quality of products and services, as well as adopting and pursuing ethical business practices, creating sustainable jobs, and creating value for all stakeholders. Similarly, Neubaum and Zahra (2006, p. 121) define CS as 'the ability of a firm to nurture and support growth over time by effectively meeting the expectation of various stakeholders'. Likewise, Montiel and Delgado-Ceballos (2014) link CSR with CS, whereas Van Marrewijk (2003) propose a hierarchical relationship between sustainability and CSR, arguing that the latter constitutes a subset of the former.

As is evident, although the concept of sustainability is much more recent than that of CSR, there seems to be a greater convergence of definitions. In most studies, the CSR paradigm appears inextricably intertwined with that of sustainable development to the point that the two terms are used almost interchangeably in practice.

To better understand the convergence between CSR and sustainability, progressively identified by scholars, it is useful to dwell on the research by Montiel (2008), who analyses the different definitions of CSR and CS over time to reveal their differences and congruence. The analysis demonstrates that the management literature utilises both CSR and CS to refer to social and environmental management challenges. However, there is no clear differentiation between the two terms, and the conceptualisations and metrics of CSR and CS seem to be converging. In addition, through a content analysis of several CSR definitions supplied between 1980 and 2003, Dahlsrud (2008) demonstrates that existing definitions are largely congruent. He identifies five common dimensions to which definitions constantly refer: the stakeholder; voluntary nature; and emphasis on the economic, social, and environmental areas.

Although the environmental dimension was neglected for the first decades and not included in CSR, as it was integrated into the concept of 'social', a more inclusive vision of the three dimensions of sustainability was subsequently established in the concept of CSR. Several researchers identify CS only in terms of environmental sustainability (i.e. Shrivastava, 1995), whereas many others position it in the triple bottom line perspective (i.e. Bansal, 2005; Hart and Milstein, 2003; Gladwin et al., 1995). Economic, social, and environmental developments are considered interconnected pillars of the economy, which is part of society and as such, part of a larger environment. In their literature review, Montiel and Delgado-Ceballos (2014) observe that although a univocal definition of sustainability is missing, the inclusion of the three dimensions (economic, social, and environmental) is common.

Essentially, both concepts (CSR and sustainability) advocate businesses' inherent need and responsibility to balance economic, social, and environmental factors. Both confirm the existence of a plurality of accountable parties beyond shareholders. Convergence between CSR and sustainability is also evident in the indicators employed in empirical studies to measure companies' degree of responsibility or sustainability, as well as in the use of the terms by for-profit and not-for-profit organisations that define their report as a 'CSR report', 'sustainability report', 'social and environmental report', or 'social responsibility report'.

Therefore, in this study, we use the terms CSR and CS interchangeably. Consequently, the terms CSR disclosure, CS disclosure, sustainability reporting, social and environmental reporting, and so on are used synonymously. Despite the diversity and partiality of the definitions identified by scholars, we consider CSR a management concept in which companies integrate social and environmental concerns into their business operations, disclosing relevant information through CSR or CS disclosure. In other words, CSR is the means by which a company balances economic, environmental, and social imperatives to meet the expectations of shareholders and stakeholders, whereas CSR disclosure is the means by which actions and impacts are communicated.

Restricting the focus on the environmental dimension, for the aim of this work, we identify environmental disclosure in the more ample field of CSR disclosure as disclosure that considers the company's activities and related impacts on the environment such as climate change, deforestation, biological resource consumption, and global warming.

A concrete definition of environmental disclosure has not been established, despite that the topic of CSR reporting, like environmental reporting, has been studied and researched by the scientific community for decades.

Therefore, it is crucial to differentiate between environmental accounting and environmental reporting. The former delivers information in the form of accounts, which set specific norms and limits on the definition, measurement, structure, and presentation of information (Van Dijk et al., 2014). Environmental accounting is a field within the natural sciences such as biology and is rooted in the concept of 'natural capital', which is a sort of capital that must be preserved to deliver ecosystem goods or services to future generations (Schumacher, 1973). This type of accounting is used to quantify the depletion or replenishment of natural capital during the provision of products and services (Weber, 2011; Costanza et al., 1997). This accounting is frequently employed at the macro-level, i.e. the country or even global level. This type of knowledge has a unique bearing on public discourse and national governments.

In contrast, 'environmental reporting' or 'environmental disclosure' often has a less formal format and discusses the environmental effects of an organisation's actions. Thus, this is the collection of results resulting from a firm-level accounting system. Azzone et al. (1996) define an environmental report as a technical document that promotes external communication and provides evidence of how a company contributes to environmental degradation and/or conservation (Gray, 1993; Ing, 1992; Owen, 1992). Contrafatto (2004) argues that environmental reporting is self-reporting by companies through which qualitative and quantitative information regarding the environmental and social effects of company activity is communicated to stakeholders through an annual report and social and environmental account.

Environmental accounting, reporting, and disclosure are concepts used interchangeably to refer to the systematic presentation of environmental information by businesses; however, these concepts are not universally accepted. Environmental information consists of quantitative and qualitative data disclosed by businesses regarding the impact of their activities on ecosystems and the availability and consumption of natural resources (e.g. water and vegetation).

Despite the differences, accounting standards have enabled environmental accounting to align with the frameworks and concepts of economic and social accounting. Consequently, company disclosure could include structured information on the impacts or contributions of a company's activities on the environment and use of natural resources.

However, because of the difficulty of precisely defining environmental disclosure, the literature frequently provides definitions that include environmental and social components.

The definitions in the literature refer to various factors including social and environmental activities and/or forms of social accounts. For instance, to define social and environmental reporting, Gray et al. (1996) rely on the notion of accountability, which states that an agent must be answerable to the principal for the acts taken and the resulting outcomes. Specifically, this reporting is defined as the process of conveying the social and environmental repercussions of an organisation's economic actions to certain interest groups in society and society at large. As such, extending the accountability of corporations beyond the traditional purpose of presenting a financial report to capital owners, specifically shareholders, is necessary. Underlying this expansion is that corporations have responsibilities beyond maximising their owners' profits. According to Gray et al. (1996), this type of reporting is distinguished by its focus, or the thematic areas on which the reporting is based: audience, or the recipients of the reporting activity; content, or the type of information reported; and preparers, or the individuals who create the report. Gray et al. (1996) add that the sources of accountability are laws that establish the minimum basis for any form of accountability (legal accountability); quasi-legal sources such as rules of conduct and codes of conduct; and philosophical-moral sources, which are based on reference values and can be improved through debate, comparison, and education.

The literature emphasises the disciplinary role of this form of accountability in the relationship between the company and society. In defining environmental balance, Bartolomeo et al. (2000), for instance, highlights it as an accounting tool that can provide an organic picture of the direct interrelationships between business and the natural environment. This is through the representation of qualitative and quantitative data on the environmental impact of company activities and the company's financial effort to protect the environment. Rusconi (1987 and 2002) also considers social reporting from a functionalist perspective as a tool designed to report information on social performance in a controlled manner to all connected centres of interest, recognising the significance of the company's connection to the entire system for its survival.

### *1.1.2 Environmental disclosure in European regulatory frameworks and in the main standards and guidance*

Beyond academic research, in recent decades, the subject of debate at the international level has been to determine the minimum essential information content of sustainability reports. There has recently been a normalisation process to determine a series of basic principles for use as a reference standard in the process of collecting, managing, and reporting socio-environmental events. Among the most important attempts here, we include the AA1000 standard (Fazio, 2005), GRI standards (Bartolomeo, 2005), and principles for drafting the Social Report defined by the GBS.

To better identify the content of environmental disclosure, considering the prescription of the NFRD regarding that disclosure could be useful. The directive requires firms to disclose information and details regarding the current and foreseen impacts of the company's operations on the environment and as applicable, on health and safety, greenhouse gas emissions, water use, air pollution, and use of renewable and/or non-renewable energy. An analysis of the Guidelines on Non-Financial Reporting issued by the EC is also useful for identifying the content of environmental disclosure. According to these guidelines, a company is expected to disclose relevant information on the actual and potential impacts of its operations on the environment, as well as how current and foreseen environmental matters may affect its development, performance, or position. This may include material disclosures on pollution prevention and control; environmental impact from energy use; direct and indirect atmospheric emissions including emissions of greenhouse gases, toxic substances, atrophying, and acidifying substances; use and protection of natural resources (e.g. water and land); related protection of biodiversity; waste management; environmental impacts from transportation or the use and disposal of products and services; development of environmentally preferable products and services; and disclosures regarding the development of environmentally preferable products and services.

The aforementioned topics are a non-exhaustive list of thematic considerations businesses are expected to consider when releasing environmental information. In addition, the guidelines emphasise the interconnection between thematic aspects. For example, an environmental concern associated with a company's operations, goods, or supply chain may also affect the safety and/or health of consumers, employees, or suppliers, and the brand's reputation. Thus, companies are expected to provide a clear, balanced, and exhaustive perspective that incorporates all pertinent aspects of an issue.

Guidelines also include examples and key performance indicators (KPIs): a corporation may disclose material information using procedures specified by relevant legislation. The annexes to Commission Recommendation 2013/179/EU, for instance, offer product environmental footprint and organisation environmental footprint methodologies. These life cycle assessment methods allow firms to determine, for each product or an entire organisation: (i) the most significant consequences and (ii) activities and emissions that contribute to those impacts along the supply chain. Environmental consequences can be reported individually or as a single score.

When applicable, companies may refer to material information submitted in accordance with specified environmental reporting standards such as obligations deriving from EU directives (Industrial Emissions Directive, Emissions Trading System, Water Framework Directive, REACH, Landfill Directive, End-of-Life Vehicles Directive, Waste Electrical and Electronic Equipment, and Restriction of Hazardous Substances Directives) and the European Pollutant Release and Transfer Register.

Energy performance and improvements therein may be among the KPIs a company considers, as well as energy consumption from non-renewable sources and energy intensity, greenhouse gas emissions in metric tonnes of $CO_2$ equivalent and greenhouse gas intensity, emissions of other pollutants, extraction of natural resources, and waste management (e.g. recycling rates).

To frame environmental disclosure/reporting in the field of CSR or CS disclosure, it may also be useful to investigate the provisions of the GRI standards,[2] the most widely recognised international guidelines that are today interrelated with the NFRD. The GRI recently published a document (*Linking the GRI Standards and the European Directive on non-financial and diversity disclosure*) to show how to fulfil the disclosure obligations of the directive using the GRI Standards.

The environmental dimension of sustainability, as defined by the GRI Standards, refers to an organisation's impact on living and non-living natural systems such as land, air, water, and ecosystems. The relevant GRI standards are as follows: 301 Materials, 302 Energy, 303 Water and Effluents, 304 Biodiversity, 305 Emissions, 306 Waste, 307 Environmental Compliance, and 308 Supplier Environmental Assessment. The Disclosures section of the Standards provides a structured method for an organisation to report information about itself and its impacts. The disclosures may include both requirements and recommendations. In accordance with the GRI Standards, the requirements list the information an organisation must report or directions it must follow. The recommendations indicate that particular information or a particular course of action is suggested but not required. Background information, explanations, and examples can all be used to aid comprehension.[3]

## 1.2 The role of disclosure as a mechanism of corporate governance

Continually fuelling the company's existence is a decision. The continuous internal and external dynamics of the company, which drive it away from the equilibrium it seeks by its own nature, necessitate continuous decision-making. According to the Italian literature on business administration, stable economic equilibrium is the overarching goal of all businesses. Economic equilibrium is the condition in which a corporation is able to thrive and meet the expectations of all its stakeholders by combining production elements, composing internal and external forces into a system, and coordinating the complex activities that comprise its life (Giannessi, 1960 and 1969).

Corporate governance and management, the board of directors, shareholders, and managers require information to make logical choices. Similarly, all stakeholders, financiers, shareholders, suppliers, and customers have the right to know information regarding the conditions of the company's life to actively participate in its affairs and adequately support their decision-making processes. In particular, they are concerned with the company's current and projected economic and financial performance; ability to meet their needs; and economic, social, and environmental sustainability of its operations. These knowledge requirements are shared by all those who contribute to the business and anticipate receiving benefits from it.

To address the aforementioned cognitive needs, organisations implement an information system, which broadly is the collection of people, structures, and procedures required for the internal and external collection, storage, processing, and distribution of data and information. An enterprise information system is a subsystem of an enterprise system (Marchi, 1993).

The concept of an information system is understood in diverse ways in the literature. Sometimes, the output of the system is emphasised, that is, the information. Other times, the inputs are highlighted, that is, the means. It could also refer to the collection of data required to meet internal and external cognitive needs (Rugiadini, 1970), or the collection of technical and human resources required to obtain that data (Sackman, 1967). The interpretations do not oppose one another; rather, they offer complementary perspectives of the same reality. To comprehend all its constituent parts, Marchi (1993) defines an information system as 'the set of elements (data, technical, and human resources, as well as information) and their relationships that determine the production of the information necessary to effectively and efficiently satisfy internal and external cognitive needs'. The information system supports the decision-making processes of both internal and external stakeholders by providing corporate governance and control processes and meeting the information requirements of all external stakeholders. Specifically, a firm's information system must be able to appropriately support the decision-making processes of individuals who provide the company with the resources it requires, including financial, human, material, and intangible resources, and who expect to be compensated. Specifically, the information system serves a crucial function not only for existing stakeholders, but also for those who may be interested in forming a relationship with the company, such as possible investors and financiers, human capital, and suppliers of other production factors.

The availability of information on CS and CSR has become vital in the sense described above. In particular, in the following pages of this chapter, we analyse the utility of environmental disclosure in influencing stakeholders' decisions, underlining its significance as a mechanism of governance.

Financial statements have always been a fundamental pillar of a company's information system. They represent the company's primary information flow to subjects participating therein, from shareholders to employees, from lenders to customers and suppliers, and from the State to other parties interested in its equity and financial performance, and income results. In this regard, a financial statement is a subsystem of the information system and principal 'product' of the accounting system.

Financial statements play a crucial role in a company's information system, but only provide a partial picture of its reality. In reality, the same concentrates solely on certain aspects of firm success—economic and financial aspects—while ignoring others that are equally important.

Since the birth of accounting, financial statements have served to demonstrate the company's ability to create income and increase its assets, indicating shareholders' ability to withdraw capital without compromising the integrity thereof. This basic purpose is flanked by others, most notably the report, which bolsters the financial statements' position as an informational instrument that enables shareholders to evaluate the performance of the board of directors (the directors). However, financial statements contain crucial information not only for shareholders tasked with evaluating the directors' performance, but also for all those who engage in corporate decision-making, in particular, the directors themselves. As such, financial statements serve an additional significant purpose as a tool for analysing and managing corporate management by internal decision-makers.

The weight of corporations in the social milieu in which they operate increases over time. In other words, they have demonstrated a growing capacity to affect the lives of society by creating and destroying resources, wealth, and jobs. As a result, the range of parties interested in a company's future has increased to include internal and external parties. These subjects require information to assess a company's capacity to protect their interests. In carrying out this external information function, traditional financial statements do not adequately satisfy information requirements. Therefore, it has become necessary to incorporate new ad hoc quantitative-qualitative data.

Corporate stakeholders' larger cognitive needs indicate that financial statements are a collection of information that can facilitate a comprehensive understanding of management beyond the company's financial performance.

This revitalised information function of financial statements is now one of the most discussed aspects in the accounting literature, and its relevance will increase as the social function of the corporation becomes more significant. In tandem with the expansion of the information role of financial statements, various communication tools that complement and supplement strict financial information have been produced. Examples include social reports, environmental reports, integrated reports, or more generally, corporate social and environmental reporting or corporate social responsibility disclosure.

Scholars' interest in social and environmental reporting is closely linked to the cultural movements of the 1960s and 1970s (Gray, 2004, 2003; Gray et al., 1996; Parker, 1986; Puxty, 1986). These years were distinguished by heated debates on topics related to environmental deterioration and business ethics (Gray, 2002). Consequently, debates and experiments in the field of social accounting and auditing developed in the academic and professional fields.

In 1975, the Accounting Standards Steering Committee in the United Kingdom adopted an accounting principle that encouraged businesses to expand the amount of social and environmental information they report. In France, Law 769 was enacted in 1977, mandating the preparation of a social report with defined indicators to enhance industrial relations (Rusconi, 1987). Employment, salaries, hygiene, safety and other working conditions, staff training and development, living circumstances, industrial relations, and the degree of worker engagement in corporate management were required to be included in the financial statements.

As one of the first legislative interventions in the realm of social and environmental reporting, Law 769 holds noteworthy symbolic significance in Europe. However, in the 1980s, not only in Europe but also in the United States, CSR issues received less attention, most likely because of Thatcher and Reagan's economic and social policies.

Beginning in the 1990s, there was a dramatic increase in environmental awareness in Europe, not only among academics, where it had been marginalised for many years, but also among business owners and executives, especially at large corporations, who adopted the first environmental accounts (Vicini, 1998). Currently, topics related to social and environmental accounting are important in both the academic and industrial-government-political spheres.

These changes in corporate communication occur in an environment that imposes an ever-increasing responsibility on businesses to satisfy the needs of all stakeholders. This responsibility extends beyond the generation of sufficient wealth flows to meet the expectations of shareholders, lenders, and other stakeholders. These responsibilities include the ability to protect the natural environment and its resources for current and future generations, protect corporate human capital, guarantee safety and health in the workplace, ensure adequate career development prospects, protect human rights, and prevent corrupt practices.

In this context, corporate disclosure refers to the set of communications linked to performance that are intended to satisfy the information needs of the numerous classes of interests converging on the company, as well as to foster external consensus and confidence. According to this viewpoint, corporate disclosure encourages establishing deeper interactions with external subjects and as a result, contributes to balancing stakeholders' physiological conflict of interest. In this way, corporate communication can serve as a source of competitive advantage by enhancing inter- and intra-organisational relationships. In other words, effective disclosure contributes to the process of producing and spreading value via a consensus circuit and the formation of relational capital.

In recent years, the corporate information system is used to collect and disseminate accounting, non-accounting, quantitative, and qualitative data and information to satisfy the cognitive needs of stakeholders and mitigate their physiological conflicts of interest, thereby enhancing the company's legitimacy.

As mentioned, the evolution of the corporate information system parallels the transformation of the corporate role in the social context. Historically, the company was primarily meant as a tool for the pursuit of private interests, that is, as a mechanism for producing commodities and wealth required to directly satisfy shareholders' requirements. However, over time, the role of the company has changed and a new conception thereof has emerged. It is no longer a mere instrument for pursuing private goals, but a reality strongly integrated into the economic and social environment, whose production is no longer directed exclusively or primarily to the members of the company, but to a larger group of people. Prior et al. (2008) argue that a stakeholder/agent perspective is adopted in which the company is no longer viewed as a bilateral relationship between shareholders and corporate management, but as a multilateral set of relationships between management and various stakeholders. In practice, the corporation influences human well-being, qualifying as an economic-social institution acting as an open system (Bertini, 1990) that operates in the economic, social, and environmental contexts to assure its own existence and that of society.

Consequent to this transition, interest in various subjects regarding a company's economic, social, and environmental sustainability performance is growing. Therefore, there has been a significant shift in the function of a financial statement from a private and internal tool (report to the company's participants) to one for accomplishing public interest goals.

This necessary evolution in corporate disclosure was recognised in the 1980s, when in relation to the company's new role, it became apparent that financial statements were insufficient to satisfy all cognitive needs, highlighting the need for a true 'accounting devolution' that emphasised the qualitative aspects of information (Bruni, 1991). Different solutions including differentiated financial statements, annexes to financial statements, and alternative accounting documents with interpretations and analyses of financial statements are offered in the literature and by practitioners.

In summary, the evolution of the relationship between the company and environment; new social role of the company; and stakeholders' changed, broad, and varied knowledge needs have led to financial statements representing only a portion of the much broader corporate information system intended to provide information to stakeholders.

In other words, there is growing awareness and interest among external stakeholders including financial market participants in understanding and evaluating a company's actual performance in various sustainability domains (Arvidsson, 2019b). Therefore, credible and accurate sustainability information is necessary.

In this regard, corporate disclosure can take the shape of financial and non-financial data and can be either mandatory or not mandatory. All forms of disclosure decrease the information asymmetries between the company and its stakeholders. As the literature notes, corporate disclosure thus serves an important function in corporate governance. With specific reference to financial disclosure, Bushman and Smith (2001, p. 295) discuss the relevance of accounting information in terms of governance.

Corporate disclosure impacts the functioning of numerous internal and external governance structures including boards of directors and management, and financial markets, and can thus affect corporate performance directly and indirectly.

First, the information communicated via corporate disclosure is a direct input to the (internal) corporate governance mechanisms designed to discipline management in selecting projects with higher added value. In fact, disclosure enables the board of directors to exercise its monitoring responsibility over the management's investment selection activity to avoid the theft of investor funds. According to Bushman and Smith (2001), disclosure disciplines management in terms of project selection and expropriation (Channel 2).

In conclusion, corporate transparency contributes directly to economic performance through its governance role, supporting the optimal selection of investments by management and decreasing the risk of management's expropriation of investors' wealth (arrow 2A). Refer to the graph (Figure 1.1).

Furthermore, effective disclosure reduces uncertainty about management's free riding opportunities and thus helps reduce the risk premium (cost of debt) required by external investors (arrow 2B). As such, corporate disclosure indirectly impacts performance.

Second, the disclosure of the company and its competitors can assist management and investors in identifying and distinguishing favourable and undesirable investment prospects. Bushman and Smith (2001) refer to this concept as 'project identification'. Here, corporate disclosure provides management and investors

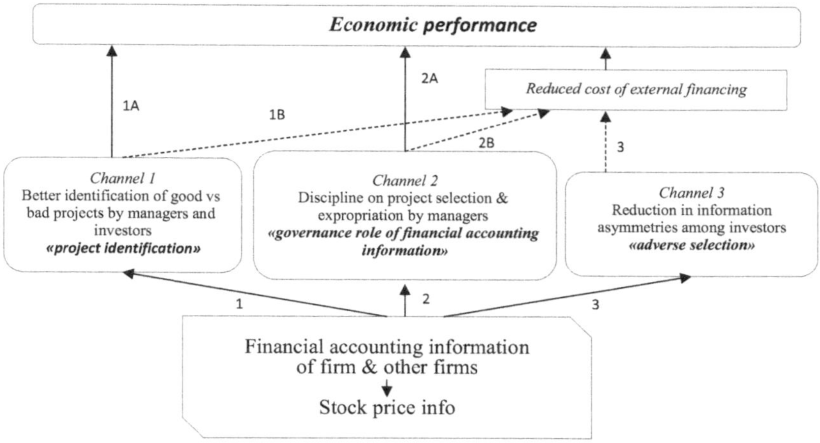


**FIGURE 1.1** Governance role of financial accounting information
*Source*: Bushman and Smith (2001)

with immediate information about investment opportunities. Using as example the high-profit margins reported by other organisations, management might find viable new investment prospects. In this sense, good disclosure also serves the monitoring function of the stock market by enhancing its efficiency and decreasing uncertainty. In practice, well-informed and well-functioning stock markets can facilitate corporate takeovers that replace underperforming managers, the mere threat of which can improve managerial incentives and reduce opportunistic behaviour (Scharfstein, 1988; Stein, 1988). However, the absence of reliable information in an economy contributes to creating uncertainty and hinders the flow of human and financial capital towards good investments. Therefore, even in the absence of agency conflicts between managers and investors, disclosure improves efficiency by giving managers and investors meaningful information that enables them to recognise possibilities for creating value with fewer mistakes. This enables investors and managers to allocate capital more precisely and profitably, as indicated by arrow 1A in the preceding image (Channel 1). Moreover, as arrow 1B shows, investors' perception of a lower level of risk is expected to result in a reduction in the cost of capital, further enhancing a company's financial performance (Channel 1). Here, corporate communication affects the functioning and efficiency of capital markets or markets for corporate control, understood as companies' external governance mechanisms.

Good disclosure also supports the information role of the share price. According to Black (2000), corporate information is likely a requirement for an active and effective stock market. In reality, such information drives analysts' behaviour, enhancing the information represented in share prices. Efficient equity markets, where share prices reflect all public information about firms' prospects and the private information of individual investors, presumably communicate this aggregate information to management and current and potential investors via share prices, thereby enhancing markets' efficiency and vitality. Therefore, effective communication can enhance performance by minimising information asymmetry between investors, adverse selection, and liquidity risk (arrow 3). Companies' commitment to the timely disclosure of high-quality accounting information minimises investors' perceived risk of loss when dealing with investors who have superior information, so attracting more capital to capital markets and lowering investor liquidity risk (Verrecchia, 2001; Leuz and Verrecchia, 2000; Baiman and Verrecchia, 1996; Diamond and Verrecchia, 1991). Capital markets with low liquidity risk for individual investors can promote the realisation of long-term, high-yielding corporate investments such as those in high-yielding technology without requiring individual investors to commit resources to long-term investments (Levine, 1997). In reality, investors can exit their holdings with relative ease. Thus, liquid and well-developed capital markets should boost economic growth by encouraging high-risk, high-return, and long-term company investments such as those in technological innovation. An important prerequisite for this capital market governance function is high-quality disclosure (Channel 3).

In summary, high-quality disclosure can improve performance through at least three channels by influencing companies' internal and external governance mechanisms.

The corporate governance literature has for several years investigated the governance role of corporate disclosure, recognising its importance (Chau and Gray, 2002; Ho and Wong, 2001; Hossain et al., 1994; Jensen and Meckling, 1976), and inducing legislators and standard setters worldwide to improve the quality of corporate disclosure.

Bushman and Smith's (2001) considerations regarding the governance function of financial accounting information summarised in the previous pages can also be made with reference to non-financial disclosure, especially in the current context wherein the focus on sustainability issues has significantly increased.

Today, it is common for companies to be mapped and ranked by capital market actors according to their sustainability work (Arvidsson, 2020). This is done based on the information companies communicate through their sustainability reports. Companies are experiencing increasing pressure to provide capital market actors with good track records regarding their sustainability performance; thus, the need for value-relevant, credible, and comparable information on sustainability performance is increasing (Arvidsson, 2019a; Arvidsson and Jonäll, 2019).

Several national, European Union, and worldwide initiatives have been implemented to increase the number and quality of corporate disclosures on sustainability. Some emphasise a particular component of sustainability, such as the Paris Agreement of 2015, which highlights environmental issues to combat climate change. EU directive 2014/95 on non-financial reporting requires the largest EU companies to disclose social and environmental information in their annual reports, whereas the launch of Agenda 2030 and the Sustainable Development

Goals (SDGs) integrates all three dimensions of sustainability: social, environmental, and economic.[4]

Regarding sustainable finance, a new scenario is emerging in which financial market participants who have demonstrated scepticism for many years are joining forces to learn how to integrate sustainability considerations into their frameworks to mobilise financial resources towards sustainable projects (Cho et al., 2015; Arvidsson, 2014; Friedman, 1970).

In this context, it is crucial for businesses to enhance the value relevance, reliability, and comparability of their sustainability reports to be considered relevant from the new perspective of financial market participants (Rimmel, 2020).

The role of corporate disclosure—mandatory and voluntary, financial and non-financial—as a governance mechanism suitable for reducing the information asymmetries existing between various market players and governing management has been the subject of numerous empirical and theoretical studies. Studies investigate various aspects of corporate disclosure, focusing on its effects on corporate performance, the relationship between disclosure and board characteristics, and relationship between ownership structure and disclosure (Lepore et al., 2022; D'Amore et al., 2021; Pisano et al., 2017; Lan et al., 2013; Patelli and Prencipe, 2007; Alsaeed, 2006; Brammer and Pavelin, 2006; Cormier et al., 2005; Chau and Gray, 2002; Haniffa and Cooke, 2002; Fama and Jensen, 1983).

In particular, research on the relationship between corporate governance and CSR disclosure has highlighted how this disclosure interacts with other governance mechanisms, mitigating or aggravating agency problems between ownership and management, majority and minority shareholders, or again, shareholders and creditors (Lepore et al., 2022; Celentano et al., 2020). However, further research is still needed, especially considering the remarkable evolution CSR disclosure is experiencing, especially environmental disclosure.

## 1.3 Environmental disclosure, relations, and stakeholder management

As anticipated in the preceding pages, environmental disclosure strives to inform internal and external stakeholders of a company's environmental performance. This information function is aimed at both primary and secondary stakeholders including financiers, customers, employees, and suppliers. Secondary stakeholders include institutions, authorities, the media, and community at large. This type of disclosure increases interlocutors' awareness of the firm's actions and environmental repercussions they cause, thereby aiding their decision-making processes and fostering their trust in the company.

Regarding internal stakeholders, if properly integrated into control systems, environmental disclosure can be useful for management to assess the efficacy of CSR initiatives, rationalising the decision-making processes that ultimately serve to redefine them, and for governance bodies in monitoring management activities. If properly integrated or paired with external accountability systems, environmental disclosure can enhance the decision-making processes of lenders, suppliers, customers, and so on, fostering confidence in the company and enhancing stakeholder relations. The indirect effect that follows the spread of trust among stakeholders is improved corporate reputation, which like trust, is an intangible asset of strategic value for the company because it can facilitate the achievement of competitive advantage and fuel the creation of long-term value, thereby strengthening relationships with all those who provide the company with resources (Fombrun, 1998).

Consequently, environmental disclosure serves a very important informational function internally and externally. Internally, it improves the effectiveness of corporate governance and control systems. Externally, it nourishes two crucial corporate assets: trust and reputation. Moreover, externally, environmental disclosure provides information to capital markets and improves the effectiveness of external governance structures. A closer look reveals that the climate of higher trust fostered by environmental disclosure can improve the quality of relationships with external and internal stakeholders, supporting a more collaborative and supportive approach. In this notion, environmental disclosure becomes a tool for stakeholder management, which constitutes the conceptual foundation for mapping various stakeholder groups. This mapping is beneficial for identifying stakeholders and the need to be prioritised, and for knowing how to balance these issues (Mitchell et al., 1997; Clarkson, 1995).

According to Carrol (1991), stakeholder mapping allows a more in-depth understanding of their characteristics and relationships with the company's mission, enabling it to select the most pertinent CSR initiatives by establishing priorities based on the strategic importance attributable to various stakeholders. From a stakeholder management and stakeholder theory perspective (Freeman, 1984), to achieve the necessary social support for success, a company must respond quickly to the pressures from the various categories of stakeholders, choosing based on power, current events, and the legitimacy of their interests (Mitchell et al., 1997).

A company's long-term survival, stability, and performance in a competitive context are closely tied to its ability to produce value for its stakeholders, particularly its key ones, without which it cannot live as a functional entity. Depending on the intensity of their interaction with the corporate mission, these topics may have a greater impact on CSR initiatives and the organisation's business model (Gangi and Mustilli, 2018; Clarkson, 1995; Carrol, 1993). Human resources, that is, managers and employees, shareholders and investors, state and government agencies, customers, and suppliers are key stakeholders. However, secondary stakeholders have no direct impact on the organisation.

This category comprises individuals and groups influenced by the company's operations while not having direct relationships with it, such as the media, natural environment, existing community, and future generations. Owing to their weaker connection to the corporate mission, they have a weaker impact on the business model of the organisation and consequently, on CSR initiatives, while still having an impact on social climate and corporate relations.

Customers play a crucial role in environmental sustainability and the related disclosure. Being the primary beneficiaries and users of the results of the company's production processes, they would also likely suffer or profit most from the environmental repercussions of the company's activity. Consider, for instance, the event in which a firm places polluting products on the market, such as automobiles, personal care products, or clothing. The first persons to be harmed by these products would be the consumers who use them.

Customers are, or should be, the subjects with the greatest interest in environmental transparency. They play a dual role because, on the one hand, they are the immediate recipients of the environmental repercussions of actions and market-placed outputs. On the other, this direct connection with corporate output could significantly impact business decisions regarding sustainability and environmental transparency. The environmental scandals that have occurred over the past decade have prompted the companies involved in the most severe cases to mitigate the negative effects on financial performance and reputation of the spread of information about the environmental damage their business caused. Consider, for instance, the Volkswagen and BMW lawsuits that blossomed over the past decade. Consequently, customers are a significant pressure factor for environmental disclosure, as they are both its primary impetus and beneficiary.

Similar arguments apply for an organisation's human capital, which consists of its employees and management. They also play a crucial role in environmental sustainability and disclosure. On the one hand, workers are the immediate recipients of the environmental effects of company activity. Human capital is frequently the most important ingredient in the generation of firm outputs, especially in labour-intensive industries; hence, workers are among the first to be harmed by toxic products alongside customers. On the other hand, human capital could considerably influence a company's decisions regarding CSR and environmental disclosure, as it is the direct recipient of certain social sustainability measures.

In fact, among other things, initiatives on sustainability in favour of human resources might involve protecting workers' health and safety on the job and quality of life more generally. Clearly, these aspects are strictly associated with environmental aspects. A polluting product is damaging to the environment and harmful to humans. Again, consider the Volkswagen diesel-gate scandal.

Therefore, polluting operations can contribute to a decline in the level of satisfaction of human resources, a loss of their motivation and trust in the firm, and a decline in worker productivity, harming the organisation's reputation and capability to attract and retain the finest personnel (Hartman et al., 2007; Greening and Turban, 2000).

In addition to customers and human capital, the group of corporate stakeholders includes lenders, suppliers, competitors, trade unions, and the broader community, which together comprise the environmental and social systems of which the firm is part.

As stated in the preceding paragraphs, the role of companies in the social milieu in which they operate has evolved substantially over the past few decades. In the past, the corporation was meant primarily as a tool for the production of commodities and wealth essential for the direct fulfilment of shareholders' demands and hence, as a means of pursuing private interests.

Subsequently, the company's role has evolved, and a new conception thereof has emerged. It is now understood as a strongly integrated reality in the economic and social environment, whose production is no longer directed primarily or exclusively to the company's owners, but to a broader group of subjects. The company is viewed as a multilateral set of relationships with various stakeholders (Prior et al., 2008), as it influences human well-being and qualifies as an economic-social institution operating as an open system (Bertini, 1990) in the economic, social, and environmental context to ensure its survival and that of society through the creation of value. It is now obvious that companies influence the existence of society by creating and destroying resources, money, and employment opportunities. As a result, the range of parties interested in the company's future has increased to include both internal and external parties.

These stakeholders require information to assess the company's capacity to protect their interests. The development of communication tools that supplement and complete financial information such as social reports, environmental reports, and environmental disclosure is predicated on corporate stakeholders' larger cognitive needs. In other words, there is a growing interest from external stakeholders including financial market actors in knowing and evaluating how a company truly performs in various sustainability domains (Arvidsson, 2019b), especially environmental sustainability.

By adequately satisfying these cognitive demands and demonstrating through environmental disclosure that corporate values are consistent with the values of all stakeholders comprising the social system in which it insists, the company obtains stakeholders' legitimacy and trust, thereby enhancing its reputation and right to citizenship. From this perspective and for these goals, environmental disclosure can be used to address the increased sensitivity of the community and institutions to environmental impacts and to develop or attract the most valuable intangible, material, human, and financial resources.

Strong corporate reputations help businesses win the struggle for talent and foster staff retention (Roberts and Dowling, 2002). Therefore, it functions as a guarantee for personnel with superior performance. For Hamori (2003), a company's reputational capital can serve as an indicator of its ability to attract outstanding personnel and investors. In general, corporate reputation connects all stakeholders, because increasing corporate reputation promotes consumer and supplier confidence in both the firm's services and companies, influencing their decisions to continue the firm's ties. According to Schwaiger (2004), organisations with a solid reputation have easier access to financial markets, which reduces the cost of capital. As mentioned, potential investors and lenders currently pay special attention to environmental concerns (Scholtens, 2009) and choose to invest in projects with reduced environmental impacts (Weber and Banks, 2012).

## 1.4 Environmental disclosure and relational capital

Although reputation has been studied extensively from various perspectives, there is no consensus on its meaning. Several authors emphasise the complexities and dimensions of business reputation. For instance, Shenkar and Yuchtman-Yaar (1997) provide a synthesis of how scholars of accounting, law, sociology, marketing, economics, and corporate management have approached the topic of reputation. They and others view it as the amalgamation of stakeholders' expectations, perceptions, and opinions of the organisation (Gangi and Mustilli, 2018; Fombrun and Van Riel, 2004). Essentially, corporate reputation is multifaceted (Dowling, 2001; Grant, 1991; Barney, 1986). The drivers of a company's reputation are firmly ingrained in the organisation itself; they are intertwined with its development and evolution in a setting that is unique and historically reliant (Dierickx and Cool, 1989). Thus, corporate reputation becomes extremely firm-specific and one of the most challenging resources to acquire. In reality, a company's current reputation is established or accumulated in a historical context under conditions that cannot be replicated. Moreover, as with all socially complex phenomena, the management of reputation is beyond the capabilities of a corporation to achieve total influence (Standifird, 2001). Deephouse (2000) notes that the development of a company's reputation is a socially complicated process that involves both internal and external players.

According to Barney (1999), reputation is a 'socially complex' capacity. For Groenland (2002), corporate reputation is an emotive construct difficult to rationalise and express. In other words, an organisation's reputation is a product of its social legitimisation. Among other things, a company's reputation and reputational capital depend on the quality and quantity of its ties with stakeholders.

To clarify the concept of reputation, Dollinger et al. (1997) emphasise its multidimensionality, stating that it comprises three distinct stakeholder-specific components: managerial reputation, financial reputation, and product reputation. de Quevedo Puente (2001) also notes the connection between stakeholders and company reputation, highlighting the existence of two primary dimensions: internal and external reputation. The first dimension relates to internal stakeholders' perception of business activities (i.e. shareholders, managers, workers, customers, and suppliers), and the second relates to the perception of firm activities by external stakeholders (i.e. society).

De Castro et al. (2006) also highlight the existence of two major elements of reputation: the business and social dimension. Business reputation encompasses various facets of corporate reputation pertaining to management and the stakeholders closely attached to the organisation's operations and processes, such as customers, suppliers, and workers. However, social reputation is the consequence of the insights and views of other stakeholders such as investors and the community who are not as close to the firm's day-to-day operations. Identifying these two primary dimensions is a significant innovation for comprehending corporate reputation as a crucial component in the legitimisation process of a corporation in the eyes of the community and society. According to the literature (De Castro et al., 2006; Fombrun, 1996; Fombrun and Shanley, 1990), numerous elements comprise corporate reputation: (i) managerial quality; (ii) financial strength; (iii) product and service quality; (iv) innovation; (v) use of corporate assets/efficiency; (vi) ability to attract, develop, and retain talented people; (vii) social responsibility; and (viii) value of long-term investments.

As emphasised in preceding sections, stakeholder management with a focus on sustainability and environmental disclosure is an indispensable tool for a company to obtain the best production inputs in a stable manner and to strengthen its competitive advantage by increasing strategic intangible assets such as the trust and reputation accorded by internal and external stakeholders (Gangi and Mustilli, 2018; Deephouse, 2000).

Stakeholders' trust is a rare and difficult-to-imitate intangible asset that forms the foundation of reputational capital. In this regard, CSR and its disclosure can be considered a driver of relational capital and consequently, of a company's reputation, as they enhance stakeholders' trust in the firm and strengthen the connections binding them to the organisation.

According to Peloza (2005), CSR can help enhance a company's reputation. As mentioned, reputational capital is the stock of a company's perceptual and social assets, which depends on the quality of a firm's relationships with its stakeholders. The literature (Oswald, 1996) views reputational capital as the value created by a company in the minds of stakeholders as a result of their relationship with the company.

Strong corporate reputation is one of the primary drivers of long-term financial performance (Roberts and Dowling, 2002). This strategic potential is a result of its inherent value-creation capabilities and intangible nature, which makes it difficult for competitors to duplicate a company's reputation, thus allowing it to maintain a better position. Thus, environmental disclosure and more generally, sustainability disclosure, which is a firm's communication with stakeholders regarding CSR efforts and performance, generates additional profits by enhancing the company's reputation (Figure 1.2).

Today, in light of the intense institutional pressure regarding environmental issues, environmental responsibility and transparency are the primary determinants of company reputation.

However, the relationship between environmental disclosure and reputation is two-way, as the company's ability to effectively communicate its actions regarding respect for the environment and its environmental performance is a driver or determinant of reputation. This is because while good environmental disclosure generates the trust of internal and external stakeholders and strengthens their relationships with the company, it is also an output of reputation (García-Sánchez et al., 2022).

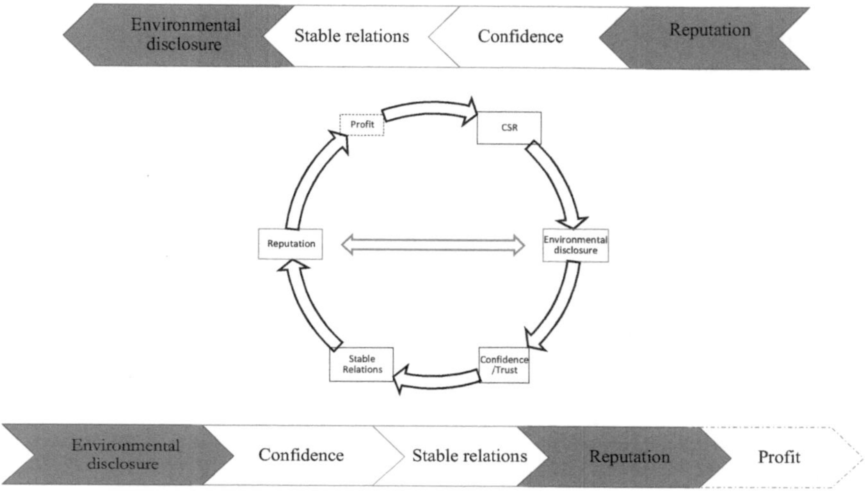


**FIGURE 1.2** The virtuous circuit
*Source*: Author's elaboration

Therefore, a virtuous cycle is generated in which socially responsible behaviour and high-quality environmental disclosure generate trust and stable relationships, reputation, competitive advantage, and long-term profitability (Orlitzky et al., 2003; Waddock and Graves, 1997).

## Notes

1 'The Functions of the Executive' by Barnard (1938) and the 'Social Control of Business' by Clark (1939) provide examples of the poor previous to 1950s literature over the social duties of corporations.

2 The latest version of the standards is that of 2021. Specifically, the GRI Standards are divided into four series, one of which is for universal standards and three series of specific standards for the three fundamental dimensions of sustainability (Economic, Environmental and Social): GRI 100 Universal Standards; GRI 101 Foundation; GRI 102 General Disclosures; GRI 103 Material Topic; GRI 200 Economic; GRI 300 Environmental; GRI 400 Social. There are also sector supplements (GRI Sector) which integrate the Guidelines with interpretations and advice on the application of the Guidelines and include sector-specific performance indicators. GRI 101 introduces the fundamental principles for defining the content and quality of the report. By applying the guidelines of GRI 101, it is possible to identify the aspects of the company that generate significant impacts on stakeholders. Once the significant impacts have been identified, it will be possible to apply the specific standards (GRI 200, 300 and 400). GRI 102 serves to report information on the context of the company and its reporting practices. This includes information on the company's profile, strategy, ethics, integrity, governance and how to involve stakeholders and the reporting process. GRI 103, however, is useful for reporting on how the company manages the material aspects, including those covered by specific GRI standards (200, 300 and

400 series). The three GRI 200, 300 and 400 series include numerous specific standards that can be used to report the company's impacts on economic, environmental and social issues.
3 Please refer to Chapter 5 for an in-depth analysis on GRI standards.
4 Rimmel (2020).

## References

Aerts, W., Cormier, D., & Magnan, M. (2006). Intra-industry imitation in corporate environmental reporting: An international perspective. *Journal of Accounting and Public Policy*, 25(3), 299–331.
Aguinis, H. (2011). Organizational responsibility: Doing good and doing well. In S. Zedeck (Ed.), *APA handbook of industrial and organizational psychology, 3 (Maintaining, expanding, and contracting the organization)* (pp. 855–879), American Psychological Association.
Alipour, M., Ghanbari, M., Jamshidinavid, B., & Taherabadi, A. (2019). Does board independence moderate the relationship between environmental disclosure quality and performance? Evidence from static and dynamic panel data. *Corporate Governance: The International Journal of Business in Society*, 19(3), 580–610.
Alsaeed, K. (2006). The association between firm-specific characteristics and disclosure: The case of Saudi Arabia. *Managerial Auditing Journal*, 21(5), 476–496.
Arvidsson, S. (2014). Corporate social responsibility and stock market actors: A comprehensive study. *Social Responsibility Journal*, 10(2), 210–225.
Arvidsson, S. (2019a). CEOs' talk of sustainability: Towards an inclusion of an embeddedness and value-creation perspective (No. 19/02). LSR Working Papers Series.
Arvidsson, S. (2019b). *The 1st SUBREA Conference Report: A focus on challenges and future knowledge needs*, Sweden: Lund University.
Arvidsson, S. (2020). Sustainability reporting from a capital market perspective. In G. Rimmel (Ed.), *Accounting for Sustainability* (pp. 159–170). London: Routledge.
Arvidsson, S., & Jonäll, K. (2019). Sustainability reporting. In S. Arvidsson (Ed.), The *1st SUBREA Conference Report: A focus on challenges and future knowledge needs*. Media Tryck: Lund University.
Azzone, G., Manzini, R., & Noci, G. (1996). Evolutionary trends in environmental reporting. *Business Strategy and the Environment*, 5(4), 219–230.
Baiman, S., & Verrecchia, R. E. (1996). The relation among capital markets, financial disclosure, production efficiency, and insider trading. *Journal of Accounting Research*, 34(1), 1–22.
Bansal, P. (2005). Evolving sustainability: A longitudinal study of corporate sustainable development. *Strategic Management Journal*, 26(3), 197–218.
Barbier, E. B. (1987). The concept of sustainable economic development. *Environmental Conservation*, 142(2), 101–110.
Barnard, C. I. ([1938] 1968). *The functions of the executive* (Vol. 11). Cambridge: Harvard University Press.
Barney, J. B. (1986). Organizational culture: Can it be a source of sustained competitive advantage? *Academy of Management Review*, 11(3), 656–665.
Barney, J. B. (1999). How a firm's capabilities affect boundary decisions. *MIT Sloan Management Review*, 40(3), 137.
Bartolomeo, M., Bennett, M., Bouma, J.J., Heydkamp, P., James, P., & Wolters T. (2000). Environmental management accounting in Europe: current practice and future potential, *European Accounting Review*, 9(1), 31–52.

Bartolomeo, M. (2005). Il framework di reporting Global Reporting Initiative (GRI). Origini, caratteristiche, critiche, in AA.VV. (edited by Rusconi G. & Dorigatti M.), Modelli di rendicontazione etico-sociale e applicazioni pratiche, collana "Persona, imprese e società" (Vol III). Milano: Franco Angeli.

Bertini, U. (1990). *Il sistema d'azienda*. Torino: Giappichelli.

Black, B. S. (2000). The legal and institutional preconditions for strong securities markets. *UCLA Law Review*, 48, 781.

Blowfield, M., & Frynas, J. G. (2005). Editorial setting new agendas: Critical perspectives on corporate social responsibility in the developing world. *International Affairs*, 81(3), 499–513.

Bowen, H. (1953). *Social Responsibilities of the businessman*. New York: Harper & Row.

Brammer, S., & Pavelin, S. (2006). Voluntary environmental disclosures by large UK companies. *Journal of Business Finance & Accounting*, 33(7–8), 1168–1188.

Bruni, G. (1991). I principi contabili generalmente accettati. In 2nd ed., E. Ardemani, (Ed.). *L'impresa*. Milano: Giuffre.

Bushman, R. M., & Smith, A. J. (2001). Financial accounting information and corporate governance. *Journal of Accounting and Economics*, 32(1–3), 237–333.

Carroll, A. B. (1979). A three-dimensional conceptual model of corporate performance. *Academy of Management Review*, 4(4), 497–505.

Carroll, A. B. (1991). The pyramid of corporate social responsibility: Toward the moral management of organizational stakeholders. *Business Horizons*, 34(4), 43.

Carroll, A. B. (1993). *Business and society: Ethics and stakeholder management*, 2nd ed. Cincinnati: South-Western Publishing Co.

Carroll, A. B. (1999). Corporate social responsibility evolution of a definitional construct. *Business & Society*, 38(3), 268–295.

Carroll, A. B. (2008). A history of corporate social responsibility: Concepts and practices. In A. M. Andrew Crane, D. Matten, J. Moon, & D. Siegel (Eds.), *The Oxford handbook of corporate social responsibility* (pp. 19–46). New York: Oxford University Press.

Carroll, A. B. (2015). Corporate social responsibility: The centerpiece of competing and complementary frameworks. *Organizational Dynamics*, 44(2), 87–96.

Celentano, A., Lepore, L., Pisano, S., D'Amore, G., & Alvino, F. (2020). The joint effect of board independence and CSR committee on CSR disclosure: Evidence from Italian listed companies. *Corporate Ownership & Control*, 17(4), 319–328.

Chaffee, E. C. (2017). The origins of corporate social responsibility. *University of Cincinnati Law Review*, 85, 347–373.

Chau, G. K., & Gray, S. J. (2002). Ownership structure and corporate voluntary disclosure in Hong Kong and Singapore. *The International Journal of Accounting*, 37(2), 247–265.

Cho, C. H., Laine, M., Roberts, R. W., & Rodrigue, M. (2015). Organized hypocrisy, organizational façades, and sustainability reporting. *Accounting, Organizations and Society*, 40, 78–94.

Clark, J. M. (1939). *Social control of business*. New York: McGraw Hill.

Clarkson, M. E. (1995). A stakeholder framework for analyzing and evaluating corporate social performance. *Academy of Management Review*, 20(1), 92–117.

Contrafatto, M. (2004). Il corporate social accounting and reporting: uno sguardo alla letteratura internazionale. In *AA.VV (a cura di Rusconi G. e Dorigatti M.) Teoria Generale del Bilancio Sociale ed applicazioni pratiche, collana "Persona, imprese* e società" (Vol. II). Milano: Franco Angeli.

Cormier, D., Magnan, M., & Van Velthoven, B. (2005). Environmental disclosure quality in large German companies: Economic incentives, public pressures or institutional conditions? *European Accounting Review*, 14(1), 3–39.

Costanza, R., d'Arge, R., De Groot, R., Farber, S., Grasso, M., Hannon, B., ... Van Den Belt, M. (1997). The value of the world's ecosystem services and natural capital. *Nature*, 387(6630), 253–260.

Dahlsrud, A. (2008). How corporate social responsibility is defined: An analysis of 37 definitions. *Corporate Social Responsibility and Environmental Management*, 15(1), 1–13.

D'Amore, G., Landriani, L., & Lepore, L. (2021). Ownership and sustainability of Italian water utilities: the stakeholder role. *Utilities Policy*, 71, 101–228.

Dalton, D. R., & Cosier, R. A. (1982). The four faces of social responsibility. *Business Horizons*, 25(3), 19–27.

Davis, K. (1960). Can business afford to ignore social responsibilities? *California Management Review*, 2(3), 70–76.

Davis, K., & Blomstrom, R. L. (1966). *Business and its environment*. New York: McGraw-Hill.

De Castro, G. M., López, J. E. N., & Sáez, P. L. (2006). Business and social reputation: Exploring the concept and main dimensions of corporate reputation. *Journal of Business Ethics*, 63(4), 361–370.

Deephouse, D. L. (2000). Media reputation as a strategic resource: An integration of mass communication and resource-based theories. *Journal of Management*, 26(6), 1091–1112.

de Quevedo Puente, E. (2001). *Reputación y creación de valor: una relación circular, aplicación al sector bancario español (1999)* (Doctoral dissertation, Universidad de Burgos).

Diamond, D. W., & Verrecchia, R. E. (1991). Disclosure, liquidity, and the cost of capital. *The Journal of Finance*, 46(4), 1325–1359.

Dierickx, I., & Cool, K. (1989). Asset stock accumulation and sustainability of competitive advantage. *Management Science*, 35(12), 1504–1511.

Dollinger, M. J., Golden, P. A., & Saxton, T. (1997). The effect of reputation on the decision to joint venture. *Strategic Management Journal*, 18(2), 127–140.

Dowling, G. (2001). *Creating corporate reputations: Identity, image, and performance*. Oxford: Oxford University Press.

Drucker, P. F. (1965). *The Practice of Management*. London: Mercury Books.

Drucker, P. F. (1984). Converting social problems into business opportunities: The new meaning of corporate social responsibility. *California Management Review* (pre-1986), 26(000002), 53.

Eells, R., & Walton, C. (1961). *Conceptual foundations of business*. Homewood: Richard D. Irwin.

Elkington, J. (1994). Towards the sustainable corporation: Win-win-win business strategies for sustainable development. *California Management Review*, 36(2), 90–100.

Fama, E. F., & Jensen, M. C. (1983). Separation of ownership and control. *The Journal of Law and Economics*, 26(2), 301–325.

Fazio, V. (2005). Lo standard Accuntability (AA)1000. Puniti di convergenza con le Guide Lines della Global Reporting Initiative (GRI) ed il modello GBS, in AA.VV (a cura di G. Rusconi e M. Dorigatti). In *Modelli di rendicontazione etico-sociale e applicazioni pratiche, collana "Persona, imprese e società"* (Vol. III). Milano: Franco Angeli.

Fombrun, C. J. (1996). *Reputation*. Boston MA: Harvard Business School Press.

Fombrun, C. J. (1998). Indices of corporate reputation: An analysis of media rankings and social monitors' ratings. *Corporate Reputation Review*, 1(4), 327–340.

Fombrun, C., & Shanley, M. (1990). What's in a name? Reputation building and corporate strategy. *Academy of Management Journal*, 33(2), 233–258.

Fombrun, C. J., & Van Riel, C. B. (2004). *Fame & fortune: How successful companies build winning reputations*. New York: FT Press.

Fonseca A., McAllister M. L., & Fitzpatrick, P. (2014). Sustainability reporting among mining corporations: A constructive critique of the GRI approach. *Journal of Cleaner Production*, 84, 70–83.

Freeman, R. E. (1984). Strategic management: A stakeholder approach. Marshfield, MA: Pittman Publishing.

Friedman, M. (1962). *Capitalism and freedom*. Chicago, IL: Chicago University Press.

Friedman, M. (1970). The social responsibility of business is to increase its profits. *New York Times Magazine*, 13 September, 32–33, 122, 124, 126.

Gangi, F., & Mustilli, M. (2018). *La responsabilità sociale dell'impresa: Principi e pratiche*. Milano: EGEA spa.

García-Sánchez, I. M., Hussain, N., Aibar-Guzmán, C., & Aibar-Guzmán, B. (2022). Assurance of corporate social responsibility reports: Does it reduce decoupling practices? *Business Ethics, the Environment & Responsibility*, 31(1), 118–138.

Giannessi, E. (1960). *Le aziende di produzione originarie*. Cursi: Pisa.

Giannessi, E. (1969). Considerazioni critiche intorno al concetto di azienda, in Scritti in onore di Giordano Dell'Amore, Saggi di discipline aziendali e sociali (Vol. I). Pisa: Pacini.

Gladwin, T. N., Kennelly, J. J., & Krause, T. S. (1995). Shifting paradigms for sustainable development: Implications for management theory and research. *Academy of Management Review*, 20(4), 874–907.

Grant, R. M. (1991). The resource-based theory of competitive advantage: Implications for strategy formulation. *California Management Review*, 33(3), 114–135.

Gray, R. (1993). Current practice in environmental reporting. *Social and Environmental Accounting Journal*, 13(1), 6–8.

Gray, R. (2002). The social accounting project and accounting organization and society: Privileging engagement, imaginings, new accountings and pragmatism over critique. *Accounting, Organizations and Society*, 27(7), 687–708.

Gray, R. (2003). *Social and environmental accounting and reporting: From ridicule to Revolution? From Hope to Hurbis?*, Glasgow: University of Glasgow (United Kingdom) ProQuest Dissertations Publishing.

Gray, R. (2004). Why is social accounting so difficult? Part I. *Social and Environmental Accounting Journal*, 24(1), 12–17.

Gray, R., Owen, D., & Adams, C. (1996). *Accounting & accountability: Changes and challenges in corporate social and environmental reporting*. Hoboken, NJ: Prentice Hall.

Greening D. W., & Turban, D. B. (2000). Corporate social performance as a competitive advantage in attracting a quality workforce. *Business & Society*, 39(3), 254–280.

Groenland, E. A. (2002). Qualitative research to validate the RQ-dimensions. *Corporate Reputation Review*, 4(4), 308–315.

Hamori, M. (2003). The impact of reputation capital on the career paths of departing employees. *Journal of Intellectual Capital*, 4(3), 304–315.

Haniffa, R. M., & Cooke, T. E. (2002). Culture, corporate governance and disclosure in Malaysian corporations. *Abacus*, 38(3), 317–349.

Hart, S. L., & Milstein, M. B. (2003). Creating sustainable value. *Academy of Management Perspectives*, 17(2), 56–67.

Hartman, L. P., Rubin, R. S., & Dhanda, K. K. (2007). The communication of corporate social responsibility: United States and European Union multinational corporations. *Journal of Business Ethics*, 74(4), 373–389.

Heald, M. (1970). *The social responsibilities of business: Company and community 1900–1960*. Cleveland, OH: Pr. of Case Western Reserve Univ.

Ho, S. S., & Wong, K. S. (2001). A study of the relationship between corporate governance structures and the extent of voluntary disclosure. *Journal of International Accounting, Auditing and Taxation*, 10(2), 139–156.

Hossain, M., Tan, L. M., & Adams, M. B. (1994), Voluntary disclosure in an emerging capital market: Some empirical evidence from companies listed on the Kuala Lumpur Stock Exchange. *International Journal of Accounting*, 29(4), 334–351.

Ing, B. (1992). *Developing green reporting systems: Some practical implications. Green reporting: Accountancy and the challenge of the nineties*. London: Chapman & Hall.

Jensen, M. C., & Meckling, W. H. (1976). Theory of the firm: Managerial behaviour, agency costs, and ownership structure. *Journal of Financial Economics*, 3(4), 305–350.

Jones, T. M. (1980). Corporate social responsibility revisited, redefined. *California Management Review*, 22(3), 59–67.

Kreps, T. J. (1940). *Measurement of the social performance of business*. Washington, DC: Government Printing Office.

Lan, Y., Wang, L., & Zhang, X. (2013). Determinants and features of voluntary disclosure in the Chinese stock market. *China Journal of Accounting Research*, 6(4), 265–285.

Latapí Agudelo, M. A., Jóhannsdóttir, L., & Davídsdóttir, B. (2019). A literature review of the history and evolution of corporate social responsibility. *International Journal of Corporate Social Responsibility*, 4(1), 1–23.

Lepore, L., Landriani, L., Pisano, S., D'Amore, G., & Pozzoli, S. (2022). Corporate governance in the digital age: The role of social media and board independence in CSR disclosure. Evidence from Italian listed companies. *Journal of Management and Governance*. https://doi.org/10.1007/s10997-021-09617-2.

Leuz, C., & Verrecchia, R. E. (2000). The economic consequences of increased disclosure. *Journal of Accounting Research*, 38, 91–124.

Levine, R. (1997). Financial development and economic growth: Views and agenda. *Journal of Economic Literature*, 35, 688–726.

Marchi, L. (1993). *I sistemi informativi aziendali*. Milano: Giuffrè.

McGuire, J. W. (1963). *Business and society*. New York: McGraw-Hill.

Mitchell, R., Agle, B., & Wood, D. (1997). Toward a theory of stakeholder identification and salience: Defining the principle of who and what really counts. *The Academy of Management Review*, 22, 853–886.

Montiel, I. (2008). Corporate social responsibility and corporate sustainability separate pasts, common futures. *Organization & Environment*, 21(3), 245–269.

Montiel, I., & Delgado-Ceballos, J. (2014). Defining and measuring corporate sustainability: Are we there yet? *Organization & Environment*, 27(2), 113–139.

Neubaum, D. O., & Zahra, S. A. (2006). Institutional ownership and corporate social performance: The moderating effects of investment horizon, activism, and coordination. *Journal of Management*, 32(1), 108–131.

Orlitzky, M., Schmidt, F. L., & Rynes, S. L. (2003). Corporate social and financial performance: A meta-analysis. *Organization Studies*, 24(3), 403–441.

Oswald, J. (1996) Human resources, scientists, and internal reputation: The role of climate and job satisfaction. *Human Relations*, 49(3), 269–293.

Owen, D. (1992). *Green Reporting*. London: Chapman & Hall.

Parker, L. D. (1986). Polemical themes in social accounting: A scenario for standard setting. *Advances in Public Interest Accounting*, 1, 67–93.

Patelli, L., & Prencipe, A. (2007). The relationship between voluntary disclosure and independent directors in the presence of a dominant shareholder. *European Accounting Review*, 16(1), 5–33.

Peloza, J. (2005). Corporate Social Responsibility as Reputational Insurance. Working Paper Series, Center of Responsible Business, UC Berkeley.

Pisano, S., Lepore, L., & Lamboglia, R. (2017). Corporate disclosure of human capital via LinkedIn and ownership structure: An empirical analysis of European companies. *Journal of Intellectual Capital*, 18(1), 102–127.

Prior, D., Surroca, J., & Tribó, J. A. (2008). Are socially responsible managers really ethical? Exploring the relationship between earnings management and corporate social responsibility. *Corporate governance: An International Review*, 16(3), 160–177.

Puxty, A. G. (1986). Social accounting as immanent legitimation: A critique of a technicist ideology. *Advances in Public Interest Accounting*, 1(6), 95–111.

Rimmel, G. (Ed.). (2020). *Accounting for sustainability*. London: Routledge.

Roberts, W. P., & Dowling, R. G. (2002). Corporate reputation and sustained superior financial performance. *Strategic Management Journal*, 23(12), 1077–1093.

Rugiadini, A. (1970). *I sistemi informativi d'impresa*. Milano: Giuffrè.

Rusconi, G. (1987). Il ruolo del bilancio sociale nel contesto dell'economia aziendale. Rivista italiana di ragioneria e di Economia aziendale.

Rusconi, G. (2002). Il bilancio sociale: origini e stato dell'arte in Italia, Unpublished.

Sackman, H. (1967). *Computers, system science and evolving society*. New York: John Wiley.

Scharfstein, D. (1988). The disciplinary role of takeovers. *The Review of Economic Studies*, 55(2), 185–199.

Scholtens, B. (2009). Corporate social responsibility in the international banking industry. *Journal of Business Ethics*, 86(2), 159–175.

Schumacher, E. F. (1973). *Small is beautiful: Economics as if people mattered*. Broadway, NY: Harper Perennial.

Schwaiger, M. (2004) Components and parameters of corporate reputation – An empirical study. *Schmalenbach Business Review*, 56(1), 46–71.

Selekman, B. M. (1959). *A moral philosophy for management*. New York: McGraw-Hill.

Shenkar, O., & Yuchtman-Yaar, E. (1997). Reputation, image, prestige, and goodwill: An interdisciplinary approach to organizational standing. *Human Relations*, 50(11), 1361–1381.

Shrivastava, P. (1995). The role of corporations in achieving ecological sustainability. *Academy of Management Review*, 20(4), 936–960.

Standifird, S. S. (2001). Reputation and e-commerce: eBay auctions and the asymmetrical impact of positive and negative ratings. *Journal of Management*, 27(3), 279–295.

Stein, H. (1988). *Presidential economics: The making of economic policy from Roosevelt to Reagan and beyond*. Simon & Schuster Books.

Székely, F., & Knirsch, M. (2005). Responsible leadership and corporate social responsibility: Metrics for sustainable performance. *European Management Journal*, 23(6), 628–647.

Van Dijk, A., Mount, R., Gibbons, P., Vardon, M., & Canadell, P. (2014). Environmental reporting and accounting in Australia: Progress, prospects and research priorities. *Science of the Total Environment*, 473, 338–349.

Van Marrewijk, M. (2003). Concepts and definitions of CSR and corporate sustainability: Between agency and communion. *Journal of Business Ethics*, 44(2), 95–105.

Verrecchia, R. E. (2001). Essays on disclosure. *Journal of Accounting and Economics*, 32(1–3), 97–180.

Vicini, G. (1998). How Italian companies deal with the environment: The results of a survey. *FEEM Newsletter*, 2, 17–18.

Viederman, S. (1994). Five capitals and three pillars of sustainability. *The Newsletter of PEGS*, 4(1), 5–12.

Waddock, S. A., & Graves, S. B. (1997). The corporate social performance–financial performance link. *Strategic Management Journal*, 18(4), 303–319.

Weber, J. L. (2011). An experimental framework for ecosystem capital accounting in Europe. *European Environment Agency*, Technical report, 13.

Weber, O., & Banks, Y. (2012). Corporate sustainability assessment in financing the extractive sector. *Journal of Sustainable Finance & Investment*, 2(1), 64–81.

# 2

# THEORETICAL FRAMEWORKS FOR ENVIRONMENTAL DISCLOSURE

Over time, scholars have used different theories to explain environmental disclosure. The theories most used to describe the release of environmental disclosure are stakeholder and legitimacy, followed by institutional, agency, and signalling theories (da Rocha Garcia et al., 2021; Mata et al., 2018). The following paragraphs describe the conceptual basis of each theory and its use in justifying companies' decision to release environmental disclosure and reporting, and critically discuss the results of relevant studies in this regard.

## 2.1 Agency theory

Agency theory investigates the function of disclosure in the bargaining process between individuals, which is established within an agency relationship (Jensen and Meckling, 1976). The latter arises when an individual (principal) delegates to another (agent) the management and performance of certain activities on his or her behalf. The consequence of this choice is that the agent has better access to the company's private information than the principal and can make decisions with greater awareness. However, the agent's decisions affect both its welfare and that of the principal. In the case of a divergence of interests between the two parties, this condition creates a conflict (agency problem). To limit the discretion of the agent, the principal has the opportunity to define specific incentives or appropriate control mechanisms (termed agency costs) that affect the behaviours of the agent.

Regarding the company, the agency relationship is found in manifold relationships. This is because companies are 'legal fictions that serve as a nexus for a set of contracting relationships among individuals' (Jensen and Meckling, 1976, p. 310). The main agency relationships investigated in the company are

DOI: 10.4324/9781003245933-3

those between shareholders (principals) and managers (agents) (Type I agency problems) or those more explanatory of the Italian context between minority shareholders/debtholders (principals) and manager/majority shareholders (agents) (Type II agency problems). In both situations, the principal represents an entity outside the company; otherwise, the agent operates within the company.

When there is a divergence of interests between the principal and agent, the agent could adopt opportunistic behaviours, assuming decisions that maximise its utility at the expense of the principal's interests. For example, in Type II agency problems, management could decide to invest resources in some projects, which could increase its utility at the expense of the shareholder distribution of dividends. This is a consequence of the separation between ownership and control (Fama and Jensen, 1983), which results in information asymmetries.

In this context, corporate disclosure is a control mechanism useful in reducing information asymmetries between the agent and principal, allowing the latter to control the behaviours of the former and consequently, to verify the quality of the investment. Furthermore, corporate disclosure can favour the agent, who can use it to signal to the principal the decisions adopted in its interests. Therefore, in agency theory, firms tend to release environmental disclosure to reduce agency problems (Barako et al., 2006).

Table 2.1 reports previous studies that investigated environmental disclosure using agency theory. Considering its focus on shareholders, when used, agency theory is often associated with other theories such as stakeholder or legitimacy theory. According to Gray et al. (1996), companies must release information not only to shareholders, but also to various other stakeholders that can influence and are influenced by firms' activities.

Reviewing previous studies that referred to agency theory to explain environmental disclosure, most scholars exclusively investigated environmental disclosure (e.g. Radu and Francoeur, 2017), while others analysed wider corporate social responsibility (CSR) disclosure (e.g. Garanina and Aray, 2021; Tibiletti et al., 2021). Most research investigated information voluntarily released by companies. However, few analysed the environmental disclosure provided after a new rule was implemented (e.g. D'Amico et al. (2016) investigated the information released after the implementation of EU Directive 51/2003,[1] and Mio et al. (2020) focused on EU Directive 95/2014). Moreover, most studies examined the information released by companies operating in developed countries (Mallin et al., 2013; Gray et al., 2001), although some analysed those in developing countries (e.g. Kalu et al., 2016). Finally, most studies were longitudinal.

Most research referring to agency theory investigated the factors affecting environmental disclosure, in particular, the relationship between the characteristics of the board of directors and corporate disclosure (e.g. Biswas et al., 2019; Fernandes et al., 2019; Hussain et al., 2018). The main characteristics analysed were board size (e.g. Kaymak and Bektas, 2017), independence (e.g. Fernández-Gago et al., 2018), gender diversity (e.g. Katmon et al., 2019), and CEO duality (e.g. Jizi et al., 2014). Essentially, an effective board of directors enhances the quantity

**TABLE 2.1** Studies that investigated environmental disclosure using the agency theory

| *Study* | *Year* | *Country* | *Sample* | *Type of disclosure* | *Aim of the study* | *Description of the aim* | *Other theory used* |
|---|---|---|---|---|---|---|---|
| Alipour et al. (2019) | 2011–2016 | Iran | 120 firms | Environmental disclosure | Effects of disclosure | To investigate the effect of environmental quality disclosure (EQD) on firm performance and the moderating role of board independence in previous relationship | Stakeholder theory |
| Biswas et al. (2019) | 1996–2011 | Bangladesh | 2,637 firm-year observations | CSR disclosure | Determinants of disclosure | To investigate how CG quality affects CSR disclosure in family and non-family firms | Socioemotional wealth theory |
| Chijoke-Mgbame et al. (2020) | 2007–2016 | Nigeria | 83 firms | CSR disclosure | Effects of disclosure | To investigate the impact of CSR disclosure on firm performance and the moderating role of corporate governance in previous relationship | Stakeholder theory, Legitimacy theory, Institutional theory, Resource dependence theory |
| D'Amico et al. (2016) | 2006 and 2009 | Italy | 170 firms | Environmental disclosure | Determinants of disclosure | To investigate the factors that influence environmental disclosures | Stakeholder theory |

(*Continued*)

**TABLE 2.1** Continued

| *Study* | *Year* | *Country* | *Sample* | *Type of disclosure* | *Aim of the study* | *Description of the aim* | *Other theory used* |
|---|---|---|---|---|---|---|---|
| Fernandes et al. (2019) | 2016 | Brasil | 152 firms | Environmental disclosure | Determinants of disclosure | To investigate the influence of the characteristics of boards of directors on the level of environmental disclosure | |
| Fernández-Gago et al. (2018) | 2009–2014 | Spain | 83 firms | CSR disclosure | Determinants of disclosure | To investigate how the background of independent directors affects CSR disclosure | Stakeholder theory, Legitimacy theory, Resource dependence theory |
| Garanina and Aray (2021) | 2012–2015 | Russia | 223 firms | CSR disclosure | Determinants of disclosure | To investigate the influence of foreign shareholders, foreign board members, and cross-listing on CSR disclosure | Legitimacy theory |
| Gerged (2021) | 2010–2014 | Jordan | 500 firm-year observations | Environmental disclosure | Determinants of disclosure | To investigate how internal corporate governance mechanisms affect corporate environmental disclosure | Stakeholder theory |
| **Gray** et al. (2001) | 1988–1995 | UK | 100 firms | CSR disclosure | Determinants of disclosure | To investigate how corporate characteristics affect social and environmental disclosure | Legitimacy theory |
| Hussain et al. (2018) | 2007–2011 | USA | 100 firms | CSR disclosure | Determinants of disclosure | To investigate the influence of the characteristics of boards of directors on CSR disclosure | Stakeholder theory |

| | | | | | | | |
|---|---|---|---|---|---|---|---|
| Injeni et al. (2021) | 2010–2018 | Kenya | 419 firm-year observations | CSR disclosure | Determinants of disclosure | To investigate how the characteristics of board of directors, ownership structure and institutional-related factors affect CSR disclosure | Institutional theory |
| Jeriji and Louhichi (2021) | 2013–2016 | World | 500 firms | CSR disclosure | Determinants of disclosure | To investigate how CSR performance affects CSR disclosure | Legitimacy theory, Stigma organisational theory |
| Jizi et al. (2014) | 2009–2011 | USA | 291 bank-year observations | CSR disclosure | Determinants of disclosure | To investigate how the characteristics of board of directors affect CSR disclosure | |
| Kalu et al. (2016) | 2013 | Malaysia | 126 real estate firms | Environmental disclosure | Determinants of disclosure | To investigate how firm characteristics and ownership structure affect environmental disclosure | Legitimacy theory |
| Karaman et al. (2018) | 2006–2015 | World | 284 aviation firms | CSR disclosure | Determinants and effects of disclosure | To investigate how firm characteristics affect CSR disclosure and how CSR disclosure affects firm value | Stakeholder theory, Legitimacy theory |

*(Continued)*

**TABLE 2.1** Continued

| *Study* | *Year* | *Country* | *Sample* | *Type of disclosure* | *Aim of the study* | *Description of the aim* | *Other theory used* |
|---|---|---|---|---|---|---|---|
| Katmon et al. (2019) | 2009–2013 | Malaysia | 200 firms | CSR disclosure | Determinants of disclosure | To investigate how board diversity affects CSR disclosure | Resource dependence theory |
| Kaymak and Bektas (2017) | | World | 80 multinational firms | CSR disclosure | Determinants of disclosure | To investigate how the characteristics of board of directors affect CSR disclosure | Stakeholder theory |
| Li et al. (2017) | 2012–2014 | China | 1179 firm-year observations | CSR disclosure | Effects of CSR disclosure | To investigate the effects of CSR disclosure on firm performance and the moderating role of government regulation and organisational slack | Institutional theory |
| Mallin et al. (2013) | 2005–2007 | USA | 100 firms | CSR disclosure | Determinants of disclosure | To investigate the effects of the corporate governance model on CSR disclosure | Stakeholder theory, Resource dependence theory |
| Mio et al. (2020) | 2016–2017 | EU countries | 253 firms | CSR disclosure | Determinants of disclosure | To investigate the ability of agency and legitimacy theory to predict companies' decision to disclose CSR after the implementation of the EU Directive | Legitimacy theory |
| Muttakin and Subramaniam (2015) | 2007–2011 | India | 100 firms | CSR disclosure | Determinants of disclosure | To investigate whether firm ownership and board characteristics affect CSR disclosure | Institutional theory |

| | | | | | | | |
|---|---|---|---|---|---|---|---|
| Ortas et al. (2015) | 2010 | World | 3931 firms | CSR disclosure | Determinants of disclosure | To investigate how corporate characteristics influence CSR disclosure | Stakeholder theory, Legitimacy theory, Signalling theory |
| Radu and Francoeur (2017) | 2011 | USA | 661 firms | Environmental disclosure | Determinants of disclosure | To investigate how environmental innovation and environmental performance influence environmental disclosure | Stakeholder theory, Legitimacy theory, Voluntary disclosure theory |
| Schiehll and Kolahgar (2020) | 1999–2014 | Canada | 520 firms | CSR disclosure | Effects of disclosure | To investigate the effects of financial materiality in CSR disclosure on stock price informativeness | Disclosure theory |
| Tibiletti et al. (2021) | 2008, 2011, 2016 | Italy | 200 firms | CSR disclosure | Determinants of disclosure | To investigate how the characteristics of board of directors impact CSR disclosure | |
| Zaid et al. (2020) | 2013–2018 | Palestine | 33 firms | CSR disclosure | Determinants of disclosure | To investigate how ownership structure influences CSR disclosure and the moderating role of board independence | |

*Source*: Author's elaboration

and quality of disclosure (Alfraih, 2016), and decreases information asymmetries between the principal and agent (Gao et al., 2016). In these studies, board of directors and environmental disclosure operate as complementary mechanisms acting together to mitigate agency problems.

In addition to the structure of the board of directors, another corporate governance mechanism investigated as a determinant of environmental disclosure according to the agency theory framework is the ownership structure (e.g. Gerged, 2021; Zaid et al., 2020). Scholars focused on how the level of ownership concentration affects environmental disclosure (e.g. Muttakin and Subramaniam, 2015). These studies used ownership diffusion as a proxy for information asymmetries between the agent and principal (i.e. shareholders). The higher the information asymmetry with the principal, the higher is the environmental disclosure released by the company to mitigate the agency problem. Similarly, scholars analysed how the level of leverage influences environmental disclosure (e.g. Ortas et al., 2015). These studies used leverage as a proxy for information asymmetry between the debtholder and manager/majority shareholder (Type II agency problems). They hypothesised that the higher the leverage, the higher is the environmental disclosure provided by the company to mitigate the agency problem.

However, few scholars used agency theory to investigate the effect of environmental disclosure on stock prices (Schiehll and Kolahgar, 2020) and company financial performance (e.g. Li et al., 2017). Regarding the influence on corporate performance, most of these studies used stakeholder theory to justify the direct association between CSR disclosure and company performance (e.g. Alipour et al., 2019; Chijoke-Mgbame et al., 2020), referring to agency theory only when introducing the moderating role of corporate governance in previous relationships. Therefore, it is more appropriate to consider these studies within the framework of stakeholder theory. Investigating the effect of CSR disclosure on firm value (measured using the market-based indicator Tobin'Q), Karaman et al. (2018) confirmed that the release of CSR disclosure shows investors a company's involvement in sustainable development and encourages the increase of firm value, as per agency theory assumptions.

In addition, some studies refer to agency theory to investigate companies' decision to assure their CSR reports. These studies consider the assurance statement a control mechanism that can reduce the information asymmetry between the principal and agent, adding more credibility to the information released (Tyson and Adams, 2020). For example, Aladwey et al. (2022) used agency theory to examine the association between specific board characteristics such as size, tenure, presence of women, and choice to engage in CSR assurance, finding a positive relationship between previous variables. Similarly, Liao et al. (2018) found a positive association between larger boards with a higher presence of female members and the assurance of CSR reports among a sample of Chinese companies. Finally, Miras-Rodriguez and Di Pietra (2018) also found a positive relationship between board independence and CSR assurance.

## 2.2 Stakeholder theory

According to stakeholder theory, each company has several counterparts apart from its shareholders, such as employees, suppliers, customers, the government, and the community in general (Freeman, 1984). These stakeholders can both influence and be influenced by the company's activities in different ways as they have diverse stakes apart from the financial ones characterising shareholders. Stakeholder theory affirms that a firm's success depends on its capacity to satisfy stakeholders' needs (Alipour et al., 2019). Therefore, the company should aim to consider the needs of all stakeholders, rather than to exclusively maximise the wealth of its shareholders, and implement good management practices that encourage the establishment of good relationships with all stakeholders. This is particularly true in recent decades, which have been characterised by an increasing influence and demand for CSR issues by all stakeholders. Stakeholders' attention to CSR issues encourages companies to integrate their strategies with social and environmental matters (Huang and Kung, 2010).

In this context, companies must be accountable to all stakeholders to satisfy their information needs and obtain their endorsement. A company's decision to release environmental data in addition to the financial information provided to shareholders could be considered a way to create a dialogue with all stakeholders, which is useful in achieving or maintaining legitimacy (Coetzee and van Staden, 2011; Gray et al., 1995) and trustworthy relationships (Abeysekera et al., 2021). Furthermore, it is useful in preventing a possible decline in forthcoming investment opportunities (Brammer and Pavelin, 2006). Here, taxonomy regulation 2020/852, aimed at boosting the allocation of private funds in green investments, will further encourage the release of environmental disclosure.[2]

According to stakeholder theory, various stakeholder groups present different stakes, and balancing their expectations influences management's decisions on environmental disclosure (Cormier et al., 2004). Stakeholder theory is classified in two branches used to explain how companies respond to stakeholders' expectations: (1) normative or ethical, and (2) managerial (Burritt et al., 2016). According to the first branch, companies consider all stakeholders in the same way, and assume decisions and release information regardless of what a specific group thereof requires (Deegan, 2002). Following the managerial branch, companies assign a different weight to stakeholders' expectations according to their capacity to influence corporate activities and act, and provide information to address the expectations of the most powerful group (Ullmann, 1985). The relevance assigned to a specific stakeholder group depends on its level of salience, which is the result of the following three attributes of its claims: (1) power, (2) legitimacy, and (3) urgency (Mitchell et al., 1997). Whether all three attributes representing their claims are present, stakeholders require priority and urgency to satisfy their needs. In contrast, stakeholders are considered 'expectant stakeholders' if they possess only two of the previous elements, or 'latent stakeholders' if they possess only one attribute (Pérez et al., 2017).

Table 2.2 reports previous studies that investigated environmental disclosure using the stakeholder theory. As the table shows, stakeholder theory is often used in conjunction with legitimacy theory. Some scholars (e.g. Garcia-Sanchez et al., 2014; Deegan, 2002) maintain that these theories are complementary, considering that both investigate a company's capacity to develop good relationships with and satisfy stakeholders' expectations (stakeholder theory) or society as a whole (legitimacy theory).

Reviewing previous studies that refer to stakeholder theory, similar to the research using agency theory, most exclusively investigated environmental disclosure (e.g. Adler et al., 2022), while others analysed wider CSR disclosure (e.g. Sannino et al., 2020; Sigurdsson and Candi, 2020). Studies examined the information released by companies operating in developed (e.g. Torelli et al., 2020) or developing countries (e.g. Weber, 2014), and some used an international sample (e.g. Vitolla et al., 2019). Finally, most studies were longitudinal.

Some research (e.g. Beske et al., 2020; Hossain et al., 2017; Depoers et al., 2016; Loh et al., 2015) used only stakeholder theory to investigate the content of environmental disclosure released by companies in different documents to manage their relationship with stakeholders, addressing their pressure and scrutiny (Thorne et al., 2014). However, most used stakeholder theory to investigate the factors affecting environmental disclosure (e.g. Pucheta-Martínez and López-Zamora, 2018; Gallego-Alvarez et al., 2017; Dong et al., 2014). In particular, the determinants investigated were proxies for the degree of attention and pressure of different stakeholder groups.

The main variables used as determinants are firm size (e.g. Garde-Sánchez et al., 2017), industry profile (e.g. Hickman, 2020; Chan et al., 2014), ownership structure (Huang and Kung, 2010), leverage (e.g. Fuhrmann, 2020), profitability (e.g. Chiu and Wang, 2015), and media exposure (e.g. Guenther et al., 2016). Firm size has been used to measure the degree of pressure exerted by stakeholders including employees, governments, and consumers (Burritt et al., 2016). Previous studies assumed that larger companies experience greater pressure from stakeholders. Likewise, it is assumed that more profitable companies receive greater pressure from stakeholders because of their visibility. As both larger and more profitable companies receive more attention from stakeholders, they should release more information to ensure they are acting coherently with stakeholders' expectations. Furthermore, industry profile has been used to measure pressure from public, government, and environmental organisations. In fact, companies operating in industries with higher environmental sensitivity attract more scrutiny and pressure from these stakeholders (Liesen et al., 2015; Liu and Anbumozhi, 2009), and should therefore release more information. Ownership concentration refers to pressure from stockholders. Similarly, leverage and media exposure proxy for debtholders and media interest in a company's activities, respectively. The value of these variables measures the degree of attention of a specific group of stakeholders to the company's activities and therefore, represents the pressure exerted on its disclosure behaviour. According to stakeholder theory, companies

**TABLE 2.2** Studies that investigated environmental disclosure using the stakeholder theory

| *Study* | *Year* | *Country* | *Sample* | *Type of disclosure* | *Aim of the study* | *Description of the aim* | *Other theory used* |
|---|---|---|---|---|---|---|---|
| Abeysekera et al. (2021) | 2008 | China | 100 firms | CSR disclosure | Determinants of disclosure | To investigate whether there is an association between financial reporting disclosure quality and CSR disclosure quality | |
| Adler et al. (2022) | 2012–2018 | India | 30 firms | Environmental disclosure | Content of disclosure | To investigate the extent of disclosure about the solid and liquid wastes released by companies | Legitimacy theory |
| Alipour et al. (2019) | 2011–2016 | Iran | 120 firms | Environmental disclosure | Effects of disclosure | To investigate the effect of environmental quality disclosure (EQD) on firm performance | Agency theory |
| Behl et al. (2022) | 2016–2019 | India | 62 energy firms | CSR disclosure | Determinants and effects of disclosure | To investigate the bidirectional causality and autoregression effects between CSR disclosure and firm value | Trade-of theory, Resource-based view, Resources theory |
| Beske et al. (2020) | 2014–2017 | Germany | 33 firms | CSR disclosure | Content of disclosure | To investigate the disclosure on materiality analysis in sustainability report | Legitimacy theory |

(*Continued*)

**TABLE 2.2** Continued

| *Study* | *Year* | *Country* | *Sample* | *Type of disclosure* | *Aim of the study* | *Description of the aim* | *Other theory used* |
|---|---|---|---|---|---|---|---|
| Burritt et al. (2016) | 2013–2014 | Japan | 100 firms | Environmental disclosure | Determinants of disclosure | To investigate different drivers of environmental disclosure | |
| Chan et al. (2014) | 2004 | Australia | 222 firms | CSR disclosure | Determinants of disclosure | To investigate how corporate governance quality, firm size, industry, profitability, leverage, ownership concentration, media exposure affect CSR disclosure | Legitimacy theory |
| Chiu and Wang (2015) | 2010–2011 | Taiwan | 246 firms | CSR disclosure | Determinants of disclosure | To investigate how stakeholder power, strategic posture, economic resources, firm size and media visibility influence CSR disclosure | |
| Cormier et al. (2004) | 2000 | World | 41 firms | Environmental disclosure | Determinants of disclosure | To investigate how management's perceptions regarding certain aspects of environmental reporting affects environmental disclosure | Legitimacy theory |
| Depoers et al. (2016) | 2007–2009 | France | 140 firms | Environmental disclosure | Content of disclosure | To investigate the environmental disclosure released in corporate reports and in the Carbon Disclosure Project | |

| | | | | | | | |
|---|---|---|---|---|---|---|---|
| Dong et al. (2014) | 2007–2010 | China | 176 mining and minerals firms | CSR disclosure | Determinants of disclosure | To investigate the influence of key stakeholder groups on CSR disclosure | |
| Fuhrmann (2020) | 2012–2016 | World | 2000 firms | CSR disclosure | Determinants of disclosure | To investigate the factors influencing the release of an integrated report, in which provide both financial and non-financial information | Voluntary disclosure, Signalling theory, Proprietary cost theory, Legitimacy theory, Institutional theory |
| Gallego-Alvarez et al. (2017) | | World | 3931 firms | Environmental disclosure | Determinants of disclosure | To investigate how different institutional constraints, stakeholder pressure and corporate governance systems affect environmental disclosure | |
| Garcia-Sanchez et al. (2014) | 2004–2010 | Spain | 98 firms | CSR disclosure | Determinants of disclosure | To investigate the moderating role of media pressure on the relation between external directors and CSR disclosure | Legitimacy theory Agenda-setting theory Stakeholder-agency theory |

*(Continued)*

**TABLE 2.2** Continued

| *Study* | *Year* | *Country* | *Sample* | *Type of disclosure* | *Aim of the study* | *Description of the aim* | *Other theory used* |
|---|---|---|---|---|---|---|---|
| García-Sánchez et al. (2019) | 2007–2016 | World | 1137 firms | CSR disclosure | Effects of disclosure | To investigate the effect of CSR disclosure on the access to financial resources | |
| Garde Sánchez et al. (2017) | 2015 | Spain | 167 state-owned firms | CSR disclosure | Determinants of disclosure | To investigate how some characteristics of the firm and its manager influence CSR disclosure | Legitimacy theory |
| Guenther et al. (2016) | 2008–2011 | World | 1120 firms | Environmental disclosure | Determinants of disclosure | To investigate how the relevance of different stakeholder groups affects environmental disclosure and moderates the relation between environmental performance and disclosure | |
| Hamrouni et al. (2020) | 2010–2015 | France | 80 firms | CSR disclosure | Effects of disclosure | To investigate the effect of CSR disclosure on the cost of debt | |
| Hickman (2020) | 2013 | USA | 478 firms | CSR disclosure | Determinants of disclosure | To investigate the effect of firm type, industry, media attention, firm size and different stakeholder importance on CSR disclosure | Legitimacy theory |
| Hossain et al. (2017) | 2010 | Bangladesh | 20 firms | CSR disclosure | Determinants of disclosure | To investigate CSR practices and motivations | |

| | | | | | | | |
|---|---|---|---|---|---|---|---|
| Huang and Kung (2010) | 2003–2005 | Taiwan | 759 firms | Environmental disclosure | Determinants of disclosure | To investigate how different stakeholder groups affect environmental disclosure | Legitimacy theory |
| Liesen et al. (2015) | 2005–2009 | Europe | 431 firms | Environmental disclosure | Determinants of disclosure | To investigate how external stakeholder pressure affects environmental disclosure | |
| Liu et al. (2021) | 2010–2018 | China | 781 firms | Environmental disclosure | Effects of disclosure | To investigate how environmental disclosure affects financial reporting quality | Signalling theory |
| Liu and Anbumozhi (2009) | 2006 | China | 175 firms | Environmental disclosure | Determinants of disclosure | To investigate how government, shareholders and creditors affect environmental disclosure | |
| Loh et al. (2015) | 1995–2009 | Australia | 2 gambling firms | CSR disclosure | Content of disclosure | To investigate the content of CSR disclosure released as a response to social pressures created around the time | Legitimacy theory, Institutional theory |

(*Continued*)

**TABLE 2.2** Continued

| *Study* | *Year* | *Country* | *Sample* | *Type of disclosure* | *Aim of the study* | *Description of the aim* | *Other theory used* |
|---|---|---|---|---|---|---|---|
| Mahjoub and Khamoussi (2013) | 2005–2010 | France | 250 firms | CSR disclosure | Effects of disclosure | To investigate the effect of CSR disclosure on earning quality | |
| Naseem et al. (2019) | 2008–2012 | China | 1500 firms | CSR disclosure | Effects of disclosure | To investigate the effect of CSR disclosure on firm value and the moderating role of financial ratio in previous relation | |
| Pérez et al. (2017) | 2013 | Spain | 84 firms | CSR disclosure | Effects of disclosure | To investigate the effect of CSR disclosure on CSR reputation | |
| Pucheta-Martínez and López-Zamora (2018) | 2004–2013 | Spain | 1092 firm-year observation | Environmental disclosure | Determinants of disclosure | To investigate how directors representing institutional investors influence environmental disclosure | Legitimacy theory |
| Radhouane et al. (2018) | 2001–2011 | France | 120 firms | Environmental disclosure | Effects of disclosure | To investigate how environmental disclosure influences firm value | |
| Rezaee et al. (2021) | 2011–2016 | Iran | 762 firm-year observations | Environmental disclosure | Effects of disclosure | To investigate how environmental disclosure affects risk and whether corporate governance practices moderate this relationship | Corporate finance theory, Agency theory, Stewardship theory |

| | | | | | | | |
|---|---|---|---|---|---|---|---|
| Sannino et al. (2020) | 2012–2018 | World | 180 OECD banks | CSR disclosure | Determinants of disclosure | To investigate the effect of cultural dimensions on GRI commitment in CSR disclosure | |
| Sigurdsson and Candi (2020) | | Europe | 355 firms | CSR disclosure | Determinants and effects of disclosure | To investigate the relationships between and among firms' commitment to social responsibility, CSR disclosure, social innovation and customer acceptance | |
| Torelli et al. (2020) | 2017 | Italy | 152 firms | CSR disclosure | Determinants of disclosure | To investigate how stakeholder engagement, industry and GRI adoption affect CSR disclosure | |
| Vitolla et al. (2019) | 2011–2018 | World | 145 firms | CSR disclosure | Determinants of disclosure | To investigate how stakeholder pressure affects integrated report, in which provide both financial and non-financial information | |
| Weber (2014) | 2005–2012 | China | 75 firms | CSR disclosure | Effects of disclosure | To investigate how CSR disclosure affects financial performance | Institutional theory |

*Source*: Author's elaboration

must satisfy the information needs of all stakeholders – internal, external, or intermediary (Huang and Kung, 2010) – by releasing corporate information.

Few studies analysed the effects of environmental disclosure on financial performance (e.g. Alipour et al., 2019; Naseem et al., 2019; Mahjoub and Khamoussi, 2013), corporate risk (Rezaee et al., 2021), firm value (e.g. Behl et al, 2022; Radhouane et al., 2018), access to financial resources (García-Sánchez et al., 2019), and the cost of debt (Hamrouni et al., 2020). According to these studies, companies release environmental disclosure to manage the expectations of different stakeholders, which can influence their activities to achieve their support and resources. By releasing environmental information, companies focus on all stakeholders, giving a positive signal to the financial market (García-Sánchez et al., 2019) and obtaining access to external financial resources. In addition, the release of environmental disclosure encourages the creation of a positive relationship with stakeholders, improving the company's financial performance (Freeman, 1984) and, therefore their financial reporting quality (Liu et al., 2021).

## 2.3 Legitimacy theory

According to legitimacy theory, companies should comply with society's expectations to achieve legitimation (Guthrie and Parker, 1989; Dowling and Pfeffer, 1975). Suchman (1995, p. 574) defined legitimacy as 'a generalized perception or assumption that the actions of an entity are desirable, proper, or appropriate within some socially constructed system of norms, values, beliefs, and definitions'. To achieve legitimacy, companies must consider what society recognises as socially acceptable behaviour and operate in response to external expectations.

Essentially, this theory contends that a social contract exists between a company and society, which indicates how the company should act to obtain legitimacy. If companies do not act in a way that satisfies society's expectations, a legitimacy gap is generated (Lindblom, 1993), which causes difficulties in obtaining human and financial resources or in selling the company's products or services (Tilling and Tilt, 2010). In addition, companies could be subject to regulatory sanctions if they do not satisfy society's legal expectations.

Therefore, legitimation can be considered a resource a company must generate, affect, or manipulate to survive in society (Deegan, 2019). In recent years, society's increasing attention to CSR issues has led companies to incorporate these matters in their activities and use different disclosure strategies to obtain legitimacy (Lu and Abeysekera, 2014; de Villiers and van Staden, 2006; Suchman, 1995).

According to legitimacy theory, companies use disclosure to achieve visibility and influence stakeholders' view of a company (Deegan, 2002. See also Patten (2020), who reported various considerations on legitimacy theory in CSR disclosure studies). Therefore, companies more visible to society tend to release greater disclosure (Cormier et al., 2004) to communicate that their activities are coherent with social values. In this way, they obtain legitimacy and support from stakeholders (Ching and Gerab, 2017; de Villiers and Marques, 2016) and enhance their reputation (Oliveira et al., 2010). Simultaneously, if companies do not perceive external pressure, they tend to not disclose too much information (Stanny, 2013; Stubbs et al., 2013).

However, the disclosure released in response to external pressure does not necessarily mean the company has decided to operate in a way useful in achieving sustainable development (Cho et al., 2012, 2014). In other words, companies could use CSR disclosure to obtain legitimacy rather than as an accountability mechanism, highlighting the opportunistic nature of CSR disclosure (Jeriji and Louhichi, 2021). In these situations, companies achieve symbolic rather than substantive legitimacy (Chelli et al., 2018). The possibility of incurring symbolic legitimacy is enhanced by the widely voluntary nature of environmental disclosure, which can further create a decoupling between the information released and companies' performance (García-Sánchez et al., 2022).

Previous considerations refer to a strategic view of legitimacy theory. The literature also investigated an institutional view of legitimacy, consisting of the company's capacity to maintain legitimacy in the context of mandatory environmental disclosure (e.g. Loh et al., 2015; Cowan and Deegan, 2011). According to the institutional view of legitimacy, regulation and other institutional pressures represent the audiences' expectations; therefore, companies should be compliant with the rules, standards, and recommendations of international organisations (Ismail et al., 2021). The institutional view of legitimacy focuses on a company's actions to maintain legitimacy, while the strategic view refers to actions to achieve or repair legitimacy (Chelli et al., 2014).

Previous studies often used legitimacy theory in conjunction with stakeholder theory, as reported in previous paragraph (see Table 2.3).

Furthermore, some studies (e.g. Adler et al., 2022; Zharfpeykan, 2021; Beske et al., 2020; Borgstedt et al., 2019; Costa et al., 2019; Lodhia and Jacobs, 2013; Cho, 2009) used legitimacy theory exclusively to explore the content of companies' environmental disclosure to identify the strategies and actions implemented to be legitimate. Pellegrino and Lodhia (2012) complemented the company-level analysis by investigating strategies implemented at the industry level. Other scholars analysed reports to understand whether they are readable and create value for stakeholders (e.g. du Toit, 2017), to measure the quality of the information released (Pitrakkos and Maroun, 2020), and after the issue of a new regulation (Yang et al., 2021).

Most studies use legitimacy theory to investigate the determinants of environmental disclosure (e.g. Antonini et al., 2021; Ballucchi et al., 2021; Oware et al., 2021). Media exposure is one of the main determinants analysed. This variable, which measures the degree of company visibility, is used to investigate whether and how public attention influences a company's environmental disclosure (Chelli et al., 2014; Islam and Deegan, 2010). Another widely used determinant is company size (e.g. Kouloukoui et al., 2019, Cho et al., 2015; Ortas et al., 2015), as larger companies have greater public profiles, face higher regulatory

**TABLE 2.3** Studies that investigated environmental disclosure using the legitimacy theory

| *Study* | *Year* | *Country* | *Sample* | *Type of disclosure* | *Aim of the study* | *Description of the aim* | *Other theory used* |
|---|---|---|---|---|---|---|---|
| Adler et al. (2022) | 2012–2018 | India | 30 firms | Environmental disclosure | Content of disclosure | To investigate the extent of disclosure about the solid and liquid wastes released by companies | Stakeholder theory |
| Antonini et al. (2021) | 2014–2015, 2017–2018 | USA | 170 firms | Environmental disclosure | Determinants of disclosure | To investigate whether changes in social and regulatory cost exposure not in sync affect environmental disclosure | |
| Ballucchi et al. (2021) | 2017 | Italy | 152 firms | Environmental disclosure | Determinants of disclosure | To investigate whether industry, SDG commitment, external pressure, experience in and stand-alone CSR report influence environmental disclosure | |
| Beske et al. (2020) | 2014–2017 | Germany | 33 firms | CSR disclosure | Content of disclosure | To investigate the disclosure on materiality analysis in sustainability report | Stakeholder theory |
| Borgstedt et al. (2019) | 2000–2014 | Germany | 30 firms | Environmental disclosure | Content of disclosure | To investigate the use of different legitimacy strategies in reporting environment information | Stakeholder theory, Institutional theory |
| Chelli et al. (2014) | 2001–2011 | France | 26 firms | Environmental disclosure | Content of disclosure | To investigate environmental disclosure released in response to the introduction of a new law | |

| | | | | | | | |
|---|---|---|---|---|---|---|---|
| Chelli et al. (2018) | 2001–2013 | France, Canada | 40 firms | Environmental disclosure | Content of disclosure | To investigate environmental disclosure released in response to the introduction of a new law | |
| Cho (2009) | 1996–2002 | France | 1 firm | Environmental disclosure | Content of disclosure | To investigate the communication strategies utilised to obtain legitimacy | |
| Cho et al. (2012) | 1996–2005 | USA | 119 firms | Environmental disclosure | Determinants of disclosure | To investigate how firm size, industry and environmental performance influence disclosure | Voluntary disclosure theory |
| Cho et al. (2015) | 1977, 2010 | USA | 71 firms | CSR disclosure | Determinants and effects of disclosure | To investigate how firm size and industry affect CSR disclosure, and how CSR disclosure influences firm value | |
| Cho and Patten (2007) | 2002 | USA | 100 firms | Environmental disclosure | Content of disclosure | To investigate differences in environmental disclosure according to industry and environmental performance | |

(*Continued*)

**TABLE 2.3** Continued

| *Study* | *Year* | *Country* | *Sample* | *Type of disclosure* | *Aim of the study* | *Description of the aim* | *Other theory used* |
|---|---|---|---|---|---|---|---|
| Cormier and Magnan (2015) | 2009 | USA, Canada | 550 firms | Environmental disclosure | Effects of disclosure | To investigate how environmental disclosure influences media coverage, which improve the relation between disclosure and financial analyst's forecasts | |
| Costa et al. (2019) | 2005–2013 | Italy | 393 cooperative banks' | CSR disclosure | Content of disclosure | To investigate the CSR disclosure released based on different "levels of empathy" towards different stakeholders | Accountability perspective |
| Cowan and Deegan (2011) | 1998–2000 | Australia | 25 firms | Environmental disclosure | Content of disclosure | To investigate the environmental disclosure released after the introduction of the emissions regulation | |
| de Villiers and van Staden (2006) | 1994–2002 | South Africa | 140 firms | Environmental disclosure | Content of disclosure | To investigate the environmental disclosure released in order to identify the trends in disclosure | |
| du Toit (2017) | 2015–2016 | South Africa | 292 firms | CSR disclosure | Content of disclosure | To investigate whether the information released in the integrated reports is readable and create value for stakeholders | Impression management theory |

| | | | | | | | |
|---|---|---|---|---|---|---|---|
| García-Sánchez et al. (2022) | 2002–2017 | World | 1939 firms | CSR disclosure | Determinants of disclosure | To investigate how external assurance and compliance to GRI influence the gap between CSR disclosure and performance | |
| Islam and Deegan (2010) | 1988–2006 | World | 2 firms | CSR disclosure | Determinants of disclosure | To investigate how media pressure influences CSR disclosure | Media agenda setting theory |
| Ismail et al. (2021) | 2002–2014 | France | 36 firms | Environmental disclosure | Determinants of disclosure | To investigate how three international sustainability initiatives influence environmental disclosure | |
| Kılıç and Kuzey (2019) | 2010–2016 | Turkey | 24 banks | Environmental disclosure | Determinants of disclosure | To investigate how size, profitability, age and listing status influence environmental disclosure | Political cost theory |
| Kouloukoui et al. (2019) | 2009–2014 | Brazil | 67 firms | Environmental disclosure | Determinants of disclosure | To investigate how size, profitability, industry, leverage and country origin influence environmental disclosure | |

(*Continued*)

**TABLE 2.3** Continued

| *Study* | *Year* | *Country* | *Sample* | *Type of disclosure* | *Aim of the study* | *Description of the aim* | *Other theory used* |
|---|---|---|---|---|---|---|---|
| Legendre and Coderre (2013) | 2009 | World | 253 firms | CSR disclosure | Determinants of disclosure | To investigate how size, profitability, country's business culture and industry influence the decision to adopt GRI and the level of GRI application | Signalling theory |
| Lodhia and Jacobs (2013) | 2003–2008 | Australia | 2 Commonwealth departments | Environmental disclosure | Content of disclosure | To investigate environmental disclosure released by Commonwealth departments | Bourdieu's theory of practice |
| Loh et al. (2015) | 1995–2009 | Australia | 2 gambling firms | CSR disclosure | Content of disclosure | To investigate how three specific interrelated government initiatives influence CSR disclosure | Stakeholder theory, Institutional theory |
| Maama (2021) | 2010–2019 | Ghana | 23 banks | CSR disclosure | Effects of disclosure | To investigate the impact of CSR disclosure on the financial sustainability | |
| Ortas et al. (2015) | 2010 | World | 3931 firms | Environmental disclosure | Determinants of disclosure | To investigate how firm specific characteristics influence environmental disclosure | Agency theory, Political costs theory, Signal theory |

| | | | | | | | |
|---|---|---|---|---|---|---|---|
| Oware et al. (2021) | 2009–2020 | India | 80 firms | Environmental disclosure | Determinants of disclosure | To investigate how female directors influences environmental disclosure in family and non-family-controlled firms | Critical mass theory |
| Pellegrino and Lodhia (2012) | 2008–2009 | Australia | 2 mining companies and two industry bodies | Environmental disclosure | Content of disclosure | To investigate the strategies implemented to be legitimate on a company and an industry level | |
| Pitrakkos and Maroun (2020) | 2016 | South Africa | 50 firms | Environmental disclosure | Content of disclosure | To investigate the quantity and quality of environmental disclosure | |
| Pucheta-Martínez and López-Zamora (2018) | 2004–2013 | Spain | 1092 firm-year observations | Environmental disclosure | Determinants of disclosure | To investigate how directors representing institutional investors influence environmental disclosure | Stakeholder theory |
| Stanny (2013) | 2016–2018 | USA | 500 firms | Environmental disclosure | Content of disclosure | To investigate the environmental disclosure released | Business case perspective, Stakeholder accountability view, Critical theory |
| Stubbs et al. (2013) | | Australia | 23 firms | CSR disclosure | Content of disclosure | To investigate why companies do not report CSR disclosure | |
| Tilling and Tilt (2010) | 1995–1999 | Australia | 1 firm | CSR disclosure | Content of disclosure | To investigate the CSR disclosure released | |

*(Continued)*

**TABLE 2.3** Continued

| *Study* | *Year* | *Country* | *Sample* | *Type of disclosure* | *Aim of the study* | *Description of the aim* | *Other theory used* |
|---|---|---|---|---|---|---|---|
| Yang et al. (2021) | 1997–2017 | Australia | 23 firms | Environmental disclosure | Content of disclosure | To investigate the quantity and quality of the environmental disclosure released after the issue of a new rule | |
| Yook et al. (2017) | 2002–2012 | Japan | 274 firms | Environmental disclosure | Determinants of disclosure | To investigate the relation between environmental performance and environmental disclosure | Voluntary disclosure theory |
| Zharfpeykan (2021) | 2011–2019 | Australia | 28 firms | CSR disclosure | Content of disclosure | To investigate the CSR disclosure released | |
| Zhou et al. (2018) | 2010–2015 | China | 334 firms | Environmental disclosure | Effects of disclosure | To investigate the impact of environmental disclosure on corporate risk-taking and the moderating role of organisational legitimacy | Signalling theory |

*Source:* Author's elaboration

pressure, and are subject to greater scrutiny (Kılıç and Kuzey, 2019; Brammer and Pavelin, 2006). Other studies investigated the relationship between profitability and environmental disclosure, hypothesising a positive association on the basis that more profitable companies tend to release more information on their performance to legitimise their activities (Legendre and Coderre, 2013). Regarding environmental performance, studies hypothesised a negative association with environmental disclosure based on the fact that those with lower performance must provide more information to legitimise their actions, supporting the idea of disclosure as a legitimising tool (Yook et al., 2017; Cho and Patten, 2007).

Few studies investigated the effects of environmental disclosure, mainly focusing on how it influences legitimacy as measured using media coverage (Cormier and Magnan, 2015). Therefore, in previous studies referring to legitimacy theory, media exposure is used both as a determinant and an effect of environmental disclosure depending on the aim of the research. Maama (2021) investigated the effect on firm performance, finding a negative association. The author justified this result by suggesting that contrary to legitimacy theory expectations, stakeholders could not give importance to the release of environmental information.

## 2.4 Institutional theory

According to institutional theory, companies are economic units whose behaviours are affected by institutions in the context in which they operate (Campbell, 2007; Roe, 1991). This theory is used to explain homogeneity among companies' behaviours (DiMaggio and Powell, 1983). The main assumption is that companies operating in countries with institutional similarities tend to assume homogeneous behaviour (La Porta et al., 1998).

The term isomorphism best describes the process of homogenisation (DiMaggio and Powell, 1983). According to Hawley's (1968) definition, isomorphism is a coercing process that induces a company to adopt the same behaviours of other companies that are subject to the same set of institutional conditions.

DiMaggio and Powell (1983) identified three types of isomorphism: mimetic, normative, and coercive. Mimetic isomorphism originates in the decision to resemble other companies. Here, companies adopt a specific behaviour to operate the same way as other companies. Normative isomorphism is the consequence of professionalisation, and occurs when companies decide to do what is considered right according to the professionalisation of a field as per the members of a profession. Normative isomorphism refers to the values, beliefs, and cultures diffused in society (Gallego-Álvarez and Pucheta-Martínez, 2020b). Finally, coercive isomorphism is attributed to political influence and occurs when companies decide to comply with the laws imposed by external forces.

Based on previous considerations, companies tend to put in place CSR activities and consequently, provide information on these CSR activities if they receive societal pressures and operate in countries characterised by greater attention and the presence of regulations regarding sustainability (Boura et al., 2020).

Here, the definitions of the sustainable development goals in Agenda 2030 by the United Nations, Non-financial Reporting Directive 95/2014/EU, and the various sustainability standards issued worldwide should encourage companies to adopt sustainable business models and release information on the CSR activities implemented. In fact, previous initiatives influence country rules, stakeholder demands for CSR activities, and corporate disclosure, and therefore, companies' reactions.

Table 2.4 reports previous studies that investigated environmental disclosure using institutional theory. Some scholars (e.g. Akbar and Deegan, 2021; Frías-Aceituno et al., 2013) investigated the content of environmental disclosure released by companies operating in different countries to understand whether and how the institutional environment influences disclosure. Others (e.g. Loh et al., 2015; Fifka and Pobizhan, 2014) focused on companies operating in just one country to explain differences or similarities in environmental disclosure using institutional factors. For example, referring to normative isomorphism, de Villiers et al. (2014) explained the invariant level of disclosure released by larger and smaller companies in the same country. Specifically, the authors sustained that similarities in environmental disclosure is due to high levels of professionalisation. On the other hand, referring to coercive isomorphism, Dong et al. (2021) explained the differences in the environmental disclosure released over time by companies operating in the same country. According to this, companies increased the information provided in response to new regulations.

Most studies used institutional theory to investigate how institutional factors influence the decision to release environmental information and performed a regression analysis (e.g. Oware and Awun-yo-Vitor, 2021; Gallego-Álvarez and Pucheta-Martínez, 2020a; García-Sánchez and Araújo-Bernardo, 2020; Kilincarslan et al., 2020; Lewis et al., 2014). These scholars measured three types of isomorphism using different measures. For example, coercive isomorphism is usually measured using the level of regulatory pressure (e.g. Mateo-Márquez et al., 2021; Boura et al., 2020; Khan et al., 2020; Situ et al., 2020), legal system (e.g. Gallego-Álvarez and Pucheta-Martínez, 2020b), or degree of investor protection (e.g. Pucheta-Martínez and Gallego-Álvarez, 2018). Normative isomorphism has been proxied using various cultural dimensions such as the degree of power distance or masculinity (e.g. Fuhrmann, 2020), and adoption of a sustainability standard (e.g. Dagiliene et al., 2020). Finally, mimetic isomorphism has been determined based on the characteristics of the industry in which the company operates (e.g. Gallego-Álvarez and Pucheta-Martínez, 2020b) or results of industrial peers (e.g. Zeng et al., 2012).

Few studies have used institutional theory to investigate the effects of environmental disclosure. However, Gerged et al. (2021), for example, referred to this theory to highlight the significant role of external institutions in stimulating environmental disclosure, which increases firm value. Furthermore, Li et al. (2017) investigated the moderating role of government regulation in the

**TABLE 2.4** Studies that investigated environmental disclosure using the institutional theory

| *Study* | *Year* | *Country* | *Sample* | *Type of disclosure* | *Aim of the study* | *Description of the aim* | *Other theory used* |
|---|---|---|---|---|---|---|---|
| Akbar and Deegan (2021) | 2011–2016 | World | 41 Apparel firms | CSR disclosure | Content of disclosure | To investigate how the institutional environment influences CSR disclosure | |
| Boura et al. (2020) | 2002–2012 | World | 2687 firms | Environmental disclosure | Determinants of disclosure | To investigate how pro-social inclination and institutional factors influence environmental disclosure | Stakeholder theory |
| Dagiliene et al. (2020) | 2016 | Europe | 226 manufacturing firms | Environmental disclosure | Determinants of disclosure | To investigate how institutional pressures affect environmental disclosure | |
| de Villiers et al. (2014) | 2007 | South Africa | 18 mining firms | CSR disclosure | Content of disclosure | To investigate the CSR disclosure released and compare the disclosures of larger firms with those of smaller firms | |
| Dong et al. (2021) | 2007–2016 | China | 57 financial firms | Environmental disclosure | Content of disclosure | To investigate the information released in response to coercive pressure from the government | |
| Fifka and Pobizhan (2014) | 2011 | Russia | 50 firms | CSR disclosure | Content of disclosure | To investigate how national and international factors influence CSR disclosure | |
| Frías-Aceituno et al. (2013) | 2008–2010 | World | 750 firms | CSR disclosure | Content of disclosure | To investigate how the legal system influences the release of an integrated report | |

(*Continued*)

**TABLE 2.4** Continued

| *Study* | *Year* | *Country* | *Sample* | *Type of disclosure* | *Aim of the study* | *Description of the aim* | *Other theory used* |
|---|---|---|---|---|---|---|---|
| Fuhrmann (2020) | 2012–2016 | World | 2000 firms | CSR disclosure | Determinants of disclosure | To investigate how firm-specific characteristics, institutional and cultural factors influence the release of an integrated report | Voluntary disclosure theory, Signalling theory, Proprietary cost theory, Legitimacy theory, Stakeholder theory |
| Gallego-Álvarez and Pucheta-Martínez (2020a) | 2005–2016 | World | 3517 firm-year observations | Environmental disclosure | Determinants of disclosure | To investigate how the varieties of capitalism framework adopted influence environmental disclosure, and the moderating role of gender diversity and board directors with specific skills | Stakeholder theory |
| Gallego-Álvarez and Pucheta-Martínez (2020b) | 2004–2015 | World | 12759 firm-year observations | Environmental disclosure | Determinants of disclosure | To investigate how cultural dimension, legal system and industry influence environmental disclosure | |

| | | | | | | | |
|---|---|---|---|---|---|---|---|
| García-Sánchez and Araújo-Bernardo (2020) | 2013, 2017, 2018 | Spain | 35 firms | | CSR disclosure | Determinants of disclosure | To investigate the level of managerial discretion in CSR disclosure, also considering mimetic isomorphism |
| Gerged et al. (2021) | 2010–2014 | World | 405 firms | | CSR disclosure | Effects of disclosure | To investigate how institutional factors influences CSR disclosure that, in turn, affects firm value |
| Khan et al. (2020) | 2001, 2006, 2011, 2017 | Pakistan | 29 firms | | CSR disclosure | Determinants of disclosure | To investigate how firm-specific characteristics and institutional factors influence CSR disclosure |
| Kilincarslan et al. (2020) | 2010–2017 | Middle East and Africa | 121 firms | | Environmental disclosure | Determinants of disclosure | To investigate the impact of board of directors' structure on environmental disclosure |
| Lewis et al. (2014) | 2002–2008 | USA | 589 firms | | Environmental disclosure | Determinants of disclosure | To investigate the influence of CEO characteristics on environmental disclosure in responses to institutional pressures |

(*Continued*)

**TABLE 2.4** Continued

| *Study* | *Year* | *Country* | *Sample* | *Type of disclosure* | *Aim of the study* | *Description of the aim* | *Other theory used* |
|---|---|---|---|---|---|---|---|
| Li et al. (2017) | 2012–2014 | China | 1179 firm-year observations | Environmental disclosure | Effects of disclosure | To investigate how environmental disclosure influences financial performance, and the moderating role of external government regulation and internal organisational slack | Agency theory |
| Loh et al. (2015) | 1995–2009 | Australia | 2 gambling firms | CSR disclosure | Content of disclosure | To investigate how three specific interrelated government initiatives influence CSR disclosure | Stakeholder theory, Legitimacy theory |
| Mateo-Márquez et al. (2021) | 2015 | World | 2327 firms | Environmental disclosure | Determinants of disclosure | To investigate how climate change-related institutional pillars influence environmental disclosure | |
| Muttakin and Subramaniam (2015) | 2007–2011 | India | 100 firms | CSR disclosure | Determinants of disclosure | To investigate whether firm owner-ship and board characteristics affect CSR disclosure | Agency theory |
| Oware and Awunyo-Vitor (2021) | 2010–2019 | India | 80 firms | Environmental disclosure | Determinants of disclosure | To investigate how CEO characteristics and reporting format influence environmental disclosure | Stakeholder theory |

| | | | | | | | |
|---|---|---|---|---|---|---|---|
| Pucheta-Martínez and Gallego-Álvarez (2018) | 2015 | World | 5293 firms | Environmental disclosure | Determinants of disclosure | To investigate whether institutional factors influence environmental disclosure | Stakeholder theory |
| Situ et al. (2020) | 2007–2011 | China | 180 firms | Environmental disclosure | Determinants of disclosure | To investigate how the government influences environmental disclosure | |
| Zeng et al. (2012) | 2006–2008 | China | 2361 firm-year observations | Environmental disclosure | Determinants of disclosure | To investigate how institutional and internal factors influence environmental disclosure | |

*Source*: Author's elaboration

**TABLE 2.5** Studies that investigated environmental disclosure using the signalling theory

| *Study* | *Year* | *Country* | *Sample* | *Type of disclosure* | *Aim of the study* | *Description of the aim* | *Other theory used* |
|---|---|---|---|---|---|---|---|
| Legendre and Coderre (2013) | 2009 | World | 253 firms | CSR disclosure | Determinants of disclosure | To investigate how size, profitability, country's business culture and industry influence the decision to adopt GRI and the level of GRI application | Legitimacy theory |
| Liu et al. (2021) | 2010–2018 | China | 781 firms | Environmental disclosure | Effects of disclosure | To investigate how environmental disclosure affects financial reporting quality | Stakeholder theory |
| Luo et al. (2019) | 2014–2016 | China | 842 firms | Environmental disclosure | Effects of disclosure | To investigate the impact of environmental disclosure and media attention on debt financing costs | |
| Paolone et al. (2021) | 2017–2018 | Italy | 122 firms | Environmental disclosure | Effects of disclosure | To investigate how environmental disclosure influences market value | |
| Zhou et al. (2018) | 2010–2015 | China | 334 firms | Environmental disclosure | Effects of disclosure | To investigate the impact of environmental disclosure on corporate risk-taking and the moderating role of organisational legitimacy | Legitimacy theory |

*Source*: Author's elaboration.

relationship between environmental disclosure and financial performance, finding that this institutional factor positively strengthens previous associations.

## 2.5 Signalling theory

Signalling theory focuses on firms' voluntary release of positive information to convey positive company attributes and reduce information asymmetry with external stakeholders (Connelly et al., 2011). According to the theory, good performers release environmental information to stakeholders to signal their good practices and results (Sun et al., 2010). Thus, companies can manage their reputation risk (Stern et al., 2014; Michelon, 2011), improve their corporate risk-taking (Zhou et al., 2018), and obtain more investments (Verrecchia, 1983). Providing environmental information encourages the reduction of investors' expectations of the company's forthcoming risks and therefore, boosts a decrease in financing costs (Liu et al., 2021).

Table 2.5 reports previous studies that investigated environmental disclosure using signalling theory. The table clarifies that Legendre and Coderre (2013) used signalling theory to investigate the determinants of environmental disclosure. Specifically, they investigated how industry influences environmental disclosure, showing that companies operating in environmentally sensitive industries receive more pressure from stakeholders. Therefore, they tend to release environmental information to reduce this pressure and manage their reputation risk.

The majority of studies used signalling theory to analyse the effects of disclosure. Liu et al. (2021), for example, used signalling theory to analyse how environmental disclosure affects financial reporting quality to signal good investment opportunities to investors. Similarly, other scholars found that the release of environmental disclosure decreases debt financing costs (Luo et al., 2019) and enhances market value (Paolone et al., 2021).

## Notes

1 EU Directive 51/2003 is a first attempt to introduce mandatory environmental disclosure by companies. In fact, it introduced a first requirement to provide environmental information, although it does not identify the specific data to release (Pisano and Alvino, 2015).
2 See Chapter 4 for an in-depth analysis of EU regulations aimed at boosting green investments.

## References

Abeysekera, I., Li, F., & Lu, Y. (2021). Financial disclosure quality and sustainability disclosure quality. A case in China. *Plos One*, 16(5), e0250884.

Adler, R., Mansi, M., & Pandey, R. (2022). Accounting for waste management: a study of the reporting practices of the top listed Indian companies. *Accounting & Finance*, 62(2), 2401–2437.

Akbar, S., & Deegan, C. (2021). Analysis of corporate social disclosures of the apparel industry following crisis: An institutional approach. *Accounting & Finance*, 61(2), 3565–3600.

Aladwey, L., Elgharbawy, A., & Ganna, M. A. (2022). Attributes of corporate boards and assurance of corporate social responsibility reporting: Evidence from the UK. *Corporate Governance: The International Journal of Business in Society*, 22(4), 748–780.

Alfraih, M. M. (2016). The effectiveness of board of directors' characteristics in mandatory disclosure compliance. *Journal of Financial Regulation and Compliance*, 24(2), 154–176.

Alipour, M., Ghanbari, M., Jamshidinavid, B., & Taherabadi, A. (2019). Does board independence moderate the relationship between environmental disclosure quality and performance? Evidence from static and dynamic panel data. *Corporate Governance: The International Journal of Business in Society*, 19(3), 580–610.

Antonini, C., Olczak, W., & Patten, D. M. (2021, April). Corporate climate change disclosure during the Trump administration: Evidence from standalone CSR reports. *In Accounting Forum*, 45(2), 118–141.

Barako, D. G., Hancock, P., & Izan, H. Y. (2006). Factors influencing voluntary corporate disclosure by Kenyan companies. *Corporate Governance: An International Review*, 14(2), 107–125.

Behl, A., Kumari, P. S., Makhija, H., & Sharma, D. (2022). Exploring the relationship of ESG score and firm value using cross-lagged panel analyses: Case of the Indian energy sector. Annals of Operations Research, 313(1), 231–256.

Beske, F., Haustein, E., & Lorson, P. C. (2020). Materiality analysis in sustainability and integrated reports. *Sustainability Accounting, Management and Policy Journal*, 11(1), 162–186.

Biswas, P. K., Roberts, H., & Whiting, R. H. (2019). The impact of family vs non-family governance contingencies on CSR reporting in Bangladesh. *Management Decision*, 57(10), 2758–2781.

Borgstedt, P., Nienaber, A. M., Liesenkötter, B., & Schewe, G. (2019). Legitimacy strategies in corporate environmental reporting: A longitudinal analysis of German DAX companies' disclosed objectives. *Journal of Business Ethics*, 158(1), 177–200.

Boura, M., Tsouknidis, D. A., & Lioukas, S. (2020). The role of pro-social orientation and national context in corporate environmental disclosure. *European Management Review*, 17(4), 1027–1040.

Brammer, S. & S. Pavelin (2006). Voluntary environmental disclosures by large UK companies. *Journal of Business Finance & Accounting*, 33(7–8), 1168–1188.

Burritt, R. L., Christ, K. L., & Omori, A. (2016). Drivers of corporate water-related disclosure: Evidence from Japan. *Journal of Cleaner Production*, 129, 65–74.

Campbell, J. L. (2007). Why would corporations behave in socially responsible ways? An institutional theory of corporate social responsibility. *Academy of Management Review*, 32(3), 946–967.

Chan, M. C., Watson, J., & Woodliff, D. (2014). Corporate governance quality and CSR disclosures. *Journal of Business Ethics*, 125(1), 59–73.

Chelli, M., Durocher, S., & Fortin, A. (2018). Normativity in environmental reporting: A comparison of three regimes. *Journal of Business Ethics*, 149(2), 285–311.

Chelli, M., Durocher, S., & Richard, J. (2014). France's new economic regulations: Insights from institutional legitimacy theory. *Accounting, Auditing & Accountability Journal*, 27(2), 283–316.

Ching, H. Y., & Gerab, F. (2017), Sustainability reports in Brazil through the lens of signaling, legitimacy and stakeholder theories. *Social Responsibility Journal*, 13(1), 95–110.

Chijoke-Mgbame, A. M., Mgbame, C. O., Akintoye, S., & Ohalehi, P. (2020). The role of corporate governance on CSR disclosure and firm performance in a voluntary environment. *Corporate Governance: The International Journal of Business in Society*, 20(2), 294–306.

Chiu, T. K., & Wang, Y. H. (2015). Determinants of social disclosure quality in Taiwan: An application of stakeholder theory. *Journal of Business Ethics*. 129(2), 379–398.

Cho, C. H. (2009). Legitimation strategies used in response to environmental disaster: A French case study of total SA's Erika and AZF incidents. *European Accounting Review*, 18(1), 33–62.

Cho, C. H., Freedman, M., & Patten, D. M. (2012). Corporate disclosure of environmental capital expenditures: A test of alternative theories. *Accounting, Auditing & Accountability Journal*, 25(3), 486–507.

Cho, C. H., Michelon, G., Patten, D. M., & Roberts, R. W. (2014), CSR report assurance in the USA: An empirical investigation of determinants and effects. *Sustainability Accounting, Management and Policy Journal*, 5(2), 130–148.

Cho, C. H., Michelon, G., Patten, D. M., & Roberts, R. W. (2015). CSR disclosure: The more things change…? *Accounting, Auditing & Accountability Journal*, 28(1), 14–35.

Cho, C. H., & Patten, D. M. (2007). The role of environmental disclosures as tools of legitimacy: A research note. *Accounting, Organizations and Society*, 32(7–8), 639–647.

Coetzee, C. M., & van Staden, C. J. (2011). Disclosure responses to mining accidents: South African evidence. *Accounting Forum*, 35(4), 232–246.

Connelly, B. L., Certo, S. T., Ireland, R. D., & Reutzel, C. R. (2011). Signalling theory: A review and assessment. *Journal of Management*, 37(1), 39–67.

Cormier, D., Gordon, I. M., & Magnan, M. (2004). Corporate environmental disclosure: Contrasting management's perceptions with reality. *Journal of Business Ethics*, 49(2), 143–165.

Cormier, D., & Magnan, M. (2015). The economic relevance of environmental disclosure and its impact on corporate legitimacy: An empirical investigation. Business Strategy and the Environment, 24(6), 431–450.

Costa, E., Pesci, C., Andreaus, M., & Taufer, E. (2019). Empathy, closeness, and distance in non-profit accountability. *Accounting, Auditing & Accountability Journal*, 32(1), 224–254.

Cowan, S., & Deegan, C. (2011). Corporate disclosure reactions to Australia's first national emission reporting scheme. *Accounting & Finance*, 51(2), 409–436.

Dagiliene, L., Frendzel, M., Sutiene, K., & Wnuk-Pel, T. (2020). Wise managers think about circular economy, wiser report and analyze it. Research of environmental reporting practices in EU manufacturing companies. *Journal of Cleaner Production*, 274, 121968.

D'Amico, E., Coluccia, D., Fontana, S., & Solimene, S. (2016). Factors influencing corporate environmental disclosure. *Business Strategy and the Environment*, 25(3), 178–192.

da Rocha Garcia, E. A., de Carvalho, G. M., Boaventura, J. M. G., & de Souza Filho, J. M. (2021). Determinants of corporate social performance disclosure: A literature review. *Social Responsibility Journal*, 17(4), 445–468.

Deegan, C. (2002). Introduction: The legitimising effect of social and environmental disclosures – a theoretical foundation. *Accounting, Auditing & Accountability Journal*, 15(3), 282–311.

Deegan, C. M. (2019). Legitimacy theory: Despite its enduring popularity and contribution, time is right for a necessary makeover. *Accounting, Auditing & Accountability Journal*, 32(8), 2307–2329.

Depoers, F., Jeanjean, T., & Jérôme, T. (2016). Voluntary disclosure of greenhouse gas emissions: Contrasting the carbon disclosure project and corporate reports. *Journal of Business Ethics*, 134(3), 445–461.

de Villiers, C., Low, M., & Samkin, G. (2014). The institutionalisation of mining company sustainability disclosures. *Journal of Cleaner Production*, 84, 51–58.

de Villiers, C., & Marques, A. (2016). Corporate social responsibility, country-level predispositions and the consequences of choosing a level of disclosure. *Accounting and Business Research*, 46(2), 167–195.

de Villiers, C., & Van Staden, C. J. (2006). Can less environmental disclosure have a legitimising effect? Evidence from Africa. *Accounting, Organizations and Society*, 31(8), 763–781.

DiMaggio, P., & Powell, W. W. (1983). The iron cage revisited: Collective rationality and institutional isomorphism in organisational fields. *American Sociological Review*, 48(2), 147–160.

Dong, S., Burritt, R., & Qian, W. (2014). Salient stakeholders in corporate social responsibility reporting by Chinese mining and minerals companies. *Journal of Cleaner Production*, 84, 59–69.

Dong, S., Xu, L., & McIver, R. (2021). China's financial sector sustainability and "green finance" disclosures. *Sustainability Accounting, Management and Policy Journal*, 12(2), 353–384.

Dowling, J., Pfeffer, J. (1975). Organisational legitimacy: Social values and organisational behavior. *Pacific Sociological Review*, 18(1), 122–136.

du Toit, E. (2017). The readability of integrated reports. Meditari Accountancy Research, 25(4), 629–653.

Fama, E. F., & Jensen, M. C. (1983). Separation of ownership and control. *The Journal of Law and Economics*, 26(2), 301–325.

Fernandes, S. M., Bornia, A. C., & Nakamura, L. R. (2019). The influence of boards of directors on environmental disclosure. *Management Decision*, 57(9), 2358–2382.

Fernández-Gago, R., Cabeza-García, L., & Nieto, M. (2018). Independent directors' background and CSR disclosure. *Corporate Social Responsibility and Environmental Management*, 25(5), 991–1001.

Fifka, M. S., & Pobizhan, M. (2014). An institutional approach to corporate social responsibility in Russia. *Journal of Cleaner Production*, 82, 192–201.

Freeman, E. (1984). *Strategic management: A stakeholder approach*. Boston, USA: Pitman Press.

Frías-Aceituno, J. V., Rodríguez-Ariza, L., & García-Sánchez, I. M. (2013). Is integrated reporting determined by a country's legal system? An exploratory study. *Journal of Cleaner Production*, 44, 45–55.

Fuhrmann, S. (2020). A multi-theoretical approach on drivers of integrated reporting– uniting firm-level and country-level associations. *Meditari Accountancy Research*, 28(1), 168–205.

Gallego-Alvarez, I., Ortas, E., Vicente-Villardón, J. L., & Alvarez Etxeberria, I. (2017). Institutional constraints, stakeholder pressure and corporate environmental reporting policies. *Business Strategy and the Environment*, 26(6), 807–825.

Gallego-Álvarez, I., & Pucheta-Martínez, M. C. (2020a). Environmental strategy in the global banking industry within the varieties of capitalism approach: The moderating role of gender diversity and board members with specific skills. *Business Strategy and the Environment*, 29(2), 347–360.

Gallego-Álvarez, I., & Pucheta-Martínez, M. C. (2020b). How cultural dimensions, legal systems, and industry affect environmental reporting? Empirical evidence from an international perspective. *Business Strategy and the Environment*, 29(5), 2037–2057.

Gao, F., Dong, Y., Ni, C., &Fu, R. (2016). Determinants and economic consequences of non-financial disclosure quality. *European Accounting Review*, 25(2), 287–317.

Garanina, T., & Aray, Y. (2021). Enhancing CSR disclosure through foreign ownership, foreign board members, and cross-listing: Does it work in Russian context? *Emerging Markets Review*, 46, 100754.

García-Sánchez, I. M., & Araújo-Bernardo, C. A. (2020). What colour is the corporate social responsibility report? Structural visual rhetoric, impression management strategies, and stakeholder engagement. *Corporate Social Responsibility and Environmental Management*, 27(2), 1117–1142.

Garcia-Sanchez, I. M., Cuadrado-Ballesteros, B., & Sepulveda, C. (2014). Does media pressure moderate CSR disclosures by external directors? *Management Decision*, 52(6), 1014–1045.

García-Sánchez, I. M., Frías-Aceituno, J. V., & Rodríguez-Domínguez, L. (2013). Determinants of corporate social disclosure in Spanish local governments. *Journal of Cleaner Production*, 39, 60–72.

García-Sánchez, I. M., Hussain, N., Aibar-Guzmán, C., & Aibar-Guzmán, B. (2022). Assurance of corporate social responsibility reports: Does it reduce decoupling practices? *Business Ethics, the Environment & Responsibility*, 31(1), 118–138.

García-Sánchez, I. M., Hussain, N., Martínez-Ferrero, J., & Ruiz-Barbadillo, E. (2019). Impact of disclosure and assurance quality of corporate sustainability reports on access to finance. *Corporate Social Responsibility and Environmental Management*, 26(4), 832–848.

Garde Sánchez, R., Rodríguez Bolívar, M. P., & López Hernández, A. M. (2017). Corporate and managerial characteristics as drivers of social responsibility disclosure by state-owned enterprises. *Review of Managerial Science*, 11(3), 633–659.

Gerged, A. M. (2021). Factors affecting corporate environmental disclosure in emerging markets: The role of corporate governance structures. *Business Strategy and the Environment*, 30(1), 609–629.

Gerged, A. M., Beddewela, E., & Cowton, C. J. (2021). Is corporate environmental disclosure associated with firm value? A multicountry study of Gulf Cooperation Council firms. *Business Strategy and the Environment*, 30(1), 185–203.

Gray, R., Javad, M., Power, D. M., & Sinclair, C. D. (2001). Social and environmental disclosure and corporate characteristics: A research note and extension. *Journal of Business Finance & Accounting*, 28(3-4), 327–356.

Gray, R., Kouhy, R., & Lavers, S. (1995). Corporate social and environmental reporting corporate social and environmental reporting: A review of the literature and a longitudinal study of UK disclosure. *Accounting, Auditing & Accountability Journal*, 8(2), 47–77.

Gray, R., Owen, D., & Adams, C. (1996). *Accounting & accountability: Changes and Challenges in Corporate Social and Environmental Reporting*, Upper Saddle River, NJ: Prentice Hall.

Guenther, E., Guenther, T., Schiemann, F., & Weber, G. (2016). Stakeholder relevance for reporting: Explanatory factors of carbon disclosure. *Business & Society*, 55(3), 361–397.

Guthrie, J., & Parker, L. D. (1989), Corporate social reporting: A rebuttal of legitimacy theory. *Accounting and Business Research*, 19(76), 343–352.

Hamrouni, A., Uyar, A., & Boussaada, R. (2020). Are corporate social responsibility disclosures relevant for lenders? Empirical evidence from France. *Management Decision*, 58(2), 267–279.

Hawley, A. (1968). Human ecology. In David L. Sills (Ed.), *International encyclopedia of the social sciences* (pp. 328–337). New York: Macmillan.

Hickman, L. E. (2020). Information asymmetry in CSR reporting: Publicly-traded versus privately-held firms. *Sustainability Accounting, Management and Policy Journal*, 11(1), 207–232.

Hossain, M. M., Momin, M. A., Rowe, A. L., & Quaddus, M. (2017). Corporate social and environmental reporting practices: A case of listed companies in Bangladesh. *Sustainability Accounting, Management and Policy Journal*, 8(2), 138–165.

Huang, C. L., & Kung, F. H. (2010). Drivers of environmental disclosure and stakeholder expectation: Evidence from Taiwan. *Journal of Business Ethics*, 96(3), 435–451.

Hussain, N., Rigoni, U., & Orij, R. P. (2018). Corporate governance and sustainability performance: Analysis of triple bottom line performance. *Journal of Business Ethics*, 149(2), 411–432.

Injeni, G., Mangena, M., Mathuva, D., & Mudida, R. (2021). Agency and institutional-related factors and the heterogeneity of sustainability and integrated report information disclosures in Kenya. *Journal of Financial Reporting and Accounting*, ahead-of-print.

Islam, M. A., & Deegan, C. (2010). Media pressures and corporate disclosure of social responsibility performance information: A study of two global clothing and sports retail companies. *Accounting and Business Research*, 40(2), 131–148.

Ismail, N. B., Alcouffe, S., Galy, N., & Ceulemans, K. (2021). The impact of international sustainability initiatives on Life Cycle Assessment voluntary disclosures: The case of France's CAC40 listed companies. *Journal of Cleaner Production*, 282, 124456.

Jensen, M. C., & Meckling, W. H. (1976). Theory of the firm: Managerial behavior, agency costs and ownership structure. *Journal of Financial Economics*, 3(4), 305–360.

Jeriji, M., & Louhichi, W. (2021). The relationship between poor CSR performance and hard, negative CSR information disclosures. *Sustainability Accounting, Management and Policy Journal*, 12(2), 410–436.

Jizi, M. I., Salama, A., Dixon, R., & Stratling, R. (2014). Corporate governance and corporate social responsibility disclosure: Evidence from the US banking sector. *Journal of Business Ethics*, 125(4), 601–615.

Kalu, J. U., Buang, A., & Aliagha, G. U. (2016). Determinants of voluntary carbon disclosure in the corporate real estate sector of Malaysia. *Journal of Environmental Management*, 182, 519–524.

Karaman, A. S., Kilic, M., & Uyar, A. (2018). Sustainability reporting in the aviation industry: Worldwide evidence. *Sustainability Accounting, Management and Policy Journal*, 9(4), 362–391.

Katmon, N., Mohamad, Z. Z., Norwani, N. M., & Al Farooque, O. (2019). Comprehensive board diversity and quality of corporate social responsibility disclosure: Evidence from an emerging market. *Journal of Business Ethics*, 157(2), 447–481.

Kaymak, T., & Bektas, E. (2017). Corporate social responsibility and governance: Information disclosure in multinational corporations. *Corporate Social Responsibility and Environmental Management*, 24(6), 555–569.

Khan, M., Lockhart, J., & Bathurst, R. (2020). A multi-level institutional perspective of corporate social responsibility reporting: A mixed-method study. *Journal of Cleaner Production*, 265, 121739.

Kılıç, M., & Kuzey, C. (2019). Determinants of climate change disclosures in the Turkish banking industry. *International Journal of Bank Marketing*, 37(3), 901–926.

Kilincarslan, E., Elmagrhi, M. H., & Li, Z. (2020). Impact of governance structures on environmental disclosures in the Middle East and Africa. *Corporate Governance: The International Journal of Business in Society*, 20(4), 739–763.

Kouloukoui, D., Sant'Anna, Â. M. O., da Silva Gomes, S. M., de Oliveira Marinho, M. M., de Jong, P., Kiperstok, A., & Torres, E. A. (2019). Factors influencing the level of environmental disclosures in sustainability reports: Case of climate risk disclosure by Brazilian companies. *Corporate Social Responsibility and Environmental Management*, 26(4), 791–804.

La Porta, R., Lopez-de-Silanes, F., Shleifer, A., & Vishny, R. W. (1998). Law and finance. *Journal of Political Economy*, 106(6), 1113–1155.

Legendre, S., & Coderre, F. (2013). Determinants of GRI G3 application levels: The case of the fortune global 500. *Corporate Social Responsibility and Environmental Management*, 20(3), 182–192.

Lewis, B. W., Walls, J. L., & Dowell, G. W. (2014). Difference in degrees: CEO characteristics and firm environmental disclosure. *Strategic Management Journal*, 35(5), 712–722.

Li, D., Cao, C., Zhang, L., Chen, X., Ren, S., & Zhao, Y. (2017). Effects of corporate environmental responsibility on financial performance: The moderating role of government regulation and organizational slack. *Journal of Cleaner Production*, 166, 1323–1334.

Liao, L., Lin, T. P., & Zhang, Y. (2018). Corporate board and corporate social responsibility assurance. *Journal of Business Ethics*, 150(1), 211–225.

Liesen, A., Hoepner, A. G., Patten, D. M., & Figge, F. (2015). Does stakeholder pressure influence corporate GHG emissions reporting? Empirical evidence from Europe. *Accounting, Auditing & Accountability Journal*, 28(7), 1047–1074.

Lindblom, C. (1993). *The Implications of organizational legitimacy for corporate social performance and disclosure*. Critical Perspectives on Accounting Conference, Nueva York, EUA.

Liu, X., & Anbumozhi, V. (2009). Determinant factors of corporate environmental information disclosure: An empirical study of Chinese listed companies. *Journal of Cleaner Production*, 17(6), 593–600.

Liu, C., Su, K., & Zhang, M. (2021). Water disclosure and financial reporting quality for social changes: Empirical evidence from China. *Technological Forecasting and Social Change*, 166, 120571.

Lodhia, S., & Jacobs, K. (2013). The practice turn in environmental reporting: A study into current practices in two Australian commonwealth departments. *Accounting, Auditing & Accountability Journal*, 26(4), 595–615.

Loh, C. M., Deegan, C., & Inglis, R. (2015). The changing trends of corporate social and environmental disclosure within the Australian gambling industry. *Accounting & Finance*, 55(3), 783–823.

Lu, Y., & Abeysekera, I. (2014). Stakeholders' power, corporate characteristics, and social and environmental disclosure: Evidence from China. *Journal of Cleaner Production*, 64, 426–436.

Luo, W., Guo, X., Zhong, S., & Wang, J. (2019). Environmental information disclosure quality, media attention and debt financing costs: Evidence from Chinese heavy polluting listed companies. *Journal of Cleaner Production*, 231, 268–277.

Maama, H. (2021). Achieving Financial Sustainability in Ghana's Banking Sector: Is Environmental, Social and Governance Reporting Contributive? *Global Business Review*, 09721509211044300.

Mahjoub, L. B., & Khamoussi, H. (2013). Environmental and social policy and earning persistence. *Business Strategy and the Environment*, 22(3), 159–172.

Mallin, C., Michelon, G., & Raggi, D. (2013). Monitoring intensity and stakeholders' orientation: How does governance affect social and environmental disclosure? *Journal of Business Ethics*, 114(1), 29–43.

Mata, C., Fialho, A., & Eugénio, T. (2018). A decade of environmental accounting reporting: What we know? *Journal of Cleaner Production*, 198, 1198–1209.

Mateo-Márquez, A. J., González-González, J. M., & Zamora-Ramírez, C. (2021). The influence of countries' climate change-related institutional profile on voluntary environmental disclosures. *Business Strategy and the Environment*, 30(2), 1357–1373.

Michelon, G. (2011). Sustainability disclosure and reputation: A comparative study. *Corporate Reputation Review*, 14(2), 79–96.

Mio, C., Fasan, M., Marcon, C., & Panfilo, S. (2020). The predictive ability of legitimacy and agency theory after the implementation of the EU directive on non-financial information. *Corporate Social Responsibility and Environmental Management*, 27(6), 2465–2476.

Miras-Rodriguez, M. D. M., & Di Pietra, R. (2018). Corporate governance mechanisms as drivers that enhance the credibility and usefulness of CSR disclosure. *Journal of Management and Governance*, 22(3), 565–588.

Mitchell, R. K., Agle, B. R., & Wood, D. J. (1997). Toward a theory of stakeholder identification and salience: Defining the principle of who and what really counts. *Academy of Management Review*, 22, 853–886.

Moseñe, J. A., Burritt, R. L., Sanagustín, M. V., Moneva, J. M., & Tingey-Holyoak, J. (2013). Environmental reporting in the Spanish wind energy sector: An institutional view. *Journal of Cleaner Production*, 40, 199–211.

Muttakin, M. B., & Subramaniam, N. (2015). Firm ownership and board characteristics: Do they matter for corporate social responsibility disclosure of Indian companies? *Sustainability Accounting, Management and Policy Journal*, 6(2), 138–165.

Naseem, M. A., Lin, J., Rehman, R. U., Ahmad, M. I., & Ali, R. (2019). Moderating role of financial ratios in corporate social responsibility disclosure and firm value. *PloS One*, 14(4), e0215430.

Oliveira, L., Rodrigues, L. L., & Craig, R. (2010), Intellectual Capital reporting in sustainability reports. *Journal of Intellectual Capital*, 11(4), 575–594.

Ortas, E., Gallego-Alvarez, I., & Álvarez Etxeberria, I. (2015). Financial factors influencing the quality of corporate social responsibility and environmental management disclosure: A quantile regression approach. *Corporate Social Responsibility and Environmental Management*, 22(6), 362–380.

Oware, K. M., & Awunyo-Vitor, D. (2021). CEO characteristics and environmental disclosure of listed firms in an emerging economy: Does sustainability reporting format matter? *Business Strategy & Development*, 4(4), 399–410.

Oware, K. M., Iddrisu, A. A., Worae, T., & Adaletey, J. E. (2021). Female and environmental disclosure of family and non-family firms. Evidence from India. *Management Research Review.*

Patten, D. M. (2020). Seeking legitimacy. *Sustainability Accounting, Management and Policy Journal*, 11(6), 1009–1021.

Paolone, F., Granà, F., Martiniello, L., & Tiscini, R. (2021). Environmental risk indicators disclosure and value relevance: An empirical analysis of Italian listed companies after the implementation of the Legislative Decree 254/2016. *Corporate Social Responsibility and Environmental Management*, 28(5), 1471–1482.

Pellegrino, C., & Lodhia, S. (2012). Climate change accounting and the Australian mining industry: Exploring the links between corporate disclosure and the generation of legitimacy. *Journal of Cleaner Production*, 36, 68–82.

Pérez, A., López, C., & del Mar García-De los Salmones, M. (2017). An empirical exploration of the link between reporting to stakeholders and corporate social responsibility reputation in the Spanish context. *Accounting, Auditing & Accountability Journal*, 30(3), 668–698.

Pisano, S. & Alvino, F. (2015). New European Union's requirements and IFRS practice statement "Management Commentary": Does MD&A disclosure quality affect analysts' forecasts? *Journal of Modern Accounting and Auditing*, 11(6), 283–301.

Pitrakkos, P., & Maroun, W. (2020). Evaluating the quality of carbon disclosures. *Sustainability Accounting, Management and Policy Journal*, 11(3), 553–589.

Pucheta-Martínez, M. C., & Gallego-Álvarez, I. (2018). Environmental reporting policy and corporate structures: An international analysis. *Corporate Social Responsibility and Environmental Management*, 25(5), 788–798.

Pucheta-Martínez, M. C., & López-Zamora, B. (2018). Engagement of directors representing institutional investors on environmental disclosure. *Corporate Social Responsibility and Environmental Management*, 25(6), 1108–1120.

Radhouane, I., Nekhili, M., Nagati, H., & Paché, G. (2018). Customer-related performance and the relevance of environmental reporting. *Journal of Cleaner Production*, 190, 315–329.

Radu, C., & Francoeur, C. (2017). Does innovation drive environmental disclosure? A new insight into sustainable development. *Business Strategy and the Environment*, 26(7), 893–911.

Rezaee, Z., Alipour, M., Faraji, O., Ghanbari, M., & Jamshidinavid, B. (2021). Environmental disclosure quality and risk: The moderating effect of corporate governance. *Sustainability Accounting, Management and Policy Journal*, 12(4), 733–766.

Roe, M. J. (1991). A political theory of American corporate finance. *Columbia Law Review*, 91(1), 10–67.

Sannino, G., Lucchese, M., Zampone, G., & Lombardi, R. (2020). Cultural dimensions, Global Reporting Initiatives commitment, and corporate social responsibility issues: New evidence from Organisation for Economic Co-operation and Development banks. *Corporate Social Responsibility and Environmental Management*, 27(4), 1653–1663.

Schiehll, E., & Kolahgar, S. (2021). Financial materiality in the informativeness of sustainability reporting. *Business Strategy and the Environment*, 30(2), 840–855.

Sigurdsson, K., & Candi, M. (2020). Saying and doing: Social responsibility declared and applied. *Creativity and Innovation Management*, 29(1), 128–140.

Situ, H., Tilt, C. A., & Seet, P. S. (2020). The influence of the government on corporate environmental reporting in China: An authoritarian capitalism perspective. *Business & Society*, 59(8), 1589–1629.

Stanny, E. (2013). Voluntary disclosures of emissions by US firms. *Business Strategy and the Environment*, 22(3), 145–158.

Stern, I., Dukerich, J. M., & Zajac, E. (2014). Unmixed signals: How reputation and status affect alliance formation. *Strategic Management Journal*, 35(4), 512–531.

Stubbs, W., Higgins, C., & Milne, M. (2013). Why do companies not produce sustainability reports? *Business Strategy and the Environment*, 22(7), 456–470.

Suchman, M. C. (1995). Managing legitimacy: Strategic and institutional approaches. *Academy of Management Review*, 20(3), 571–610.

Sun, N., Salama, A., Hussainey, K., & Habbash, M. (2010). Corporate environmental disclosure, corporate governance and earnings management. *Managerial Auditing Journal*, 25(7), 679–700.

Thorne, L., Mahoney, L. S., & Manetti, G. (2014), Motivations for issuing standalone CSR reports: A survey of Canadian firms. *Accounting, Auditing and Accountability Journal*, 27, 686–714.

Tibiletti, V., Marchini, P. L., Furlotti, K., & Medioli, A. (2021). Does corporate governance matter in corporate social responsibility disclosure? Evidence from Italy in the "era of sustainability". *Corporate Social Responsibility and Environmental Management*, 28(2), 896–907.

Tilling, M. V., & Tilt, C. A. (2010). The edge of legitimacy: Voluntary social and environmental reporting in Rothmans' 1956-1999 annual reports. *Accounting, Auditing & Accountability Journal*, 23(1), 55–81.

Torelli, R., Balluchi, F., & Furlotti, K. (2020). The materiality assessment and stakeholder engagement: A content analysis of sustainability reports. *Corporate Social Responsibility and Environmental Management*, 27(2), 470–484.

Tyson, T., & Adams, C. A. (2020). Increasing the scope of assurance research: New lines of inquiry and novel theoretical perspectives. *Sustainability Accounting, Management and Policy Journal*, 11(2), 291–316.

Ullmann, A. A. (1985). Data in search of a theory: A critical examination of the relationship among social performance, social disclosure, and economic performance of U.S. Firms. *Academy of Management Review*, 10(3), 540–557.

Verrecchia, R. E. (1983). Discretionary disclosure. *Journal of Accounting and Economics*, 5, 179–194.

Vitolla, F., Raimo, N., Rubino, M., & Garzoni, A. (2019). How pressure from stakeholders affects integrated reporting quality. *Corporate Social Responsibility and Environmental Management*, 26(6), 1591–1606.

Weber, O. (2014). Environmental, social and governance reporting in China. *Business Strategy and the Environment*, 23(5), 303–317.

Yang, H., Le Luo, L., & Bhattacharyya, A. (2021). Mandatory environmental reporting in Australia: An in-depth analysis of quantity and quality. *Abacus*, 57(4), 737–779.

Yook, K. H., Song, H., Patten, D. M., & Kim, I. W. (2017). The disclosure of environmental conservation costs and its relation to eco-efficiency: Evidence from Japan. *Sustainability Accounting, Management and Policy Journal*, 8(1), 20–42.

Zaid, M. A., Abuhijleh, S. T., & Pucheta-Martínez, M. C. (2020). Ownership structure, stakeholder engagement, and corporate social responsibility policies: The moderating effect of board independence. *Corporate Social Responsibility and Environmental Management*, 27(3), 1344–1360.

Zeng, S. X., Xu, X. D., Yin, H. T., & Tam, C. M. (2012). Factors that drive Chinese listed companies in voluntary disclosure of environmental information. *Journal of Business Ethics*, 109(3), 309–321.

Zharfpeykan, R. (2021). Representative account or greenwashing? Voluntary sustainability reports in Australia's mining/metals and financial services industries. *Business Strategy and the Environment*, 30(4), 2209–2223.

Zhou, Z., Liu, L., Zeng, H., & Chen, X. (2018). Does water disclosure cause a rise in corporate risk-taking? – Evidence from Chinese high water-risk industries. *Journal of Cleaner Production*, 195, 1313–1325.

# 3

# DETERMINANTS AND EFFECTS OF ENVIRONMENTAL DISCLOSURE

Research conducted on environmental disclosure mainly developed empirical models useful in explaining the factors influencing the release of environmental information or effects of such data on external stakeholders. While most studies analysed the determinants of a company's decision to provide environmental disclosure (Zhang and Liu, 2020; Mata et al., 2018), few studies address the effects of such information.

## 3.1 Determinants of disclosure

Studies investigating the determinants of disclosure mainly conducted an empirical analysis, with environmental disclosure as the dependent variable. To measure environmental disclosure, most scholars used data collected by databases such as Bloomberg ESG (Delgado-Márquez and Pedauga, 2017), Thomson Reuters Eikon (e.g. Pucheta-Martínez and Gallego-Álvarez, 2018), and GRI Sustainability Disclosure (e.g. Alberici and Querci, 2016). Other studies employed diffused scores such as the carbon disclosure score (Hsueh, 2019), and some assessed environmental disclosure based on the preparation of CSR reports following the GRI and level of adherence to these standards (e.g. Fernández-Gago et al., 2018). However, most research has measured environmental disclosure by content analysing company documents (e.g. Dinca et al., 2019; Vormedal and Ruud, 2009).

The factors affecting environmental disclosure can be categorised in two groups: (1) internal or firm-specific, and (2) external or institutional.

### *3.1.1 Internal or firm-specific factors*

Internal factors typically investigated in the literature include company characteristics such as size, profitability, industry, leverage, and corporate governance

DOI: 10.4324/9781003245933-4

characteristics. Next, for each variable, we briefly describe the theoretical framework used in hypothesising the relationship with environmental disclosure, proxies to measure the variable, and main findings of previous studies investigating the association. For some variables such as company size, scholars refer to different theories to formulate hypotheses (Fuhrmann, 2020). In these cases, we briefly describe all theoretical frameworks. Table 3.1 reports the sign and significance of the regression coefficients of the relationship between internal or firm-specific factors and environmental disclosure.

### *3.1.1.1 Company characteristics*

#### 3.1.1.1.1 Size

Size is the most investigated determinant of environmental disclosure. Most studies investigated the relationship between company size and environmental disclosure with reference to legitimacy or stakeholder theories. The main argument is that larger companies, which attract interest from a multitude of stakeholder groups, release more data because of their greater visibility (de Villiers et al., 2014). In other words, larger companies disclose more information because they are under greater scrutiny from external stakeholders. Legitimacy theory suggests that bigger companies must release more information to satisfy the social expectations of a multitude of stakeholders (D'Amico et al., 2016). In addition, larger companies have more resources to invest in the communication process because of their size (Skouloudis et al., 2014). Therefore, they are able to release more information, in addition to the mandatory data required by law, spending lower costs than smaller companies (D'Amico et al., 2016).

Stakeholder theory suggests that company size is used as a proxy for different stakeholder pressures. Researchers apply this theory to investigate how different stakeholder pressures and interests, computed using company size, influence the level and quality of environmental disclosure. For example, Huang and Kung (2010) used company size to measure government pressure.

The relationship between company size and environmental disclosure is also studied based on agency theory. According to this theoretical framework, larger companies tend to release higher levels of environmental disclosure to reduce the higher agency costs derived from the stronger information asymmetries between the principal and agent (Jensen and Meckling, 1976).

Independent of the theoretical framework used, all the studies hypothesised a positive association between company size and environmental disclosure. Most research measured company size using total assets (e.g. Karaman et al., 2018) or the natural logarithm of total assets (e.g. Abeysekera et al., 2021; Garanina and Aray, 2021; Fernandez-Gago et al., 2018). However, scholars have also used other measures such as the total number of employees (e.g. Sánchez et al., 2017; Gray et al., 2001), market capitalisation (e.g. Chan et al., 2014), company revenues (e.g. Mio et al., 2020), and the natural logarithm of total sales (e.g. Ismail

**TABLE 3.1** Studies that investigated the internal or firm-specific factors influencing environmental disclosure

| Study | Year | Country | Dependent variable | *Determinants (Sign and significance of the regression coefficients)* | | | | | | | | | | | | |
|---|---|---|---|---|---|---|---|---|---|---|---|---|---|---|---|---|
| | | | | *Company characteristics* | | | | *Ownership structure* | | | *Board of directors' composition* | | | | | |
| | | | | *SIZE* | *PROF* | *IND* | *LEV* | *FAM* | *OUTINV* | *OWCON* | *BSIZE* | *BIND* | *BGDIV* | *CEOD* | *BMEET* | *CSRC* |
| Abeysekera et al. (2021) | 2008 | China | CSRdisc | + | | | ns | | | | | | | | | |
| Antonini et al. (2021) | 2014–2015, 2017–2018 | USA | ED | ns | | + | | | | | | | | | | |
| Balluchi et al. (2021) | 2017 | Italy | ED | ns | ns | | ns | | | | | | | | | |
| Biswas et al. (2019) | 1996–2011 | Bangladesh | CSRdisc | + | + | + | ns | - | ns | | + | ns | | + | | |
| Boura et al. (2020) | 2002–2012 | World | ED | + | + | + | | | | | | | | | | |
| Burritt et al. (2016) | 2013–2014 | Japan | ED | + | ns | + | | | | - | | | | | | |
| Chan et al. (2014) | 2004 | Australia | CSRdisc | + | ns | + | + | | | ns | | | | | | |
| Chiu and Wang (2015) | 2010–2011 | Taiwan | CSRdisc | + | ns | | ns | | | | | | | | | |
| Cho et al. (2012) | 1996–2005 | USA | ED | ns | ns | + | ns | | | | | | | | | |
| Cho et al. (2015) | 1977, 2010 | USA | CSRdisc | + | + | | - | | | | | | | | | |
| Cormier et al. (2004) | 2000 | World | ED | ns | ns | | ns | | | | | | | | | |
| D'Amico et al. (2016) | 2006 and 2009 | Italy | ED | + | + | + | + | | + | - | | | | | | |
| Fernández-Gago et al. (2018) | 2009–2014 | Spain | CSRdisc | + | + | ns | ns | | | | + | ns | | | | |

(*Continued*)

**TABLE 3.1** Continued

| Study | Year | Country | Dependent variable | Determinants (Sign and significance of the regression coefficients) | | | | | | | | | | | | |
|---|---|---|---|---|---|---|---|---|---|---|---|---|---|---|---|---|
| | | | | *Company characteristics* | | | | *Ownership structure* | | | *Board of directors' composition* | | | | | |
| | | | | *SIZE* | *PROF* | *IND* | *LEV* | *FAM* | *OUTINV* | *OWCON* | *BSIZE* | *BIND* | *BGDIV* | *CEOD* | *BMEET* | *CSRC* |
| Fuhrmann (2020) | 2012–2016 | World | CSRdisc | ns | - | | - | | | | | | | | | |
| Gallego-Álvarez and Pucheta-Martínez (2020a) | 2005–2016 | World | ED | ns | ns | | | | | | - | ns | ns | + | | + |
| Gallego-Álvarez and Pucheta-Martínez (2020b) | 2004–2015 | World | ED | ns | +/- | | ns | | | | + | + | | | | + |
| Gallego-Alvarez et al. (2017) | | World | ED | + | ns | + | ns | | | | | | | | | |
| Garanina and Aray (2021) | 2012–2015 | Russia | CSRdisc | + | ns | + | ns | | - | | + | ns | ns | | | |
| Garcia-Sanchez et al. (2014) | 2004–2010 | Spain | CSRdisc | + | ns | | | | | | ns | + | + | | ns | |
| García-Sánchez et al. (2022) | 2002–2017 | World | CSRdisc | + | + | ns | ns | | + | | - | ns | + | ns | ns | ns |
| Garde Sánchez et al. (2017) | 2015 | Spain | CSRdisc | + | | + | | | ns | | | | ns | | | |
| Gerged 2021 | 2010–2014 | Jordan | ED | - | + | | + | | +/- | - | + | + | | + | | |
| Gray et al. (2001) | 1988–1995 | UK | CSRdisc | + | + | | | | | | | | | | | |

| | | | | | | | | | | | | | | | |
|---|---|---|---|---|---|---|---|---|---|---|---|---|---|---|---|
| Huang and Kung (2010) | 2003–2005 | Taiwan | ED | + | - | + | + | | - | | | | | | |
| Hussain et al. (2018) | 2007–2011 | USA | CSRdisc | ns | + | ns | ns | | | ns | + | ns | - | ns | + |
| Injeni et al. (2021) | 2010–2018 | Kenya | CSRdisc | + | ns | + | ns | + | ns | | ns | + | | | |
| Ismail et al. (2021) | 2002–2014 | France | ED | ns | ns | ns | ns | | | | | | | | |
| Jeriji and Louhichi 2021 | 2013–2016 | World | CSRdisc | + | + | + | - | + | ns | - | - | | | - | |
| Jizi et al. (2014) | 2009–2011 | USA | CSRdisc | + | + | | ns | | | + | + | | + | + | |
| Karaman et al. (2018) | 2006–2015 | World | CSRdisc | + | ns | | + | | + | | | | | | |
| Katmon et al. (2019) | 2009–2013 | Malaysia | CSRdisc | + | | + | + | | | ns | + | ns | | + | |
| Kaymak and Bektas (2017) | | World | CSRdisc | ns | ns | - | | | | ns | + | | ns | | |
| Kılıç and Kuzey (2019) | 2010–2016 | Turkey | ED | + | + | | | - | - | | | | | | |
| Kilincarslan et al. (2020) | 2010–2017 | Middle East and Africa | ED | + | - | + | - | - | | ns | - | + | + | | |
| Kouloukoui et al. (2019) | 2009–2014 | Brazil | ED | + | + | ns | - | | | | | | | | |
| Legendre and Coderre (2013) | 2009 | World | CSRdisc | ns | ns | - | | | | | | | | | |

*(Continued)*

**TABLE 3.1** Continued

| *Study* | *Year* | *Country* | *Dependent variable* | *Determinants (Sign and significance of the regression coefficients)* | | | | | | | | | | | | |
|---|---|---|---|---|---|---|---|---|---|---|---|---|---|---|---|---|
| | | | | *Company characteristics* | | | | *Ownership structure* | | | *Board of directors' composition* | | | | | |
| | | | | *SIZE* | *PROF* | *IND* | *LEV* | *FAM* | *OUTINV* | *OWCON* | *BSIZE* | *BIND* | *BGDIV* | *CEOD* | *BMEET* | *CSRC* |
| Liesen et al. (2015) | 2005–2009 | Europe | ED | + | + | + | ns | | ns | | | | | | | |
| Liu and Anbumozhi (2009) | 2006 | China | ED | + | ns | + | ns | | | ns | | | | | | |
| Mateo-Márquez et al. (2021) | 2015 | World | ED | + | ns | | ns | | | | | | | | | |
| Mio et al. (2020) | 2016–2017 | EU countries | CSRdisc | + | ns | + | ns | | | - | + | | | | | |
| Muttakin and Subramaniam (2015) | 2007–2011 | India | CSRdisc | + | + | + | - | | + | | | + | | - | | |
| Ortas et al. (2015) | 2010 | World | CSRdisc | + | ns | +/- | ns | | | | | | | | | |
| Oware and Awunyo-Vitor (2021) | 2010–2019 | India | ED | + | | ns | + | | | | ns | ns | | | | ns |
| Oware et al. (2022) | 2009–2020 | India | ED | ns | | | ns | | | | | | ns | | | |
| Pucheta-Martínez and Gallego-Álvarez (2018) | 2015 | World | ED | + | - | + | ns | | | - | | | | | | |

| | | | | | | | | | | | | | | | | |
|---|---|---|---|---|---|---|---|---|---|---|---|---|---|---|---|---|
| Pucheta-Martínez and López-Zamora (2018) | 2004–2013 | Spain | ED | + | ns | ns | + | | | | | ns | + | | | ns |
| Radu and Francoeur (2017) | 2011 | USA | ED | + | ns | ns | ns | | | | | | | | | |
| Sannino et al. (2020) | 2012–2018 | World | CSRdisc | + | ns | | ns | | | | | | | | | |
| Tibiletti et al. (2021) | 2008, 2011, 2016 | Italy | CSRdisc | - | ns | | | | | | | ns | - | | - | |
| Torelli et al. (2020) | 2017 | Italy | CSRdisc | ns | ns | - | ns | | | | | | | | | |
| Yook et al. (2017) | 2002–2012 | Japan | ED | ns | | | - | | | | | | | | | |
| Zaid et al. (2020) | 2013–2018 | Palestine | CSRdisc | + | + | + | + | | + | | | + | + | | | |
| Zeng et al. (2012) | 2006–2008 | China | ED | + | ns | + | + | | + | | | | | | | |

*Source*: Author's elaboration

*Notes*: + = positive and significant, - = negative and significant, ns = no significant, CSRdisc = CSR disclosure, ED = Environmental Disclosure, SIZE = Firm Size, PROF = Profitability, IND = Industry, LEV = Leverage, FAM = Family Firm, OUTINV = Outside Investors (institutional shareholders, government, foreign investors and general public), OWCON = Ownership Concentration, BSIZE = Board Size, BIND = Board Independence, BGDIV = Board Gender Diversity, CEOD = CEO Duality, BMEET = Board Meetings, CSRC = CSR Committee et al., 2021). Excepting some studies that found no significant relationship (e.g. Balluchi et al., 2021), most confirmed a positive association between company size and the level of environmental disclosure released (e.g. Liu and Anbumozhi, 2009), level of adherence to GRI (e.g. Fuente et al., 2017), and decision to prepare a CSR report (e.g. Haddock-Fraser and Fraser, 2008). This confirms the hypothesis developed according to the theoretical frameworks.

#### 3.1.1.1.2 Profitability

Scholars primarily investigated the relationship between profitability and environmental disclosure with reference to stakeholder theory. According to this theoretical framework, more profitable companies that experience more visibility are more exposed to social pressure from stakeholders and must guarantee they are acting in accordance with stakeholders' expectations. Thus, they release a higher level of disclosure (Gamerschlag et al., 2011). In addition, more profitable companies have more resources to devote to the production and dissemination of environmental disclosure to make their activities known to stakeholders (Frias-Aceituno et al., 2013).

Some researchers referred to legitimacy theory, which states that companies with better profitability release more information on their environmental performance to legitimise their operations (Legendre and Coderre, 2013). Few researchers refer to signalling theory, according to which companies with better profitability release higher information to send a signal to their shareholders on their stronger capacity to produce higher performance (e.g. Fuhrmann, 2020; Ortas et al., 2015).

Regarding the proxies used to measure profitability, scholars mainly utilise return on assets (ROA) (e.g. Gerged, 2021; Biswas et al., 2019; Fernandez-Gago et al., 2018). Some also employed return on equity (ROE) (e.g. Chan et al., 2014), return on investment (ROI) (e.g. Kouloukoui et al., 2019), and NEBIT (e.g. Gray et al., 2001).

Although the theoretical frameworks support a positive relationship between profitability and environmental disclosure, and the results of most studies confirmed this hypothesis (e.g. Boura et al., 2020), some research found no significant (e.g. Mateo-Márquez et al., 2021; Sannino et al., 2020) or negative association (e.g. Kilincarslan et al., 2020; Pucheta-Martínez and Gallego-Álvarez, 2018). These results were justified based on the higher expected proprietary costs supported by more profitable companies because of the decision to release further disclosure (Fuhrmann, 2020). According to these authors, higher proprietary costs bring more profitable companies to the decision to not provide higher levels of environmental disclosure.

#### 3.1.1.1.3 Industry

The literature suggests a strong industry effect on environmental disclosure because of the degree of attention paid to environmental issues by key stakeholders of the sector in which the company operates (Sinclair-Desgagné and Gozlan, 2003). According to stakeholder theory, companies operating in more environmentally sensitive industries typically receive greater attention from environmentalists, politicians, and the wider public opinion (Gamerschlag et al., 2011). Therefore, these companies tend to release higher levels of environmental disclosure. Similarly, according to legitimacy theory, companies operating in more environmentally sensitive sectors receive more pressure to operate in conformity with society's values and therefore, disclose more environmental information to legitimise their activities (Chan et al., 2014). Investigating the relationship between industry and environmental disclosure, some scholars referred to signalling theory, according to which companies operating in more environmentally sensitive industries are under more pressure from stakeholders and release environmental information to manage their reputation risk (Legendre and Coderre, 2013).

All discussed theoretical frameworks support a positive relationship between industry and environmental disclosure. Scholars computed industry by dividing all sectors into two groups (environmentally sensitive industry and not an environmentally sensitive industry) and assigning a score of one when the company belongs to an environmentally sensitive industry and 0 otherwise (e.g. Antonini et al., 2021; Fernandez-Gago et al., 2018). Few researchers determined industry using dummy variables for all sectors. Aligned with the theoretical arguments, most research found that companies operating in high environmentally sensitive industries tend to release more environmental disclosure (e.g. Zaid et al., 2020; Cho et al. 2012).

### 3.1.1.1.4 Leverage

Leverage is another company characteristic widely investigated as a determinant of environmental disclosure. The more commonly used theoretical frameworks are agency and stakeholder theories. According to agency theory, companies characterised by higher levels of leverage support more agency costs because of information asymmetries between managers and debtholders. In these companies, it might be possible for the manager to assume decisions that could expropriate the wealth of creditors, increasing shareholder wealth (Pisano et al., 2015; Crutchley and Hansen, 1989). These companies tend to release higher levels of disclosure to mitigate agency costs with debtholders (Type II agency problems) (Jensen and Meckling, 1976), which also decreases the cost of financial capital. According to stakeholder theory, companies characterised by higher levels of leverage tend to provide more disclosure to satisfy the information needs of debtholders, who are considered among the most significant stakeholder groups whose influence has to be adequately managed (Chan et al., 2014). Aligned with these considerations, Liesen et al. (2015) and Huang and Kung (2010) employed leverage to measure debtors' pressure and attention to the information released by companies.

Previous theoretical arguments suggest a positive association between leverage and environmental disclosure. However, some studies hypothesised a negative relationship between leverage and environmental disclosure. The main idea is that companies operating in bank-oriented countries tend to pay more attention to the information privately released to banks, reducing the corporate disclosure publicly provided to all stakeholders (D'Amico et al., 2016).

Furthermore, scholars have determined leverage using different proxies. The most commonly used measures are the ratio between total liabilities and total assets (e.g. Gerged, 2021; Biswas et al., 2019), total debt over total assets (Fernandez-Gago et al., 2018), and the debt/equity ratio (e.g. D'Amico et al., 2016).

In line with the theoretical arguments supporting both positive and negative associations, research has produced mixed results for the relationship between leverage and environmental disclosure. Specifically, although several scholars found a positive relationship with environmental disclosure (e.g. Oware and Awunyo-Vitor, 2021; Chan et al., 2014), others demonstrated a negative (e.g. Kouloukoui et al., 2019; Cho et al., 2015) or non-significant (e.g. Abeysekera et al., 2021) relationship.

### *3.1.1.2 Corporate governance characteristics*

Regarding corporate governance characteristics, previous studies focused on the ownership structure and composition of the board of directors. Within the ownership structure, the main aspects investigated were the level of ownership concentration (or dispersion) and identity of shareholders. For the board of directors, the main aspects investigated concern its dimension, independence, level of gender diversity, CEO duality, number of board meetings, and presence of a CSR committee.

#### 3.1.1.2.1 Ownership structure

*3.1.1.2.1.1 Ownership concentration*

Most studies investigated the influence of level of ownership concentration on environmental disclosure with reference to agency and stakeholder theories. Based on agency theory, scholars stated that companies with lower levels of ownership concentration pay more attention to external pressure due to higher levels of agent-principal conflicts, enhancing the disclosure released to achieve greater consensus among shareholders (Brammer and Pavelin, 2008; Cormier et al., 2005; Cormier and Magnan, 1999). However, companies with higher degrees of ownership concentration present lower levels of agency conflict and are less interested in releasing information to external stakeholders. Therefore, these studies employed ownership concentration as a proxy for the level of agency conflicts. They also hypothesised a negative association between ownership concentration and environmental disclosure, considering that the greater are agency conflicts, the higher is the disclosure. According to stakeholder theory, the degree of ownership concentration (or dispersion) influences the level of disclosure released (Gamerschlag et al., 2011) because of shareholders' pressure on management to satisfy their expectations (Cormier et al., 2004). Specifically, in companies characterised by diffused ownership, managers receive more pressure from external shareholders to release higher levels of disclosure. On the other hand, in companies characterised by concentrated ownership, management receives less pressure to disclose information because the controlling owner can satisfy information needs through other and more direct (private) channels. Therefore, according to stakeholder theory, the more concentrated the ownership, the lower the disclosure level released to external stakeholders. Studies applying a stakeholder theory framework used ownership concentration as a proxy for the level of shareholder pressure (e.g. Chiu and Wang, 2015; Huang and Kung, 2010; Liu and Anbumozhi, 2009), hypothesising a negative association with the level of disclosure.

In conclusion, both the agency and stakeholder theories support a negative association between ownership concentration and environmental disclosure. Most research measures ownership concentration using the percentage of shares held by the largest shareholders (e.g. Gerged, 2021). Some also measure the level of ownership dispersion (e.g. Kiliç and Kuzey, 2019), for example, computing the percentage of shares traded on the stock market (e.g. Karaman et al., 2018) or total number of shareholders (e.g. Mio et al., 2020). For these last studies, we changed the sign of the coefficient in Table 3.1. Furthermore, most studies found a negative relationship between ownership concentration and environmental disclosure, confirming the theoretical arguments previously reported.

*3.1.1.2.1.2 Identity of shareholders*

Several studies investigated the influence of shareholder identity on environmental disclosure. Using an agency theory framework, Biswas et al. (2019) investigated how the presence of a family in the ownership structure influences the level of CSR disclosure released by companies. They found that family companies disclose a lower level of information than non-family companies, which indicates that family ownership decreases controlling shareholders attention to stakeholder expectations, reducing CSR disclosure. Other scholars investigated how the percentage of shares held by an outside investor (i.e. institutional shareholders, government, foreign investors) affects environmental disclosure, finding a positive association (e.g. Injeni et al., 2021; Zaid et al., 2020; D'Amico et al., 2016). It is argued that outside investors bring companies to assume decisions in all shareholders' interests because of their greater power in monitoring management's behaviours (Gerged et al., 2021). Rather than investigating overall outside investors (e.g. Zaid et al., 2020; Biswas et al., 2019), some research focused on the shares held by the government (e.g. D'Amico et al., 2016; Muttakin and Subramaniam, 2015), foreign investors (e.g. Garanina and Aray, 2021; Injeni et al., 2021) or institutional shareholders (e.g. Gerged, 2021; Jeriji and Louhichi, 2021). Most of these studies found a positive association with environmental disclosure, confirming the theoretical arguments.

### 3.1.1.2.2 Composition of the board of directors

To investigate the association between the characteristics of the board of directors and environmental disclosure, most studies applied agency theory (e.g. Gerged, 2021; Katmon et al., 2019; Jizi et al., 2014). According to this theory, the board of directors is effective when the information released is improved (Alfraih, 2016), which reduces principal-agent asymmetries (Gao et al., 2016). The most investigated board aspects are dimension, independence, presence of women, CEO duality, number of meetings, and presence of a CSR committee. For these characteristics, we largely referred to the agency theory framework to explain the theoretical arguments supporting hypotheses of their association with environmental disclosure.

*3.1.1.2.2.1 Board size*

Board size is considered a fundamental characteristic that can enhance environmental disclosure because of the presence of various expertise and know-how held by numerous directors (Fernandes et al., 2019). The literature supports a positive association between board size and environmental disclosure (e.g. Jizi et al., 2014). However, it also suggests a contrasting position, contending that smaller boards are more efficient in reducing information asymmetries, resulting in a higher level of disclosure due to better group dynamics and joint decision-making (Prado-Lorenzo and Garcia-Sanchez, 2010; Ahmed et al., 2006).

Research has measured board size using the number of directors on the board (e.g. Gerged, 2021; Fernandez-Gago et al., 2018; Hussain et al., 2018). However, other proxies such as the natural logarithm of the number of members on the board (e.g. Biswas et al., 2019; Kaymak and Bektas, 2017) have also been employed.

Aligned with theoretical arguments supporting both positive and negative associations, the empirical evidence is mixed. The majority of research (e.g. Garanina and Aray, 2021; Jizi et al., 2014) found a positive relationship between board size and environmental disclosure, confirming the effectiveness of a larger board size. However, studies have also demonstrated a negative association between board size and environmental disclosure (e.g. García-Sánchez et al., 2022; Gallego-Álvarez and Pucheta-Martínez, 2020a), supporting the theoretical argument of group dynamics that maintains it is better to have smaller boards.

*3.1.1.2.2.2 Board independence*

The level of directors' independence is another board aspect usually analysed in disclosure studies. The literature indicates that the presence of independent members on the board promotes the effective monitoring of opportunistic managerial behaviours (Fama, 1980; Hillman and Dalziel, 2003), enhancing the information released to external stakeholders (Garcia-Meca and Sanchez-Ballesta, 2010). Previous arguments are generally based on the agency theory framework. Using the stakeholder theory framework, independent members are expected to encourage higher levels of environmental disclosure, considering that they receive less pressure from controlling owners and managers compared to other directors, and are thus more likely to satisfy all stakeholders' expectations (Hussain et al., 2018). Finally, for their role, independent directors have higher reputational concerns, which induce them to act in the interest of a larger number of stakeholders (Armstrong et al., 2010; Prado-Lorenzo and Garcia-Sanchez, 2010). From an institutional perspective, in companies characterised by higher levels of external pressure to operate according to society's values, independent members are more prone to satisfying social expectations to maintain their professional reputation and increase the level of disclosure released (Muttikan and Subramaniam, 2015).

Most scholars calculated board independence as the percentage of independent members (e.g. Gerged, 2021; Injeni et al., 2021; Fernandez-Gago et al., 2018).

Although all previous theoretical arguments support a positive association between independent directors and environmental disclosure, and the majority of empirical evidence confirms this hypothesis (e.g. Zaid et al., 2020; Katmon et al., 2019), some demonstrated a negative relationship (e.g. Jeriji and Louhichi 2021; Tibiletti et al., 2021). This result was justified by attributing the negative association to formal independent directors appointed exclusively for symbolic motivations (Kilincarslan et al., 2020). In these situations, independent directors could be less motivated to control opportunistic managerial behaviours (Lambert et al., 1993) and therefore, negatively influence the level of disclosure.

#### *3.1.1.2.2.3 Gender diversity*

In addition to male members, the presence of female members on boards is widely considered a measure of gender diversity (Hussain et al., 2018). The literature suggests that more diversified boards are more effective (Jizi, 2017). According to the literature, gender diversity encourages the disclosure of higher levels of environmental information, as women pay greater attention to CSR questions (Matsa and Miller, 2013; Williams, 2003). This greater engagement in CSR issues could be a consequence of some female characteristics such as being supportive, respectful, kind, and empathetic (Katmon et al., 2019).

Most studies measured gender diversity using the percentage of female directors sitting on the board (e.g. Injeni et al., 2021; Hussain et al., 2018). Others have used different measures including the presence of women in executive positions (Tibiletti et al., 2021) or a dummy variable equal to one when there are three or more female directors on the board and 0 otherwise (Oware et al., 2022).

Aligned with the theoretical arguments, most studies found a positive association between gender diversity and environmental disclosure (e.g. Injeni et al., 2021; Garcia-Sanchez et al., 2014).

#### *3.1.1.2.2.4 CEO duality*

CEO duality occurs when the same person holds the positions of the CEO and chairman of the board, which could potentially significantly affect board decisions. This condition could enhance the risk that the CEO assumes decisions exclusively in his/her interests, thus reducing the effectiveness of board monitoring activities (Cerbioni and Parbonetti, 2007). For example, if the CEO believes CSR is not important, he/she could decrease these activities and reduce the level of disclosure to external stakeholders (Sundarasen et al., 2016). However, the literature suggests the CEO could also increase disclosure when considering the release of environmental information as successful or able to benefit its tenure or remuneration (Jizi et al., 2014).

Most studies measured CEO duality using a dummy variable, which was equal to one when the CEO is also the chairman of the board and 0 otherwise (e.g. Gerged, 2021; Biswas et al., 2019; Hussain et al., 2018).

Aligned with previous arguments, empirical evidence further indicates both a positive (e.g. Gallego-Álvarez and Pucheta-Martínez, 2020a; Jizi et al., 2014) and negative (e.g. Hussain et al., 2018; Muttakin and Subramaniam, 2015) association between CEO duality and environmental disclosure.

*3.1.1.2.2.5 Board meetings*

Board meetings are typically used as a proxy for the level of board activities. The literature outlines two positions concerning the effectiveness of board meetings on board functioning. First, directors who meet more frequently are less effective with lower levels of disclosure (Frias-Aceituno et al., 2013; Prado-Lorenzo and Garcia-Sanchez, 2010; Vafeas, 1999). According to the second viewpoint, more frequent meetings indicate that the board is more effective because directors are better able to monitor companies' activities, resulting in higher levels of disclosure (Allegrini and Greco, 2013; Lipton and Lorsch, 1992).

All studies measured board meetings as the number of meetings held during the year (e.g. Hussain et al., 2018).

Aligned with these theoretical arguments, empirical evidence confirms both a positive (e.g. Katmon et al., 2019; Jizi et al., 2014) and negative (e.g. Jeriji and Louhichi, 2021) association between board meetings and environmental disclosure.

*3.1.1.2.2.6 CSR committee*

Companies frequently create a CSR committee as part of the board of directors, which focuses on CSR matters. The literature suggests that the establishment of a CSR committee signals a company's orientation and attention to CSR issues (Gennari and Salvioni, 2019). Theoretical arguments support a positive relationship between the presence of a CSR committee and environmental disclosure (Ricart et al., 2005).

All scholars measured this variable using a dummy variable equal to one when the company established a CSR committee within the board and 0 otherwise (e.g. Hussain et al., 2018).

Aligned with the theoretical arguments, empirical evidence reveals a positive association between the presence of a CSR committee and environmental disclosure (e.g. Gallego-Álvarez and Pucheta-Martínez, 2020b).

### 3.1.2 External or institutional factors

External or institutional factors refer to elements external to the company that can influence its decision to release environmental disclosure. One of the main factors widely investigated by scholars is pressure by the media, which can affect a company's disclosure behaviour. In addition, scholars investigated how different country-level factors, distinctive of the context in which the company operates, influence the level of environmental disclosure. These studies mainly referred to institutional theory, according to which companies operating in countries with institutional similarities tend to assume homogeneous behaviours (La Porta et al., 1998). Referring to DiMaggio and Powell's (1983) classification of the three types of isomorphism, we grouped these institutional determinants as: (1) mimetic factors, (2) normative factors, and (3) coercive factors. Next, for each variable, we briefly describe the theoretical framework applied in hypothesising the relationship with environmental disclosure, the proxies used to measure the variable, and main findings of previous studies investigating the association.

#### 3.1.2.1 Media exposure

Media exposure has been widely investigated as a determinant of environmental disclosure. Previous studies exploring the relationship between media exposure and environmental disclosure tend to apply stakeholder theory. According to this theoretical framework, enhanced visibility due to higher levels of media pressure brings greater scrutiny from environmentalists, politicians, and the wider public opinion, leading companies to release higher levels of disclosure to external stakeholders to satisfy their expectations (Reverte, 2009). Some scholars also referred to legitimacy theory, according to which companies more exposed to media pressure release more environmental information to demonstrate that they are operating in conformity with society's values, thus gaining legitimacy (e.g. Garcia-Sanchez et al., 2014; Islam and Deegan, 2010).

Previous theoretical arguments support the positive relationship between media exposure and environmental disclosure. Scholars usually measure media pressure as the amount of news on a company in a predefined period (e.g. Burritt et al., 2016; Garcia-Sanchez et al., 2014). Some calculate media pressure as the sum of all controversies faced by a company (e.g. Guenther et al., 2016).

Aligned with theoretical arguments, most scholars demonstrated a positive and significant association between media pressure and environmental disclosure (e.g. Hickman, 2020; Chiu and Wang, 2015; Garcia-Sanchez et al., 2014). Islam and Deegan (2010) focused on negative media attention, finding that companies exposed to negative media coverage release higher disclosure to demonstrate to the public that they are addressing community concerns.

Contrary to expectations, Burritt et al. (2016) showed a negative and significant association between media pressure and environmental disclosure. They justified this result by considering that too much disclosure can 'kill information'

(Farvaque et al., 2011). In other words, when companies release too much disclosure, both bad and good, it could happen that bad information is hidden by good data. This case of data overload makes it difficult for stakeholders to distinguish between bad and good disclosure to identify relevant information, reducing the media's attention on the company. Furthermore, companies characterised by a low level of media pressure and more subject to negative press, increase the level of information released.

### *3.1.2.2 Institutional factors*

Most studies investigated the influence of institutional factors on environmental disclosure based on the fact that CSR information varies according to country (Gray et al., 2001). Applying institutional theory, these studies investigated how mimetic, normative, and coercive pressures influence the level of environmental disclosure companies released. Scholars measured these three isomorphic pressures using various proxies. Next, we identify the main variables used to proxy for isomorphic pressures and report the results of previous studies.

#### 3.1.2.2.1 Mimetic pressure

Mimetic isomorphism occurs when companies act in a way similar to other more successful companies. Therefore, companies tend to implement the processes and activities carried out by influential companies operating in the same industry. Simultaneously, these leading companies can influence practices adopted in a specific field (Ferdous et al., 2019). Regarding disclosure behaviour, according to mimetic isomorphism, companies will release environmental disclosure if the leading industry's companies report this kind of information.

Few empirical studies specifically investigated the relationship between mimetic pressure and environmental disclosure, and they measured the independent variable in different ways. For example, Dagiliene et al. (2020) verified whether the presence within a sector of companies that disclose environmental information positively affects the environmental disclosure released by other companies operating in the same industry. They empirically confirmed this hypothesis. Earlier, Zeng et al. (2012) investigated how the communication behaviours of other companies operating in the same industry influenced both the decision to disclose environmental information and the level of disclosure to release. They measured mimetic pressure as the mean level of corporate environmental disclosure released in each sector each year, showing that the presence of other companies in the same industry that release environmental information influences the decision to provide environmental data. However, the variable used to capture mimetic pressure exhibits weak explanatory power for decisions pertaining to the extent of environmental disclosure to release. Therefore, the communication behaviours of other companies operating in the same industry influence the decision to release environmental disclosure, leading companies to provide information. However, they do not affect decisions regarding the content of the environmental information.

In contrast to previous studies, Boura et al. (2020) explored whether the degree of openness to international trade positively influences environmental disclosure. They contended that companies operating in the broader international environment tend to implement the practices and actions of leading companies both at the national and international levels. These companies pay more attention to environmental demands from international and national stakeholders, and thus release higher levels of environmental information. They measured mimetic pressure via international trade activity, which was equal to the ratio between imports plus exports and the gross domestic product of each country, finding a positive association with environmental disclosure. This result confirms their hypothesis that companies operating in open economies are susceptible to international pressures regarding the environmental information to disclose and therefore, report higher levels of environmental information.

#### 3.1.2.2.2 Normative pressure

Normative isomorphism occurs when companies decide to do what is considered right by the professionalisation of a field according to the members of a profession. Normative isomorphism also refers to the diffusion of values, beliefs, and cultures in society (Gallego-Álvarez and Pucheta-Martínez, 2020b). According to Mateo-Márquez et al. (2021), normative isomorphism can be identified via actions considered morally correct. Therefore, it refers to both the standards and guidelines issued by professional organisations and the norms and values considered worthwhile in a society that are strengthened through social practices and actions (Ferdous et al., 2019). Regarding disclosure behaviour, the development of specific reporting standards (Bebbington et al., 2012) and society's orientation towards specific values as disseminated through education processes are considered sources of normative pressure (Dagiliene et al., 2020). Companies should release environmental disclosure to follow the standards and act in a morally correct way (Mateo-Márquez et al., 2021).

Previous studies on the relationship between normative pressure and environmental disclosure focused on different aspects of normative isomorphism. For example, Dagiliene et al. (2020) investigated whether the adoption of a sustainability reporting standard and decision to receive external assurance positively influence environmental disclosure, confirming both hypotheses. Boura et al. (2020) explored whether the country's environmental performance index, used as a proxy for the level of environmental policies and consciousness in the country in which the company operates, positively influences environmental disclosure, confirming the hypothesis. Mateo-Márquez et al. (2021) analysed whether the proportion of companies that answered the Carbon Disclosure Project questionnaire in the preceding year in a specific country, used as a proxy for normative pressure, positively affects the propensity of companies to disclose and quality of the environmental information reported. They also found support for their hypothesis. In addition, the authors explored whether countries' climate change concerns, used as a proxy for the country's cultural dimension, positively influence the propensity of companies to disclose and quality of the environmental information reported. The results showed that the country's cultural dimension positively influences disclosure quality but has no effect on the company's decision to disclose environmental information.

Furthermore, Mateo-Márquez et al. (2021) distinguished between cultural dimensions and normative pressure. However, most studies considered the cultural dimension a proxy for normative isomorphism and investigated its role in environmental disclosure.

For example, Gallego-Álvarez and Pucheta-Martínez (2020b) explored the influence of certain cultural dimensions on environmental disclosure. They measured cultural dimensions using Hofstede's (1980, 2001) model, finding that (1) individualism and indulgence negatively influence environmental disclosure, and (2) uncertainty avoidance and long-term orientation positively influence environmental disclosure.

#### 3.1.2.2.3 Coercive pressure

Coercive isomorphism is attributed to political influence and occurs when companies decide to comply with the laws imposed by external forces. Therefore, the issue of new rules requiring companies to disclose specific information (i.e. Directive 95/2014/EU) is considered the main source of coercive isomorphism, leading companies to release environmental disclosure (Ferdous et al., 2019). Other factors considered sources of coercive isomorphism are the country's legal system and market regulations (Dagiliene et al., 2020).

Although theoretical arguments support a positive association between coercive pressure and environmental disclosure, some studies investigating whether regulation influences environmental disclosure yielded mixed results. For example, Boura et al. (2020) indicated that country-level regulatory quality positively affects environmental disclosure. Similarly, Khan et al. (2020) found that country-level regulatory influence positively affects environmental disclosure, and Zeng et al. (2012) confirmed that companies with more regulatory pressure release higher levels of environmental disclosure. Mateo-Márquez et al. (2021) demonstrated that the stringency of a country's environmental policy positively influences the decision to release environmental disclosure, but has no effect on disclosure quality. However, Dagiliene et al. (2020) noted that neither the country's regulation nor market regulation influence environmental disclosure.

In addition, most studies explored the influence of a country's legal system on environmental disclosure. Gallego-Álvarez and Pucheta-Martínez (2020b), for example, measured the legal system as the ratio between different aspects such as the rule of law, protection of property rights, and level of law enforcement, finding that this coercive factor positively influences environmental disclosure. Frías-Aceituno et al. (2013) revealed that companies situated in civil law countries, which are characterised by higher indices of law and order, tend to publish a wide range of integrated reports. Fuhrmann (2020) noted that the country-level features of civil law settings and level of investor protection influence the probability of releasing an integrated report. However, Pucheta-Martínez and Gallego-Álvarez (2018) observed that companies located in countries with strong investor protection are not associated with environmental disclosure policies.

Other variables used as proxies for coercive pressure are the level of corruption, which has been found to negatively influence environmental disclosure (Boura et al., 2020), and the capitalist approach. Regarding the latter, Gallego-Álvarez and Pucheta-Martínez (2020a) indicated that companies operating in co-ordinated market economy countries are involved in more environmental issues than those in liberal market economy countries. Similarly, Pucheta-Martínez and Gallego-Álvarez (2018) found that companies operating in countries where the most important capital providers are capital markets rather than banks are most likely to disclose environmental issues.

## 3.2 Effects of disclosure

Studies investigating the effects of environmental disclosure can be categorised into two groups: (1) usefulness of disclosure for stakeholders and (2) impact on company performance and financial markets.

The first group of studies conducted interviews and distributed questionnaires to understand the differences between stakeholders' informational needs (Lodhia and Martin, 2014). For example, Spence (2009) found that investors and employees are the most critical audiences targeted by firms. Other scholars focused on the usefulness of environmental information to managers (Eagan and Joeres, 2002) or fund managers (Said et al., 2013).

Most research has been conducted on the impact of environmental disclosure on company performance and financial markets. The second group of studies mainly performed empirical analyses employing environmental disclosure as the independent variable. To measure environmental disclosure, most scholars used data collected by databases such as Bloomberg ESG (e.g. Xie et al., 2019) or EIRIS (García-Sánchez and García-Meca, 2017). Others used diffused scores such as Rankins CSR Ratings (Luo et al., 2019). Furthermore, some studies assessed environmental disclosure based on the preparation of CSR reports and the level of adherence to GRI (e.g. Weber, 2014; Berthelot et al., 2012). However, most measured environmental disclosure by content analysing company documents (e.g. Camodeca et al., 2019; Sampong et al., 2018). In the next sections, we briefly illustrate scholars' theoretical arguments regarding the effects of environmental disclosure on company performance and financial markets, and report the results of these studies.

### *3.2.1 Company performance*

Most studies investigated the effect of environmental disclosure on company performance by applying stakeholder theory. Essentially, it is contended that companies that disclose environmental information can improve their reputation (Pérez et al., 2017) and consensus among stakeholders, thereby enhancing their performance (Alipour et al., 2019). Globally, an increasing focus on ethical investments reveals stakeholders' interest in companies implementing CSR practices (Karaman et al., 2018). This increased interest in CSR issues increases the value of companies involved in CSR practices and that disclose information thereon. According to stakeholder theory, companies release environmental information to satisfy the information needs of different stakeholders. Therefore, by enhancing transparency regarding CSR issues, companies create positive relationships with their key stakeholders, improving their profitability.

Scholars measure company performance using accounting-based indicators such as ROA, ROE, and ROS (e.g. Chijoke-Mgbame et al., 2020; Li et al., 2017), and market-based measures such as Tobin's Q (e.g. Naseem et al., 2019; Karaman et al., 2018; Radhouane et al., 2018). The difference between these measures is that market-based indicators express the expectations of the future effects of a company's activities and policies, while accounting-based measures express the results of past events. Considering the different functions of accounting- and market-based measures, some scholars used both to compute company performance (e.g. Gerged et al., 2021; Alipour et al., 2019).

Although theoretical arguments support the positive association between environmental disclosure and company performance, there are contrasting results. Most scholars (e.g. Gerged et al., 2021; Alcaide González et al., 2020; Alipour et al., 2019; Li et al., 2017) confirmed the positive effect of environmental disclosure on company performance. However, others showed a negative (e.g. Maama, 2021; Wasara and Ganda, 2019) or insignificant (e.g. Karaman et al., 2018; Gallego-Álvarez, 2012) relationship, or indicated that previous associations take different forms depending on the type of environmental disclosure (Chen et al., 2016). A possible reason for the negative relationship between environmental disclosure and performance could be that the necessity for companies to comply with different rules in releasing environmental disclosure negatively affects their profitability, as it increases costs for the production and dissemination of information (Alipour et al., 2019). For Carnevale et al. (2012), the insignificant association between environmental disclosure and performance could indicate investors' low interest in environmental disclosure, mainly due to their incapacity to understand this type of information because of the lack of standardisation among reports.

Other scholars revealed a positive association between environmental performance and environmental disclosure (e.g. Hora and Subamanian, 2019; Hassan and Romilly, 2018; Arena et al., 2015), which is aligned with the abovementioned theoretical arguments.

### 3.2.2 *Financial markets*

Research has investigated the effect of environmental disclosure on financial markets, focusing on the assessments of financial stakeholders such as investors, financial analysts, and debtholders. Theoretical arguments are based on disclosure theory (Dye, 1985; Verrecchia, 1983), according to which credible and extended disclosure is an essential mechanism companies use to share their information with financial markets to more easily access external financial resources (Healy and Palepu, 2001). Companies' decision to release information benefits financial markets, for example, by enhancing the level of stock price information on the company's forthcoming performance (Schiehll and Kolahgar, 2021) or reducing financing costs (Hamrouni et al., 2020). According to signalling theory, releasing environmental information is intended as a way to communicate the company's involvement in CSR issues to financial markets to enhance its reputation (Paolone et al., 2021) and attract investors to invest their resources in the company (Verrecchia, 1983).

Previous arguments support a positive association between environmental disclosure and assessments conducted by different stakeholders operating in financial markets.

Empirical research on this association can be grouped according to the investigated financial stakeholders. Most studies confirm a positive association between environmental disclosure and financial markets.

Most research focused on shareholders and measured the investors' assessments using different measures. For example, Yao and Liang (2019) indicated that environmental disclosure reduces equity costs. Others demonstrated that it positively influences market value (e.g. Hassan, 2018), stock market returns (e.g. Weber, 2014), the degree to which stock prices reveal company information (e.g. Schiehll and Kolahgar, 2021), capacity to access finances (e.g. García-Sánchez et al., 2019a) and trading strategies adopted by institutional investors (e.g. Wei et al., 2020).

Furthermore, studies examined the effects on analysts, finding that environmental disclosure positively affects analysts' coverage and the accuracy of their forecasts (e.g. García-Sánchez et al., 2019b; Cormier and Magnan, 2015).

Finally, some have investigated the influence on debtholders, revealing that the higher the environmental disclosure, the lower the cost of debt financing (e.g. Hamrouni et al., 2020; Luo et al., 2019). Aligned with the abovementioned theoretical arguments, this result indicates that when companies release higher levels of environmental disclosure, creditors reduce the costs of debt because they have to sustain lower costs for searching for information considering that their information needs are satisfied by the companies' disclosure.

## References

Abeysekera, I., Li, F., & Lu, Y. (2021). Financial disclosure quality and sustainability disclosure quality. A case in China. *Plos One*, 16(5), e0250884.

Alberici, A., & Querci, F. (2016). The quality of disclosures on environmental policy: The profile of financial intermediaries. *Corporate Social Responsibility and Environmental Management*, 23(5), 283–296.

Alcaide González, M. Á., De La Poza Plaza, E., & Guadalajara Olmeda, N. (2020). The impact of corporate social responsibility transparency on the financial performance, brand value, and sustainability level of IT companies. *Corporate Social Responsibility and Environmental Management*, 27(2), 642–654.

Alfraih, M. M. (2016). The effectiveness of board of directors' characteristics in mandatory disclosure compliance. *Journal of Financial Regulation and Compliance*, 24(2), 154–176.

Alipour, M., Ghanbari, M., Jamshidinavid, B., & Taherabadi, A. (2019). Does board independence moderate the relationship between environmental disclosure quality and performance? Evidence from static and dynamic panel data. *Corporate Governance: The International Journal of Business in Society*, 19(3), 580–610.

Allegrini, M., & Greco, G. (2013). Corporate boards, audit committees and voluntary disclosure: Evidence from Italian Listed Companies. *Journal of Management and Governance*, 17(1), 187–216.

Antonini, C., Olczak, W., & Patten, D. M. (2021, April). Corporate climate change disclosure during the Trump administration: Evidence from standalone CSR reports. *In Accounting Forum*, 45(2), 118–141.

Arena, C., Bozzolan, S., & Michelon, G. (2015). Environmental reporting: Transparency to stakeholders or stakeholder manipulation? An analysis of disclosure tone and the role of the board of directors. *Corporate Social Responsibility and Environmental Management*, 22(6), 346–361.

Armstrong, C. S., Guay, W. R., & Weber, J. P. (2010). The role of information and financial reporting in corporate governance and debt contracting. *Journal of Accounting and Economics*, 50(2), 179–234.

Balluchi, F., Lazzini, A., & Torelli, R. (2021). Credibility of environmental issues in non-financial mandatory disclosure: Measurement and determinants. *Journal of Cleaner Production*, 288, 125744.

Bebbington, J., Kirk, E. A., & Larrinaga, C. (2012). The production of normativity: A comparison of reporting regimes in Spain and the UK. *Accounting, Organizations and Society*, 37(2), 78–94.

Berthelot, S., Coulmont, M., & Serret, V. (2012). Do investors value sustainability reports? A Canadian study. *Corporate Social Responsibility and Environmental Management*, 19(6), 355–363.

Biswas, P. K., Roberts, H., & Whiting, R. H. (2019). The impact of family vs non-family governance contingencies on CSR reporting in Bangladesh. *Management Decision*, 57(10), 2758–2781.

Boura, M., Tsouknidis, D. A., & Lioukas, S. (2020). The role of pro-social orientation and national context in corporate environmental disclosure. *European Management Review*, 17(4), 1027–1040.

Brammer, S., & Pavelin, S. (2008). Factors influencing the quality of corporate environmental disclosure. *Business Strategy and the Environment*, 17(2), 120–136.

Burritt, R. L., Christ, K. L., & Omori, A. (2016). Drivers of corporate water-related disclosure: Evidence from Japan. *Journal of Cleaner Production*, 129, 65–74.

Camodeca, R., Almici, A., & Sagliaschi, U. (2019). Strategic information disclosure, integrated reporting and the role of intellectual capital. *Journal of Intellectual Capital*, 20(1), 125–143.

Carnevale, C., Mazzuca, M., & Venturini, S. (2012). Corporate social reporting in European banks: The effects on a firm's market value. *Corporate Social Responsibility and Environmental Management*, 19(3), 159–177.

Cerbioni, F., & Parbonetti, A. (2007). Exploring the effects of corporate governance on intellectual capital disclosure: An analysis of European biotechnology companies. *European Accounting Review*, 16(4), 791–826.

Chan, M. C., Watson, J., & Woodliff, D. (2014). Corporate governance quality and CSR disclosures. *Journal of Business Ethics*, 125(1), 59–73.

Chen, L., Srinidhi, B., Tsang, A., & Yu, W. (2016). Audited financial reporting and voluntary disclosure of corporate social responsibility (CSR) reports. *Journal of Management Accounting Research*, 28(2), 53–76.

Chijoke-Mgbame, A. M., Mgbame, C. O., Akintoye, S., & Ohalehi, P. (2020). The role of corporate governance on CSR disclosure and firm performance in a voluntary environment. *Corporate Governance: The International Journal of Business in Society*, 20(2), 294–306.

Chiu, T. K., & Wang, Y. H. (2015). Determinants of social disclosure quality in Taiwan: An application of stakeholder theory. *Journal of Business Ethics*, 129(2), 379–398.

Cho, C. H., Freedman, M., & Patten, D. M. (2012). Corporate disclosure of environmental capital expenditures: A test of alternative theories. *Accounting, Auditing & Accountability Journal*, 25(3), 486–507.

Cho, C. H., Michelon, G., Patten, D. M., & Roberts, R. W. (2015). CSR disclosure: The more things change…?. *Accounting, Auditing & Accountability Journal*, 28(1), 14–35.

Cormier, D., Gordon, I. M., & Magnan, M. (2004). Corporate environmental disclosure: Contrasting management's perceptions with reality. *Journal of Business Ethics*, 49(2), 143–165.

Cormier, D., & Magnan, M. (1999). Corporate environmental disclosure strategies: Determinants, costs and benefits. *Journal of Accounting, Auditing and Finance*, 14, 429–451.

Cormier, D., & Magnan, M. (2015). The economic relevance of environmental disclosure and its impact on corporate legitimacy: An empirical investigation. *Business Strategy and the Environment*, 24(6), 431–450.

Cormier, D., Magnan, M., & Van Velthoven, B. (2005). Environmental disclosure quality in large German companies: Economic incentives, public pressures or institutional conditions? *European Accounting Review*, 14(1), 3–39.

Crutchley, C. E., & Hansen, R. S. (1989). A test of the agency theory of managerial ownership, corporate leverage, and corporate dividends. *Financial Management*, 18(4), 36–46.

D'Amico, E., Coluccia, D., Fontana, S., & Solimene, S. (2016). Factors influencing corporate environmental disclosure. *Business Strategy and the Environment*, 25(3), 178–192.

Dagiliene, L., Frendzel, M., Sutiene, K., & Wnuk-Pel, T. (2020). Wise managers think about circular economy, wiser report and analyze it. Research of environmental reporting practices in EU manufacturing companies. *Journal of Cleaner Production*, 274, 121968.

de Villiers, C., Low, M., & Samkin, G. (2014). The institutionalisation of mining company sustainability disclosures. *Journal of Cleaner Production*, 84, 51–58.

Delgado-Márquez, B. L., Pedauga, L. E., & Cordón-Pozo, E. (2017). Industries regulation and firm environmental Disclosure: A stakeholders' perspective on the importance of legitimation and international activities. *Organization & Environment*, 30(2), 103–121.

DiMaggio, P., & Powell, W. W. (1983). The iron cage revisited: Collective rationality and institutional isomorphism in organisational fields. *American Sociological Review*, 48(2), 147–160.

Dinca, M. S., Madaleno, M., Baba, M. C., & Dinca, G. (2019). Environmental information transparency-Evidence from Romanian companies. *Sustainability*, 11(18), 1–22.

Dye, R. A. (1985). Disclosure of nonproprietary information. *Journal of Accounting Research*, 23, 123–145.

Eagan, P. D., & Joeres, E. (2002). The utility of environmental impact information: a manufacturing case study. *Journal of Cleaner Production*, 10(1), 75–83.

Esteban-Sanchez, P., de la Cuesta-Gonzalez, M., & Paredes-Gazquez, J. D. (2017). Corporate social performance and its relation with corporate financial performance: International evidence in the banking industry. *Journal of Cleaner Production*, 162, 1102–1110.

Fama, E. F., & Jensen, M. C. (1983). Separation of ownership and control. *The Journal of Law and Economics*, 26(2), 301–325.

Farvaque, E., Refait-Alexandre, C., & Saïdane, D. (2011). Corporate disclosure: A review of its (direct and indirect) benefits and costs. *International economics*, 128, 5–31.

Ferdous, M. I., Adams, C. A., & Boyce, G. (2019). Institutional drivers of environmental management accounting adoption in public sector water organisations. *Accounting, Auditing & Accountability Journal*, 32, 984–1012.

Fernández-Gago, R., Cabeza-García, L., & Nieto, M. (2018). Independent directors' background and CSR disclosure. *Corporate Social Responsibility and Environmental Management*, 25(5), 991–1001.

Frias-Aceituno, J. V., Rodriguez-Ariza, L., & Garcia-Sanchez, I. M. (2013). The role of the board in the dissemination of integrated corporate social reporting. *Corporate Social Responsibility and Environmental Management*, 20(4), 219–233.

Fuente, J. A., García-Sánchez, I. M., & Lozano, M. B. (2017). The role of the board of directors in the adoption of GRI guidelines for the disclosure of CSR information. *Journal of Cleaner Production*, 141, 737–750.

Fuhrmann, S. (2020). A multi-theoretical approach on drivers of integrated reporting–uniting firm-level and country-level associations. *Meditari Accountancy Research*, 28(1), 168–205.

Gallego-Álvarez, I. (2012). Indicators for sustainable development: Relationship between indicators related to climate change and explanatory factors. *Sustainable Development*, 20(4), 276–292.

Gallego-Álvarez, I., & Pucheta-Martínez, M. C. (2020a). Environmental strategy in the global banking industry within the varieties of capitalism approach: The moderating role of gender diversity and board members with specific skills. *Business Strategy and the Environment*, 29(2), 347–360.

Gallego-Álvarez, I., & Pucheta-Martínez, M. C. (2020b). How cultural dimensions, legal systems, and industry affect environmental reporting? Empirical evidence from an international perspective. *Business Strategy and the Environment*, 29(5), 2037–2057.

Gamerschlag, R., Möller, K., & Verbeeten, F. (2011). Determinants of voluntary CSR disclosure: Empirical evidence from Germany. *Review of Management Science*, 5, 233–262.

Garanina, T., & Aray, Y. (2021). Enhancing CSR disclosure through foreign ownership, foreign board members, and cross-listing: Does it work in Russian context? *Emerging Markets Review*, 46, 100754.

Garcia-Meca, E., & Sanchez-Ballesta, J. P. (2010). The association of board independence and ownership concentration with voluntary disclosure: A meta-analysis. *European Accounting Review*, 19(3), 603–627.

Garcia-Sanchez, I. M., Cuadrado-Ballesteros, B., & Sepulveda, C. (2014). Does media pressure moderate CSR disclosures by external directors? *Management Decision*, 52(6), 1014–1045.

García-Sánchez, I. M., & García-Meca, E. (2017). CSR engagement and earnings quality in banks. The moderating role of institutional factors. *Corporate Social Responsibility and Environmental Management*, 24(2), 145–158.

García-Sánchez, I. M., Hussain, N., Martínez-Ferrero, J., & Ruiz-Barbadillo, E. (2019a). Impact of disclosure and assurance quality of corporate sustainability reports on access to finance. *Corporate Social Responsibility and Environmental Management*, 26(4), 832–848.

García-Sánchez, I. M., Gómez-Miranda, M. E., David, F., & Rodríguez-Ariza, L. (2019b). Analyst coverage and forecast accuracy when CSR reports improve stakeholder engagement: The Global Reporting Initiative-International Finance Corporation disclosure strategy. *Corporate Social Responsibility and Environmental Management*, 26(6), 1392–1406.

García-Sánchez, I. M., Hussain, N., Khan, S. A., & Martínez-Ferrero, J. (2022). Assurance of corporate social responsibility reports: Examining the role of internal and external corporate governance mechanisms. *Corporate Social Responsibility and Environmental Management*, 29(1), 89–106.

Garde Sánchez, R., Rodríguez Bolívar, M. P., & López Hernández, A. M. (2017). Corporate and managerial characteristics as drivers of social responsibility disclosure by state-owned enterprises. *Review of Managerial Science*, 11(3), 633–659.

Gennari, F., & Salvioni, D. M. (2019). CSR committees on boards: The impact of the external country level factors. *Journal of Management and Governance*, 23(3), 759–785.

Gerged, A. M. (2021). Factors affecting corporate environmental disclosure in emerging markets: The role of corporate governance structures. *Business Strategy and the Environment*, 30(1), 609–629.

Gerged, A. M., Beddewela, E., & Cowton, C. J. (2021). Is corporate environmental disclosure associated with firm value? A multicountry study of Gulf Cooperation Council firms. *Business Strategy and the Environment*, 30(1), 185–203.

Gray, R., Javad, M., Power, D. M., & Sinclair, C. D. (2001). Social and environmental disclosure and corporate characteristics: A research note and extension. *Journal of Business Finance & Accounting*, 28(3–4), 327–356.

Guenther, E., Guenther, T., Schiemann, F., & Weber, G. (2016). Stakeholder relevance for reporting: Explanatory factors of carbon disclosure. *Business & Society*, 55(3), 361–397.

Haddock-Fraser, J., & Fraser, I. (2008). Assessing corporate environmental reporting motivations: Differences between 'close-to-market' and 'business-to-business' companies. *Corporate Social Responsibility and Environmental Management*, 15(3), 140–155.

Hamrouni, A., Uyar, A., & Boussaada, R. (2020). Are corporate social responsibility disclosures relevant for lenders? Empirical evidence from France. *Management Decision*, 58(2), 267–279.

Hassan, O. A. (2018). The impact of voluntary environmental disclosure on firm value: Does organizational visibility play a mediation role? *Business strategy and the Environment*, 27(8), 1569–1582.

Hassan, O. A., & Romilly, P. (2018). Relations between corporate economic performance, environmental disclosure and greenhouse gas emissions: New insights. *Business Strategy and the Environment*, 27(7), 893–909.

Healy, P. M., & Palepu, K. G. (2001). Information asymmetry, corporate disclosure, and the capital markets: A review of the empirical disclosure literature. *Journal of Accounting and Economics*, 31(1–3), 405–440.

Hickman, L. E. (2020). Information asymmetry in CSR reporting: Publicly-traded versus privately-held firms. *Sustainability Accounting, Management and Policy Journal*, 11(1), 207–232.

Hillman, A., & Dalziel, T. (2003). Boards of directors and firm performance: Integrating agency and resource dependence perspectives. *Academy of Management Review*, 28(3), 383–396.

Hofstede, G. (1980). *Culture's consequences: International differences in work-related values*. Newbury Park: Sage Publications.

Hofstede, G. (2001). *Culture's consequences: Comparing values, behaviors, institutions, and organizations across nations*. Thousand Oaks: Sage Publications.

Hora, M., & Subramanian, R. (2019). Relationship between positive environmental disclosures and environmental performance: An empirical investigation of the greenwashing sin of the hidden trade-off. *Journal of Industrial Ecology*, 23(4), 855–868.

Hsueh, L. (2019). Opening up the firm: What explains participation and effort in voluntary carbon disclosure by global businesses? An analysis of internal firm factors and dynamics. *Business Strategy and the Environment*. 28(7), 1302–1322.

Huang, C. L., & Kung, F. H. (2010). Drivers of environmental disclosure and stakeholder expectation: Evidence from Taiwan. *Journal of Business Ethics*, 96(3), 435–451.

Hussain, N., Rigoni, U., & Orij, R. P. (2018). Corporate governance and sustainability performance: Analysis of triple bottom line performance. *Journal of Business Ethics*, 149(2), 411–432.

Injeni, G., Mangena, M., Mathuva, D., & Mudida, R. (2021). Agency and institutional-related factors and the heterogeneity of sustainability and integrated report information disclosures in Kenya. *Journal of Financial Reporting and Accounting*, ahead-of-print.

Ismail, N. B., Alcouffe, S., Galy, N., & Ceulemans, K. (2021). The impact of international sustainability initiatives on Life Cycle Assessment voluntary disclosures: The case of France's CAC40 listed companies. *Journal of Cleaner Production*, 282, 124456.

Islam, M. A., & Deegan, C. (2010). Media pressures and corporate disclosure of social responsibility performance information: A study of two global clothing and sports retail companies. *Accounting and Business Research*, 40(2), 131–148.

Jensen, M. C., & Meckling, W. H. (1976). Theory of the firm: Managerial behavior, agency costs and ownership structure. *Journal of Financial Economics*, 3(4), 305–360.

Jeriji, M., & Louhichi, W. (2021). The relationship between poor CSR performance and hard, negative CSR information disclosures. *Sustainability Accounting, Management and Policy Journal*, 12(2), 410–436.

Jizi, M. (2017). The influence of board composition on sustainable development disclosure. *Business Strategy and the Environment*, 26(5), 640–655.

Jizi, M. I., Salama, A., Dixon, R., & Stratling, R. (2014). Corporate governance and corporate social responsibility disclosure: Evidence from the US banking sector. *Journal of Business Ethics*, 125(4), 601–615.

Karaman, A. S., Kilic, M., & Uyar, A. (2018). Sustainability reporting in the aviation industry: Worldwide evidence. *Sustainability Accounting, Management and Policy Journal*, 9(4), 362–391.

Katmon, N., Mohamad, Z. Z., Norwani, N. M., & Al Farooque, O. (2019). Comprehensive board diversity and quality of corporate social responsibility disclosure: Evidence from an emerging market. *Journal of Business Ethics*, 157(2), 447–481.

Kaymak, T., & Bektas, E. (2017). Corporate social responsibility and governance: Information disclosure in multinational corporations. *Corporate Social Responsibility and Environmental Management*, 24(6), 555–569.

Khan, M., Lockhart, J., & Bathurst, R. (2020). A multi-level institutional perspective of corporate social responsibility reporting: A mixed-method study. *Journal of Cleaner Production*, 265. DOI: 10.1016/j.jclepro.2020.121739.

Kılıç, M., & Kuzey, C. (2019). Determinants of climate change disclosures in the Turkish banking industry. *International Journal of Bank Marketing*, 37(3), 901–926.

Kilincarslan, E., Elmagrhi, M. H., & Li, Z. (2020). Impact of governance structures on environmental disclosures in the Middle East and Africa. *Corporate Governance: The International Journal of Business in Society*, 20(4), 739–763.

Kouloukoui, D., Sant'Anna, Â. M. O., da Silva Gomes, S. M., de Oliveira Marinho, M. M., de Jong, P., Kiperstok, A., & Torres, E. A. (2019). Factors influencing the level of environmental disclosures in sustainability reports: Case of climate risk disclosure by Brazilian companies. *Corporate Social Responsibility and Environmental Management*, 26(4), 791–804.

La Porta, R., Lopez-de-Silanes, F., Shleifer, A., & Vishny, R. W. (1998). Law and finance. *Journal of Political Economy*, 106(6), 1113–1155.

Lambert, R. A., Larcker, D. F., & Weigelt, K. (1993). The structure of organizational incentives. *Administrative Science Quarterly*, 38(2), 438–461.

Legendre, S., & Coderre, F. (2013). Determinants of GRI G3 application levels: The case of the fortune global 500. *Corporate Social Responsibility and Environmental Management*, 20(3), 182–192.

Li, D., Zhao, Y., Sun, Y., & Yin, D. (2017). Corporate environmental performance, environmental information disclosure, and financial performance: Evidence from China. *Human and Ecological Risk Assessment: An International Journal*, 23(2), 323–339.

Liesen, A., Hoepner, A. G., Patten, D. M., & Figge, F. (2015). Does stakeholder pressure influence corporate GHG emissions reporting? Empirical evidence from Europe. *Accounting, Auditing & Accountability Journal*, 28(7), 1047–1074.

Lipton, M., & Lorsch, J. W. (1992). A modest proposal for improved corporate governance. *The Business Lawyer*, 59–77.

Liu, X., & Anbumozhi, V. (2009). Determinant factors of corporate environmental information disclosure: An empirical study of Chinese listed companies. *Journal of Cleaner Production*, 17(6), 593–600.

Lodhia, S., & Martin, N. (2014). Corporate sustainability indicators: An Australian mining case study. *Journal of Cleaner Production*, 84, 107–115.

Luo, J. M., Huang, G. Q., & Lam, C. F. (2019). Barriers to the implementation of corporate social responsibility in gaming industry. *Journal of Quality Assurance in Hospitality & Tourism*, 20(5), 528–551.

Maama, H. (2021). Achieving financial sustainability in Ghana's banking sector: Is environmental, social and governance reporting contributive? *Global Business Review*. DOI: 10.1177/09721509211044300.

Mata, C., Fialho, A., & Eugénio, T. (2018). A decade of environmental accounting reporting: What we know? *Journal of Cleaner Production*, 198, 1198–1209.

Mateo-Márquez, A. J., González-González, J. M., & Zamora-Ramírez, C. (2021). The influence of countries' climate change-related institutional profile on voluntary environmental disclosures. *Business Strategy and the Environment*, 30(2), 1357–1373.

Mio, C., Fasan, M., Marcon, C., & Panfilo, S. (2020). The predictive ability of legitimacy and agency theory after the implementation of the EU directive on non-financial information. *Corporate Social Responsibility and Environmental Management*, 27(6), 2465–2476.

Muttakin, M. B., & Subramaniam, N. (2015). Firm ownership and board characteristics: Do they matter for corporate social responsibility disclosure of Indian companies? *Sustainability Accounting, Management and Policy Journal*, 6(2), 138–165.

Naseem, M. A., Lin, J., Rehman, R. U., Ahmad, M. I., & Ali, R. (2019). Moderating role of financial ratios in corporate social responsibility disclosure and firm value. *PloS One*, 14(4), e0215430.

Ortas, E., Gallego-Alvarez, I., & Álvarez Etxeberria, I. (2015). Financial factors influencing the quality of corporate social responsibility and environmental management disclosure: A quantile regression approach. *Corporate Social Responsibility and Environmental Management*, 22(6), 362–380.

Oware, K. M., & Awunyo-Vitor, D. (2021). CEO characteristics and environmental disclosure of listed firms in an emerging economy: Does sustainability reporting format matter? *Business Strategy & Development*, 4(4), 399–410.

Oware, K. M., Iddrisu, A. A., Worae, T., & Adaletey, J. E. (2022). Female and environmental disclosure of family and non-family firms. Evidence from India. *Management Research Review*, 45(6), 760–780.

Paolone, F., Granà, F., Martiniello, L., & Tiscini, R. (2021). Environmental risk indicators disclosure and value relevance: An empirical analysis of Italian listed companies after the implementation of the Legislative Decree 254/2016. *Corporate Social Responsibility and Environmental Management*, 28(5), 1471–1482.

Pérez, A., López, C., & del Mar García-De los Salmones, M. (2017). An empirical exploration of the link between reporting to stakeholders and corporate social responsibility reputation in the Spanish context. *Accounting, Auditing & Accountability Journal*, 30(3), 668–698.

Pisano, S., Lepore, L., & Agrifoglio, R. (2015). Corporate governance and information asymmetry between shareholders and lenders: An analysis of Italian listed companies. *Financial Reporting*, 2, 27–53.

Prado-Lorenzo, J. M., & Garcia-Sanchez, I.-M. (2010). The role of the board of directors in disseminating relevant information on greenhouse gases. *Journal of Business Ethics*, 97(3), 391–424.

Pucheta-Martínez, M. C., & Gallego-Álvarez, I. (2018). Environmental reporting policy and corporate structures: An international analysis. *Corporate Social Responsibility and Environmental Management*, 25(5), 788–798.

Pucheta-Martínez, M. C., & López-Zamora, B. (2018). Engagement of directors representing institutional investors on environmental disclosure. *Corporate Social Responsibility and Environmental Management*, 25(6), 1108–1120.

Radu, C., & Francoeur, C. (2017). Does innovation drive environmental disclosure? A new insight into sustainable development. *Business Strategy and the Environment*, 26(7), 893–911.

Radhouane, I., Nekhili, M., Nagati, H., & Paché, G. (2018). The impact of corporate environmental reporting on customer-related performance and market value. *Management Decision*, 56(7), 1630–1659.

Reverte, C. (2009). Determinants of corporate social responsibility disclosure ratings by Spanish listed firms. *Journal of Business Ethics*, 88, 351–366.

Ricart, J. E., Rodríguez, M. Á., & Sánchez, P. (2005). Sustainability in the boardroom. *Corporate Governance: The International Journal of Business in Society*, 5(3), 24–41.
Said, R. M., Sulaiman, M., & Ahmad, N. N. N. (2013). Do fund managers perceive environmental information useful? An empirical study from Malaysia. *Journal of Cleaner Production*, 52, 281–288.
Sampong, F., Song, N., Boahene, K. O., & Wadie, K. A. (2018). Disclosure of CSR performance and firm value: New evidence from South Africa on the basis of the GRI guidelines for sustainability disclosure. *Sustainability*, 10(12), 4518.
Sannino, G., Lucchese, M., Zampone, G., & Lombardi, R. (2020). Cultural dimensions, Global Reporting Initiatives commitment, and corporate social responsibility issues: New evidence from Organisation for Economic Co-operation and Development banks. *Corporate Social Responsibility and Environmental Management*, 27(4), 1653–1663.
Schiehll, E., & Kolahgar, S. (2021). Financial materiality in the informativeness of sustainability reporting. *Business Strategy and the Environment*, 30(2), 840–855.
Sinclair-Desgagné, B., & Gozlan, E. (2003). A theory of environmental risk disclosure. *Journal of Environmental Economics and Management*, 45, 377–393.
Skouloudis, A., Jones, N., Malesios, C., & Evangelinos, K. (2014). Trends and determinants of corporate non-financial disclosure in Greece. *Journal of Cleaner Production*, 68, 174–188.
Spence, C. (2009). Social and environmental reporting and the corporate ego. *Business Strategy and the Environment*, 18(4), 254–265.
Tibiletti, V., Marchini, P. L., Furlotti, K., & Medioli, A. (2021). Does corporate governance matter in corporate social responsibility disclosure? Evidence from Italy in the "era of sustainability". *Corporate Social Responsibility and Environmental Management*, 28(2), 896–907.
Torelli, R., Balluchi, F., & Furlotti, K. (2020). The materiality assessment and stakeholder engagement: A content analysis of sustainability reports. *Corporate Social Responsibility and Environmental Management*, 27(2), 470–484.
Vafeas, N. (1999). Board meeting frequency and firm performance. *Journal of Financial Economics*, 53(1), 113–142.
Verrecchia, R. E. (1983). Discretionary disclosure. *Journal of Accounting and Economics*, 5, 179–194.
Vormedal, I. H., & Ruud, A. (2009). Sustainability reporting in Norway - An assessment of performance in the context of legal demands and socio-political drivers. *Business Strategy and the Environment*, 18(4), 207–222.
Wasara, T. M., & Ganda, F. (2019). The relationship between corporate sustainability disclosure and firm financial performance in Johannesburg Stock Exchange (JSE) listed mining companies. *Sustainability*, 11(16), 4496.
Weber, O. (2014). Environmental, social and governance reporting in China. *Business Strategy and the Environment*, 23(5), 303–317.
Wei, P., Mao, X., & Chen, X. (2020). Institutional investors' attention to environmental information, trading strategies, and market impacts: Evidence from China. *Business Strategy and the Environment*, 29(2), 566–591.
Williams, R. (2003). Women on corporate boards of directors and their influence on corporate philanthropy. *Journal of Business Ethics*, 42(1), 1–10.
Xie, K., Mao, Z. E., & Wu, J. (2019). Learning from peers: The effect of sales history disclosure on peer-to-peer short-term rental purchases. *International Journal of Hospitality Management*, 76, 173–183.

Yao, S., & Liang, H. (2019). Analyst following, environmental disclosure and cost of equity: Research based on industry classification. *Sustainability*, 11(2), 300.

Yook, K. H., Song, H., Patten, D. M., & Kim, I. W. (2017). The disclosure of environmental conservation costs and its relation to eco-efficiency: Evidence from Japan. *Sustainability Accounting, Management and Policy Journal*, 8(1), 20–42.

Zaid, M. A., Abuhijleh, S. T., & Pucheta-Martínez, M. C. (2020). Ownership structure, stakeholder engagement, and corporate social responsibility policies: The moderating effect of board independence. *Corporate Social Responsibility and Environmental Management*, 27(3), 1344–1360.

Zeng, S. X., Xu, X. D., Yin, H. T., & Tam, C. M. (2012). Factors that drive Chinese listed companies in voluntary disclosure of environmental information. *Journal of Business Ethics*, 109(3), 309–321.

Zhang, Y. J., & Liu, J. Y. (2020). Overview of research on carbon information disclosure. *Frontiers of Engineering Management*, 7(1), 47–62.

# 4

# REGULATORY FRAMEWORKS FOR ENVIRONMENTAL DISCLOSURE

Over the years, the number of companies releasing environmental information has increased (KPMG, 2020). Most companies have voluntarily decided to prepare a sustainability report to address stakeholders' increasing demand for corporate social responsibility (CSR) disclosure (Fiandrino, 2019). However, the growth in the number of companies preparing sustainability reports is also motivated by the increasing number of legal requirements, which shifted environmental information from voluntary to mandatory disclosure. Based on these considerations, this chapter aims to illustrate the evolution of regulatory frameworks on environmental disclosure, emphasising the transition from voluntary to mandatory disclosure. This passage can primarily be attributed to Directive 2014/95/EU. Therefore, after delineating the European Union's focus on environmental issues by describing the key rules and programs pertaining to environmental matters since its foundation, the chapter focuses on environmental disclosure regulations and, in particular, on Directive 2014/95/EU. The chapter concludes with an illustration of the proposal Corporate Sustainability Reporting Directive, which will amend Directive 2014/95/EU, encouraging overcoming some of its critical issues.

## 4.1 The European Union's attention to environmental issues

Since its foundation, the European Union (EU) has focused on CSR issues, considering sustainability one of its primary aims. Promoting an 'economic and social progress which is balanced and sustainable' was a key objective in the Maastricht Treaty on EU (1992, art B – Title I Common Provisions).

The Lisbon Treaty, issued in 2007, amended the Treaty on EU by introducing a reference to environmental issues. Specifically, Article 3 of the Treaty on

DOI: 10.4324/9781003245933-5

EU states that the Union 'shall contribute to the sustainable development of the Earth' (Article 3 of the Treaty on EU).

Over time, the EU has indicated its focus on environmental issues by defining various types of funding and issuing rules, communications, and programs covering matters including pollution, waste management, nature protection, and environmental impact estimates. Through these policies, the EU aims to achieve the following objectives (Article 191 of the Treaty on the Functioning of the EU):

- To defend, preserve, and improve the EU's natural capital and, in general, the quality of the environment
- To achieve efficient use of natural resources, making the EU a resource-efficient, green, and competitive low-carbon economy
- To combat climate change
- To prevent environment-related risks, which can affect the health and well-being of EU populations

Regarding funding, Article 177 of the Treaty on the Functioning of the EU states that specific funds finance projects in environmental fields. Recent data show that in recent years, the EU has allocated about 30% of both the EU budget for 2021–2027 and the Recovery Instrument Next Generation EU, equal to almost €550 billion, to finance the transition to climate neutrality. Specifically, EU funding has been allocated to finance: (1) member states, companies, and the public sector to implement different climate actions; (2) the development of innovation and research programs; and (3) protection of the environment. Concerning point (1), the EU allocated funding to finance investments aiming to boost the transition to clean and renewable energy, introduce circular economy paradigms, and reduce emissions. For (2), the EU financed innovation in low-carbon technologies or renewables, and research programs useful in achieving the Sustainable Development Goals (SDGs), tackling climate change, and boosting the EU's environmentally sustainable economic growth. Concerning (3), the EU allocated funding to the protection of nature, biodiversity, and quality of life.

EU policy and legislation are based on Articles 11 and 191–193 of the Treaty on the Functioning of the EU. Article 11 focuses on actions to ensure environmental protection, guaranteeing these activities are integrated into EU policies, and to promote and achieve sustainability. Article 191 recognises the main objectives of EU environmental policy and regulation, such as combating climate change. In addition, it identifies the principles that refer to EU environmental policy, which state that (1) it is necessary to adopt precautionary actions to prevent environmental damage; (2) when done, environmental damage should be modified at the source; and (3) the polluter should pay for the environmental damage. Furthermore, member states shall finance and implement the EU environmental policy (Article 192 of the Treaty on the Functioning of the EU), and can maintain or introduce more stringent measures (Article 193 of the Treaty on the Functioning of the EU). According to Article 4 of the Treaty on the Functioning of the EU, dealing with environmental issues is a competence shared between the Union and member states.

Since its founding, the EU has issued numerous policies and regulations on environmental issues. One of the most important recent policies, considered a reference point for other policies, is the *European Green Deal* issued by the European Commission in December 2019. With this communication, the European Commission aimed to make Europe the first climate-neutral continent in the world, in part through the transition to clean energy and development of green technologies. To achieve this aim, the European Green Deal identified the following concrete actions: (1) reduce net greenhouse gas emissions by at least 55% by 2030, compared to the 1990 levels, and achieve no net emissions by 2050; (2) encourage the efficient use of resources by adopting circular economy paradigms; and (3) re-establish biodiversity and reduce pollution. All actions are perfectly aligned with the EU objectives in Article 191 of the Treaty on the Functioning of the EU.

These actions pertain to different areas ranging from clean energy to climate change, and have been implemented through the issuing of numerous other policies and regulations (Figure 4.1 lists the main EU policies and regulations on environmental matters issued since the European Green Deal). For example, to reduce pollution, the European Commission adopted the Communication *Pathway to a Healthy Planet for All EU Action Plan: 'Towards Zero Pollution for Air, Water, and Soil'* in 2021. To introduce the circular economy paradigm, the European Commission in 2020 issued the Communication *A new Circular Economy Action Plan For a cleaner and more competitive Europe.*

In addition to the European Commission's communications, in 2022, the European Parliament and Council issued the *8th Environmental Action Programme*[1] (Decision EU 2022/591), which identifies objectives for 2030 to boost the transition to a climate-neutral and resource-efficient economy as defined in the European Green Deal. Moreover, the 8th Environmental Action Programme suggests increasing stakeholder involvement to foster the effective implementation of EU environmental policies and laws. To this end, to encourage citizens and stakeholders to engage in defining actions to combat climate change, the Commission launched the *European Climate Pact* in 2020. This initiative helps stakeholders (e.g. citizens, communities, and organisations) share ideas, information, actions, and measures to develop solutions useful in tackling climate change.

To ensure the effective implementation of EU policies, the European Parliament and Council added the objectives defined in the European Green Deal to a rule via the *European Climate Law* (Regulation EU 2021/1119). The law identifies legally binding targets to reduce net greenhouse gas emissions by at least 55% by 2030, compared to the 1990 levels, and to eliminate greenhouse gas emissions by 2050. The European Climate Law also includes measures to better understand advances in the actions implemented and if necessary, to correct them. With the issuing of a rule, EU member states are obliged to implement all measures to

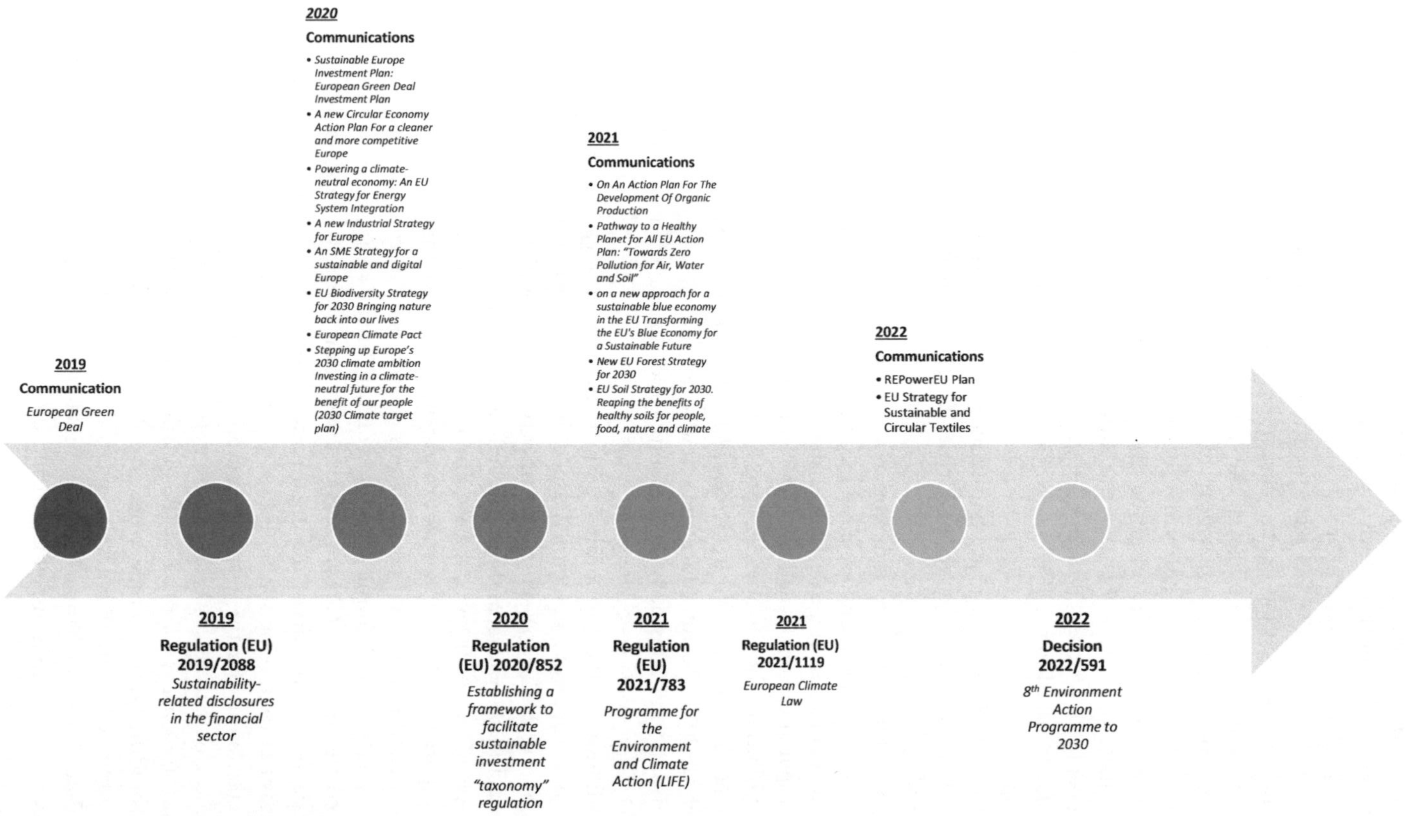


**FIGURE 4.1** The EU policies and regulations on environmental matters since the issue of the European Green Deal

achieve the targets stipulated in the European Climate Law. Thus, the objectives defined in the European Green Deal are likely to be realised.

To achieve the European Green Deal objectives, the EU had to obtain further investments and other funding. Thus, in 2020, the European Commission issued the Communication *Sustainable Europe Investment Plan: European Green Deal Investment Plan*, which acknowledges the investments and funding necessary to implement the actions identified in the European Green Deal. As reported, the EU allocated approximately 30% of both the EU budget for 2021–2027 and the Next Generation EU Recovery Plan, equal to almost €550 billion, to finance the European Green Deal actions.

In addition to previous funding, the EU also aimed to allocate private capital flows into green investments to facilitate the transition to climate neutrality. To this end, regulation 2019/2088 was issued on *sustainability-related disclosures in the financial sector*, which was successively amended by regulation 2020/852 on *establishing a framework to facilitate sustainable investment*, better known as the 'taxonomy' regulation. The 'taxonomy' regulation contains several indications for recognising the environmental sustainability of an economic activity. This helps investors who want to allocate their private funds to sustainable activities, as it enables them to identify green investments. Indeed, the ultimate objective of the regulation is to boost the allocation of capital flows to sustainable investments that foster sustainable growth.

All previous EU policies and legislation shall encourage environmentally sustainable economic growth. The EU plays a significant role in boosting sustainable development (Papa et al., 2022). As reported in the European Green Deal and other EU policies such as the 8th Environmental Action Programme, Communication is part of the wider EU strategy to implement the SDGs.

In 2015, all United Nations member states issued the *2030 Agenda for Sustainable Development*, in which they defined 17 goals and 169 targets to achieve by 2030 to render the world more sustainable. These SDGs are based on the eight Millennium Development Goals (MDGs) defined by the United Nations in 2000 and aim to finalise what the MDGs did not realise. Concerning environmental issues, the main objective of the SDGs is to defend the planet and its natural resources from degradation and guarantee sustainable economic growth that can satisfy both present and future generations' needs. To achieve this aim, the SDGs boost sustainable consumption and production, and the implementation of actions to combat climate change. Numerous SDGs are devoted to environmental issues as follows:

- SDG 6: Ensure availability and sustainable management of water and sanitation for all
- SDG 7: Ensure access to affordable, reliable, sustainable and modern energy for all
- SDG 8: Promote sustained, inclusive and sustainable economic growth, full and productive employment and decent work for all

- SDG 9: Build resilient infrastructure, promote inclusive and sustainable industrialisation and foster innovation
- SDG 12: Ensure sustainable consumption and production patterns
- SDG 13: Take urgent action to combat climate change and its impacts
- SDG 14: Conserve and sustainably use the oceans, seas and marine resources for sustainable development
- SDG 15: Protect, restore and promote sustainable use of terrestrial ecosystems, sustainably manage forests, combat desertification, and halt and reverse land degradation and halt biodiversity loss

Various actors including citizens, public administrations, companies, and States should aim to achieve the SDGs. For companies, the SDGs identify various actions to implement to achieve sustainable development, such as improving resource efficiency in production (Target 8.4). In addition to adopting sustainable business models, companies must communicate the actions implemented to external stakeholders. In this way, companies can increase their transparency; enhance their image, trust, and stakeholder engagement; and improve their decision-making processes on sustainability issues (Global Reporting Initiative and United Nations Global Compact, 2018).

The relevance of disclosing CSR information –or with specific reference to the object of this monograph, environmental information –is also recognised by the EU, which over the years, has issued different rules regarding identifying the information companies should release. The first attempt to introduce environmental disclosure in companies' annual reports was in the *5th Action Programme on the Environment 'Towards Sustainability'* issued by the European Commission in 1993. It suggested that companies need to provide information on financial aspects relating to the environment. Similarly, in 1995, the Accounting Advisory Forum (AAF) suggested incorporating environmental issues into the fourth and seventh Council Directives in the paper *Environmental Issues in Financial Reporting.* In 2001, the European Commission followed the AAF's suggestion by issuing the *6th Environment Action Programme 'Environment 2010: Our future, Our choice'.*

The first rule was Directive 2003/51/EC, with which the EU suggested companies release environmental information in their annual report if these data help in better understanding the company's growth and performance. This directive was the first attempt to introduce a mandatory requirement to provide environmental information. However, the EU legislator did not identify the specific topics or items of information to release, giving a great margin of discretion to companies in deciding what information to disclose. Thus, the key passage introducing mandatory environmental disclosure was first included in 2014 in Directive 2014/95/EU. Herein, EU legislators mandated larger companies to prepare a non-financial statement containing, among others, environmental information. In February 2020, the EU launched a public consultation to obtain stakeholders' views on possible revisions to Directive 2014/95/EU. The consultation ended in June 2020. The primary issues identified include a deficiency in the information

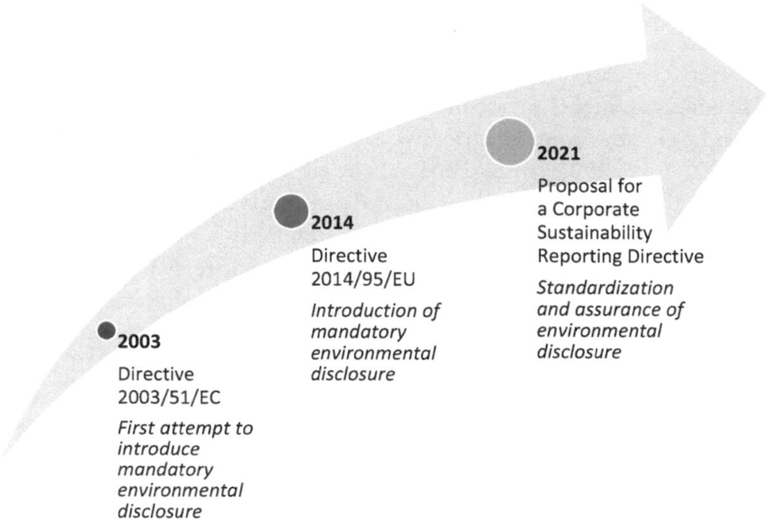


**FIGURE 4.2** The evolution of EU regulation on environmental disclosure
*Source*: Author's elaboration

released in terms of comparability and reliability, necessity to disclose the materiality assessment process, digitalisation of environmental disclosure, and expansion of the scope thereof. In 2021, the European Commission issued a proposal for a new directive on Corporate Sustainability Reporting, which will amend Directive 2014/95/EU to overcome some issues such as the poor level of comparability and reliability of the information released. Therefore, in addition to the requirement to release environmental information, the new directive on Corporate Sustainability Reporting aims to increase the level of standardisation and assure the information provided.

Figure 4.2 shows the evolution of EU regulations on environmental disclosure. The following section explores the main aspects of each directive.

## 4.2 Modernisation Directive 2003/51/EC

In 2003, the European Parliament and Council issued the Modernisation Directive 2003/51/EC on *the annual and consolidated accounts of certain types of companies, banks, and other financial institutions and insurance undertakings*. This Directive amended the Fourth Council Directive 78/660/EEC on the annual accounts of certain types of companies; the Seventh Council Directive 83/349/EEC on consolidated accounts; and Directives 86/635/EEC and 91/674/EEC on the annual accounts and consolidated accounts of banks, other financial institutions, and insurance undertakings.

The main objective of the Directive was to enhance the comparability of financial statements formulated by companies operating in EU member states. In fact, after Regulation (EC) 1606/2002 was issued, EU companies prepared their financial statements in accordance with the IAS/IFRS standards and the Fourth and Seventh Council Directives. Specifically, according to IAS Regulation (EC) 1606/2002, since 2005, all listed companies must prepare their consolidated financial statements in accordance with the IAS/IFRS standards. Companies that did not adopt the IAS/IFRS standards (i.e. listed companies for the preparation of their annual accounts if they do not refer to the IAS/IFRS, and all non-listed companies) must prepare their financial statements following the Fourth and the Seventh Council Directives. In this context, Directive 2003/51/EC aimed to introduce the developments in the IAS/IFRS standards in the Fourth and Seventh Council Directives to reduce differences between the financial statements prepared by companies who are IAS/IFRS compliant and those who are not.[2]

In addition to the previous objective, Directive 2003/51/EC aimed to improve the requirement to include in the annual report 'at least a fair review of the development of the company's business and of its position' contained in Article 46 of the Fourth Council Directive. A similar requirement was included in Article 36 of the Seventh Council Directive for the consolidated annual report. This description was contained in a document prepared by directors, namely the management discussion and analysis, management commentary, management report, or directors' report. According to Directive 2003/51/EC, to provide a fair review, companies must release other information in addition to financial data. Specifically, companies are required to provide, where appropriate, a description of both the environmental and social aspects beneficial in comprehending the company's development, performance, or position.

The requirement to include environmental information in the annual report in Directive 2003/51/EC was consequent to Commission Recommendation 2001/453/EC issued in 2001 on *the recognition, measurement, and disclosure of environmental issues in the annual accounts and annual reports of companies*. With this recommendation, the EU acknowledged that companies' environmental disclosure was unable to satisfy the information needs of users of financial statements. In fact, companies voluntarily release environmental disclosures because of the absence of rules. In addition, the lack of explicit guidance has resulted in information that cannot be compared between companies. Therefore, the environmental information released did not facilitate understanding the effects of environmental risks on the company's position or of the company's environmental actions, which could influence its performance. Commission Recommendation 2001/453/EC overcame previous criticalities by identifying the environmental disclosure companies should have released in their annual reports to provide significant and comparable information on environmental matters to financial statement users. In response to Recommendation 2001/453/EC, numerous EU member states (e.g. Denmark, Finland, France, Portugal, Sweden, and Spain) modified their national rules, introducing the requirement to report environmental information in their annual reports (Criado-Jiménez et al., 2008).

Directive 2003/51/EC introduced the requirement to release previous environmental disclosure in the annual report or consolidated annual report. This represents the first attempt to introduce mandatory environmental disclosure at the EU level. Specifically, Directive 2003/51/CE amended the Fourth and Seventh Council Directives, replacing the first paragraph on the contents of both the annual report and consolidated annual report. Concerning the Fourth Council Directive, Directive 2003/51/EC replaced the first paragraph of Article 46 as follows:

a *The annual report shall include at least a fair review of the development and performance of the company's business and of its position, together with a description of the principal risks and uncertainties that it faces.*

*The review shall be a balanced and comprehensive analysis of the development and performance of the company's business and of its position, consistent with the size and complexity of the business.*

b *To the extent necessary for an understanding of the company's development, performance or position, the analysis shall include both financial and, where appropriate, non-financial key performance indicators relevant to the particular business, including **information relating to environmental** and employee **matters**.*

c *In providing its analysis, the annual report shall, where appropriate, include references to and additional explanations of amounts reported in the annual accounts.*[3]

Despite the requirement to release environmental information in the annual report, noteworthy is that Directive 2003/51/EC does not specify the information to disclose or format thereof (Knopf et al., 2010). The EU legislator opted for a rule with a low level of detail (Bini et al., 2017). In addition, the Directive offered the possibility to each member state to exempt smaller companies from the obligation to release environmental information. Therefore, the EU legislator left great margins of discretion to EU member states in transposing the directive into national laws and companies in defining the type and format of environmental information to release (Pisano and Alvino, 2015). This high degree of discretion led to a low level of comparability of the environmental information released by companies operating in different states and those in the same country.

Member states should have transposed Directive 2003/51/EU into national law by January 2005. Most did so by 2005 and some by 2007. In addition, most member states transposed the Directive as is without amendment (Knopf et al., 2010). Some governments and national organisations issued guidance to support companies in releasing environmental information (Williamson et al., 2014). For example, in 2009, the Italian National Council of Chartered Accountants (Consiglio Nazionale dei Dottori Commercialisti e degli Esperti Contabili) issued two guidelines to support companies in releasing environmental information after the transposition of Directive 2003/51/EU into national law under

Legislative Decree 32/2007.[4] Furthermore, in 2010, the IASB formulated the IFRS Practice Statement 'Management Commentary', non-binding guidelines for companies for the preparation of their management commentary according to the new requirements introduced with Directive 2003/51/EU. Specifically, the guidelines provide principles directors should respect and topics that should be reported in the management commentary. The 'Management Commentary' provides suggestions for most information to release therein according to Directive 2003/51/EU. However, although useful, it did not make recommendations regarding the required environmental information.

To simplify the preparation of the annual report for smaller companies, in 2013, the EU issued Accounting Directive 2013/34/EU on *the annual financial statements, consolidated financial statements, and related reports of certain types of undertakings*, which repealed the Fourth and Seventh Council Directives. Based on the 'think small first' principle, the Directive allowed smaller companies to prepare a simplified financial statement to reduce their administrative burden. However, Directive 2013/34/EU did not modify the contents on the management report. Therefore, the disclosure of environmental information was still required when needed to comprehend a company's development, performance, or position. It also confirmed the possibility of each member state to exempt smaller companies from the obligation to release environmental information.

## 4.3 Non-Financial Reporting Directive 2014/95/EU

In 2014, the EU issued the Non-Financial Reporting Directive 2014/95/EU *disclosure of non-financial and diversity information by certain large undertakings and groups*, which introduced the requirement for larger companies to release, among others, information on environmental aspects in a document named the non-financial statement. Specifically, according to Directive 2014/95/EU, larger companies must prepare a non-financial statement in which information must be reported on the activities carried out, risks supported and results concerning environmental aspects, social and employee-related matters, respect for human rights, anti-corruption and bribery issues, and diversity of the board of directors.

Directive 2014/95/EU represents an important step in achieving sustainable development (Muserra et al., 2020). It is the result of a long process to introduce the requirement for companies to release information on environmental and social aspects to permit external stakeholders to understand the company's development, performance, and position. As mentioned, this process started with Directive 2003/51/EU, which introduced the requirement to release environmental and employee information in the management report when needed to comprehend the company's development, performance, or position. It did not specify the topics to include. The following years, the European Commission highlighted the need to enhance the level of social and environmental information released by companies, considering that higher levels of disclosure are key elements in achieving a greater focus on CSR issues. These aspects were included in the Communications *Single Market Act. Twelve levers to boost growth and strengthen confidence: Working together to create new growth* and *A renewed strategy 2011–2014 for Corporate Social Responsibility* issued by the European Commission in 2011. In February 2013, the European Parliament issued two resolutions[5] in which it further recognised the need to enhance the information released on environmental and social aspects. It also asked the European Commission to develop a legislative proposal. In April 2013, after a process of consultation with interested parties, the European Commission issued the proposal *For a Directive as regards disclosure of non-financial and diversity information by certain large companies and groups* to improve company disclosure on social and environmental aspects, and greater comparability of the information released by different companies. In the proposal, the European Commission noted that only a few EU companies habitually released non-financial disclosures on environmental and social issues, and that the information provided did not satisfy stakeholders' needs. Moreover, companies adopted a great margin of discretion in disclosing this kind of information, making it difficult for external stakeholders to compare that of various companies. Finally, the European Commission noted the fragmentation of legislative frameworks across EU member states. Previous considerations brought the European Commission to affirm that the requirement to provide environmental and social information contained in the Directives in force at the time was not sufficiently effective, and that it was necessary to introduce clearer and stronger requirements for adoption in all EU member states in the same way.

The issuing of Directive 2014/95/EU addresses previous needs and marks an important moment in the transition from an environmental disclosure released voluntarily and in a discretionary way to the mandatory provision of information (La Torre et al., 2018). In contrast to Directive 2003/51/EU, Directive 2014/95/EU identifies specific environmental arguments to include in the non-financial statement. Here, the implementation of Directive 2014/95/EU represents a key passage for increasing the release of environmental information, especially in countries where no disclosure requirements previously existed (Bini and Bellucci, 2020). The necessity to release environmental information mandated by legal requirements could have induced companies to incorporate environmental issues into their business models, increasing their commitment to CSR matters and achieving the SDGs. However, to be effective, it is important that the information released does not simply remain words, but that environmental practices and activities are fully incorporated in the business model (Bini and Bellucci, 2020).

Considering this monograph's focus on environmental information, the two paragraphs below illustrate the environmental disclosure requirements introduced by Directive 2014/95/EUand included in the guidelines issued by the EU to help companies release this information. Then, the transposition of Directive 2014/95/EU into the national laws of EU member states is described to clarify whether EU countries introduced the same environmental disclosure requirements.

### 4.3.1 Environmental disclosure requirements according to Directive 2014/95/EU

Directive 2014/95/EU amended Directive 2013/34/EU by inserting a new article (Article 19a) that required larger companies to prepare a non-financial statement. Directive 2014/95/EU requires that:

> *Large undertakings which are public-interest entities exceeding on their balance sheet dates the criterion of the average number of 500 employees during the financial year shall include in the management report a non-financial statement [...]*

The concept of a public-interest entity is defined in Directive 2013/34/EU, according to which it is: (1) a company with trading transferable securities on an EU member state's regulated market, (2) a financial company (credit institute or insurance), or (3) a company designated as a public-interest entity by the EU member state.

Directive 2013/34/EU also defines the concept of a large undertaking, stating that it exceeds at least two of the following three criteria: (1) total balance sheet: € 20 million, (2) net turnover: € 40 million, (3) average number of employees: 250.

Therefore, companies with more than 500 employees that present a total balance sheet higher than € 20 million or net turnover higher than € 40 million must prepare a non-financial statement. A similar requirement has been introduced for bigger groups, which have to prepare a consolidated non-financial statement if they have more than 500 employees on average and present a total balance sheet higher than € 20 million or net turnover higher than € 40 million.

Consistent with the 'think small first' principle, Directive 2014/95/EU must be applied exclusively by bigger companies, because the EU legislator considered it too onerous for small and medium-sized enterprises (SMEs) to prepare the non-financial statement. In the proposal issued in 2013, the European Commission estimated that the new disclosure requirements would affect around 18,000 large companies and groups in the EU.

In addition, Directive 2014/95/EU identifies where this statement must be inserted, requiring a non-financial statement in the management report. Furthermore, if the company prepares another separate report containing the same information required by Directive 2014/95/EU, the EU member states have the possibility to exempt that company from preparing the non-financial statement. However, the company must make a separate report available at the same time as the management report, or no later than six months after, on the company's website.

Directive 2014/95/EU identifies both the thematic aspects companies must discuss in the non-financial statement and the reporting areas for each thematic aspect. The Directive 2014/95/EU requires companies to report the following in the non-financial statement:

> *Information to the extent necessary for an understanding of the undertaking's development, performance, position and impact of its activity, relating to, as a minimum, environmental, social and employee matters, respect for human rights, anti-corruption and bribery matters, including:*
>
> a *a brief description of the undertaking's business model;*
> b *a description of the policies pursued by the undertaking in relation to those matters, including due diligence processes implemented;*
> c *the outcome of those policies;*
> d *the principal risks related to those matters linked to the undertaking's operations including, where relevant and proportionate, its business relationships, products or services which are likely to cause adverse impacts in those areas, and how the undertaking manages those risks;*
> e *non-financial key performance indicators relevant to the particular business.*
>
> *Where the undertaking does not pursue policies in relation to one or more of those matters, the non-financial statement shall provide a clear and reasoned explanation for not doing so.*

Therefore, Directive 2014/95/EU identifies four thematic aspects on which the company must provide information: (1) environmental issues, (2) social and employee matters, (3) respect for human rights, and (4) anti-corruption and bribery matters. In addition, the company must provide information on the diversity policies adopted in defining the composition of the board of directors. For each thematic aspect, the company must describe the business model implemented, activities carried out, results achieved, main risks, and the most important non-financial key performance indicators (KPIs). Finally, according to the 'comply or explain' principle, Directive 2014/95/EU requires companies that do not provide some information to explain the reason for non-disclosure.

In contrast to Directive 2003/51/EU, Directive 2014/95/EU provides clear and stringent disclosure requirements. However, it does not specify the format in which to present this information. It also identifies the reporting areas for each thematic aspect in a generic way, without defining the specific items of information to release for describing, for example, the business model implemented, results achieved, or KPIs (Lepore et al., 2022). Therefore, companies continue to report environmental information with great margins of discretion.

Some indications are contained in Recital 7 of Directive 2014/95/EU, which stipulates the main elements to describe in the non-financial statement for each thematic aspect. For example, concerning environmental information, Recital 7 states the following:

> *Where undertakings are required to prepare a non-financial statement, that statement should contain, as regards environmental matters, details of the current and foreseeable impacts of the undertaking's operations on the environment, and, as appropriate,*

> *on health and safety, the use of renewable and/or non-renewable energy, greenhouse gas emissions, water use and air pollution.*

As such, Directive 2014/95/EU encourages the release of key environmental performance indicators on the use of renewable or non-renewable energy, greenhouse gas emissions, air pollution, and so on (Camilleri, 2015).

However, the great margin of discretion given to companies is remarked in the same Directive 2014/95/EU, which states companies should refer to national, European, or international guidelines in preparing their non-financial statements, such as the GRI, Eco-Management and Audit Scheme (EMAS), UN Global Compact, and ISO 26000. While most companies prepared their non-financial statements with reference to the GRI standards (De Groen et al., 2020; KPMG, 2020; Doni et al., 2019), the option contained in Directive 2014/95/EU does not exclude the possibility that different companies adopt different guidelines, thereby rendering the information released non-comparable (Papa et al., 2022; La Torre et al., 2020).

### *4.3.2 European Commission Guidelines*

Although it stipulates clearer and more stringent disclosure requirements than previous Directives, Directive 2014/95/EU gives companies great margins of discretion in defining the specific items of information to release for all reporting areas within each thematic aspect identified, presentation format, and guidelines to refer to when disclosing the information.

To reduce this flexibility and help companies in releasing information, Directive 2014/95/EU imposes the European Commission to issue guidance in 2016. Specifically, Article 2 of Directive 2014/95/EU states:

> *The Commission shall prepare non-binding guidelines on methodology for reporting non-financial information, including non-financial key performance indicators, general and sectoral, with a view to facilitating relevant, useful and comparable disclosure of non-financial information by undertakings. In doing so, the Commission shall consult relevant stakeholders.*
>
> *The Commission shall publish the guidelines by 6 December 2016.*

Therefore, unlike previous Directives for which the EU did not issue guidance to support companies in releasing the information required (Bini et al., 2007), in Directive 2014/95/EU, the EU legislator imposed the European Commission to develop non-binding guidelines based on existing EU and international best practices (Arif et al., 2021).

The European Commission developed two non-binding guidelines on how to disclose environmental and social information. The first guideline, published in 2017, concerned non-financial information, environmental and social. The second, issued in 2019, referred to the disclosure of climate-related information.

### 4.3.2.1 Guidelines on non-financial reporting (methodology for reporting non-financial information)

The objective of the first guidance is to support companies in releasing material, significant and comparable information on both environmental and social matters, which is useful for external stakeholders in their decisions. As reported in the 'purpose' section of the guidance:

> *The aim of these guidelines is to help companies disclose high quality, relevant, useful, consistent and more comparable non-financial (environmental, social and governance-related) information in a way that fosters resilient and sustainable growth and employment, and provides transparency to stakeholders. These non-binding guidelines are proposed within the remit of the reporting requirements provided for under the Directive. They are intended to help companies draw up relevant, useful concise non-financial statements according to the requirements of the Directive. Significant efforts have been made to avoid undue administrative burden, boilerplate disclosures, or a mere box-ticking exercise.*

To achieve the objective, the guidance provides a principle-based methodology to release information on environmental and social issues. Aligned with the approach in Directive 2014/95/EU, the guidelines confirm the great flexibility afforded to companies in providing non-financial information. It defines the key principles according to which companies should report information in the non-financial statement, and the content to provide for the five reporting areas and four thematic aspects (i.e. environmental issues, social and employee matters, respect for human rights, anti-corruption, and bribery matters) specified in Directive 2014/95/EU. The guidelines provide explanations, examples, and KPIs. However, they do not stipulate the information to be released, giving companies the discretion to define the specific items of information to disclose and format of its presentation.

To prepare the guidelines, the European Commission reviewed existing national, EU, and international frameworks on non-financial information, such as the Climate Disclosure Standards Board, EMAS, GRI, International Integrated Reporting Framework, and Sustainability Accounting Standards Board. In addition, in 2016, the European Commission conducted a public consultation by submitting an online questionnaire to obtain stakeholders' opinions on the non-binding guidance to issue. The questionnaire received 355 responses, highlighting the perceived importance of the content of Directive 2014/95/EU.

The guidelines identify the following key principles to consider when defining the information to release:

- Disclose material information
- Fair, balanced, and understandable
- Comprehensive but concise
- Strategic and forward-looking

- Stakeholder orientated
- Consistent and coherent

For each key principle, the guidelines provide a definition, explanation to understand the application of the principle, and examples and KPIs. For example, concerning the first key principle, namely to disclose material information, the guidelines define material information as follows:

> *The status of information where its omission or misstatement could reasonably be expected to influence decisions that users make on the basis of the financial statements of the undertaking. The materiality of individual items shall be assessed in the context of other similar items.*

In addition, as an explanation, they specify the concept of environmental and social materiality from the double materiality perspective as follows:

> *The impact of a company's activity is a relevant consideration when making non-financial disclosures. Impacts may be positive or adverse. Material disclosures should cover both in a clear and balanced way. The non-financial statement is expected to reflect a company's fair view of the information needed by relevant stakeholders.*

Finally, the guidance provides some examples and KPIs, for example:

> *A bank may consider that its own water consumption in offices and branches is not a material issue to be included in its management report. In contrast, the bank may assess that the social and environmental impacts of projects that it funds and its role in supporting the real economy of a city, a region or a country are material information.*

Concerning the content of the non-financial statement, the guidelines resume the five reporting areas identified for each thematic aspect in Directive 2014/95/EU:

- Description of the business model
- Description of policies and due diligence
- Outcomes of the policies
- Principal risks
- Non-financial KPIs

For each reporting area, the guidelines provide explanations, recommendations on what companies can disclose, and examples. For example, concerning the first reporting area, namely the description of the business model, the guidelines include the following explanation:

> *A company's business model describes how it generates and preserves value through its products or services over the longer term. The business model provides context*

> *for the management report as a whole. It provides an overview of how a company operates and the rationale of its structure, by describing how it transforms inputs into outputs through its business activities. In more simple terms, what a company does, how and why it does it.*

In addition, it suggests the information that could be reported to describe the business model: '*Disclosures relating to: their business environment; their organisation and structure; the markets where they operate; their objectives and strategies; and main trends and factors that may affect their future development*'. Finally, the guidelines include examples such as:

> *A company may consider specific disclosures explaining: the main products it makes, and how they meet the needs of consumers/customers; how these products are made, and what makes its production approach competitive and sustainable; the characteristics of the market where it operates, and how it may evolve.*

They also provide recommendations and examples of information items companies should report for each thematic aspect. Concerning environmental issues, for example, the guidelines suggest the following:

> *A company is expected to disclose relevant information on the actual and potential impacts of its operations on the environment, and on how current and foreseeable environmental matters may affect the company's development, performance or position.*
>
> *This may include:*
>
> - *material disclosures on pollution prevention and control;*
> - *environmental impact from energy use;*
> - *direct and indirect atmospheric emissions;*
> - *use and protection of natural resources (e.g. water, land) and related protection of biodiversity;*
> - *waste management;*
> - *environmental impacts from transportation or from the use and disposal of products and services; and*
> - *development of green products and services.*

Finally, guidelines indicate KPIs companies can report in the non-financial statement for each thematic aspect. For example, concerning environmental matters, the guidelines suggest the following KPIs:

- Energy performance and improvements in energy performance
- Energy consumption from non-renewable sources and energy intensity
- Greenhouse gas emissions in metric tonnes of $CO_2$ equivalent and greenhouse gas intensity
- Emissions of other pollutants (measured in absolute value and as intensity)

- Extraction of natural resources
- Impacts and dependences on natural capital and biodiversity
- Waste management (e.g. recycling rates)

#### *4.3.2.2 Guidelines on non-financial reporting: Supplement on reporting climate-related information*

In 2019, the European Commission issued a second guidance focusing on the disclosure of climate-related information.

These guidelines resulted from an online consultation in 2019, and are based on the recommendations of the Task Force on Climate-related Financial Disclosures (TCFD) in 2017 and Technical Expert Group on Sustainable Finance in 2018. Both these aimed to encourage companies to release climate-related information to boost the allocation of private funds in sustainable investments. To formulate the guidelines, the European Commission referred to existing frameworks including the GRI, Climate Disclosure Standards Board, Sustainability Accounting Standards Board, International Integrated Reporting Council, and EMAS.

Aligned with previous guidelines, this one also adopted a flexible approach, giving companies a great margin of discretion in providing climate-related information. Moreover, it supports companies in releasing environmental information by deepening the key principle of materiality and suggesting what information to disclose for each reporting area identified by Directive 2014/95/EU.

Concerning the first point, the second guidelines do not illustrate all the key principles but focus on the first, namely to disclose material information, better specifying the double materiality perspective in reporting climate-related information. When discussing environmental and social disclosure, the principle of materiality assumes two perspectives: a financial perspective (or 'outside-in' perspective) and an environmental and social perspective (or 'inside-out' perspective). Therefore, it is common to talk about the double materiality perspective, according to which the company should release climate-related information to understand its development, performance, and position (financial materiality), and its external impacts on people and the environment (environmental and social materiality). Users of the information released following the double materiality perspective include investors, the primary audience of the information released from a financial perspective, and other stakeholders (i.e. citizens, employees, and society), the primary audience of the information regarding environmental and social perspectives (see Figure 4.3).

Furthermore, from a double materiality perspective, the environmental information reported should discuss both the risks of the negative impacts of climate change on the company's development, performance, and position, and risks of the negative impacts of the company's activities on climate. In addition to the risks, the company should also report opportunities for the company and climate based on the implementation of actions to mitigate climate change.

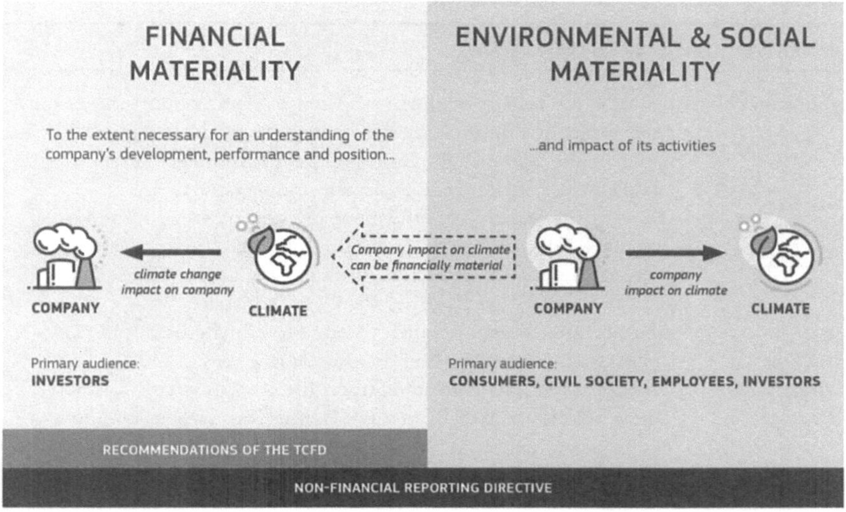


**FIGURE 4.3** The double materiality perspective in releasing environmental disclosure

Then, based on the double materiality perspective, the guidelines resume the reporting areas of Directive 2014/95/EU, focusing on the thematic aspect of environmental matters. For each reporting area, the guidelines list climate-related disclosures companies could report to improve understanding of their development, performance, position, and impact of their activities, providing for each disclosure further guidance and explanation on the information to release (see Table 4.1).

### *4.3.3 Transposition of Directive 2014/95/EU into the laws of EU member states*

Directive 2014/95/EU was effective on 5 December 2014. It required larger companies to prepare a non-financial statement disclosing environmental and social information for the first time in 2018, referred to as financial year 2017. EU member states had to transpose the Directive into national law by 6 December 2016.

Member states generally have considerable flexibility in the transposition of a directive into national law. Regarding Directive 2014/95/EU, the following are the main aspects for which EU member states can define different requirements:

- Company scope
- Reporting features
- Auditor's involvement
- Penalties for non-compliance

**TABLE 4.1** The climate-related disclosure for each reporting area

| *Reporting area* | *Climate-related disclosures* |
|---|---|
| Business model | - Describe the impact of climate-related risks and opportunities on the company's business model, strategy and financial planning.<br>- Describe the ways in which the company's business model can impact the climate, both positively and negatively.<br>- Describe the resilience of the company's business model and strategy, taking into consideration different climate-related scenarios over different time horizons, including at least a 2 °C or lower scenario and a greater than 2 °C scenario. |
| Policies and Due Diligence Processes | - Describe any company policies related to climate, including any climate change mitigation or adaptation policy.<br>- Describe any climate-related targets the company has set as part of its policies, especially any GHG emissions targets, and how company targets relate to national and international targets and to the Paris Agreement, in particular.<br>- Describe the board's oversight of climate-related risks and opportunities.<br>- Describe management's role in assessing and managing climate-related risks and opportunities and explain the rationale for the approach. |
| Outcomes | - Describe the outcomes of the company's policy on climate change, including the performance of the company against the indicators used and targets set to manage climate-related risks and opportunities.<br>- Describe the development of GHG emissions against the targets set and the related risks over time. |
| Principal Risks and their Management | - Describe the company's processes for identifying and assessing climate-related risks over the short, medium, and long term and disclose how the company defines short, medium, and long term.<br>- Describe the principal climate-related risks the company has identified over the short, medium, and long term throughout the value chain, and any assumptions that have been made when identifying these risks. This description should include the principal risks resulting from any dependencies on natural capitals threatened by climate change, such as water, land, ecosystems, or biodiversity.<br>- Describe processes for managing climate-related risks (if applicable how they make decisions to mitigate, transfer, accept, or control those risks), and how the company is managing the particular climate-related risks that it has identified.<br>- Describe how processes for identifying, assessing, and managing climate-related risks are integrated into the company's overall risk management. An important aspect of this description is how the company determines the relative significance of climate-related risks in relation to other risks. |

| | |
|---|---|
| Key Performance Indicators | ***GHG emissions***<br>- Direct GHG emissions from sources owned or controlled by the company.<br>- Indirect GHG emissions from the generation of acquired and consumed electricity, steam, heat, or cooling (collectively referred to as "electricity").<br>- All indirect GHG emissions that occur in the value chain of the reporting company, including both upstream and downstream emissions.<br>- GHG absolute emissions target.<br>***Energy***<br>- Total energy consumption and/or production from renewable and non-renewable sources.<br>- Energy efficiency target.<br>- Renewable energy consumption and/or production target.<br>***Physical risks***<br>- Assets committed in regions likely to become more exposed to acute or chronic physical climate risks.<br>***Products and services***<br>- Percent turnover in the reporting year from products or services associated with activities that meet the criteria for substantially contributing to mitigation of or adaptation to climate change as set out in the Regulation on the establishment of a framework to facilitate sustainable investment (EU taxonomy).<br>- Percent investment (CapEx) and/or expenditures (OpEx) in the reporting year for assets or processes associated with activities that meet the criteria for substantially contributing to mitigation of or adaptation to climate change as set out in the Regulation on the establishment of a framework to facilitate sustainable investment (EU taxonomy).<br>***Green Finance***<br>- Climate-related Green Bond Ratio (Total amount of green bonds outstanding (at year-end) divided by (a 5-year rolling average of) total amount of bonds outstanding).<br>- Climate-related Green Debt Ratio (Total amount of all green debt instruments outstanding (at year-end) divided by (a 5-year rolling average of) total amount of all debt outstanding). |

*Source*: Guidelines on non-financial reporting: Supplement on reporting climate-related information (2019a)

Company scope refers to the identification of companies that must prepare a non-financial statement. According to Directive 2014/95/EU, large undertakings that are public-interest entities with more than 500 employees must prepare a non-financial statement. In transposing the Directive into national law, EU member states had flexibility in the definition of a large undertaking and public-interest entity. Therefore, the typology and number of companies that must prepare non-financial statements differ based on the definition of large undertaking and public interest entities by EU member states at the time of transposition.

Reporting features refer to the definition of the content to report and identification of the reporting framework and document in which to disclose information. The content to report refers to the four thematic aspects and five reporting areas identified in Directive 2014/95/EU, which EU member states could adapt when transposing the Directive into national law. Specifically, some EU member states could repeat all the content identified in the Directive, while some may require companies to release information not included in the Directive. EU member states could also define different requirements regarding reporting frameworks in preparing the non-financial statement (i.e. national, Union-based, or international) and for the disclosure format (i.e. separate report or in the management report). Although the EU legislator's intention was to encourage the release of comparable information on environmental and social issues, possibly, the disclosure provided by companies operating in different states would be not comparable because the EU member states defined different reporting features when they transposed the Directive.

Auditor involvement refers to the possibility that EU member states require an independent auditor to verify the presence of the non-financial statement and/or content reported in it. Different transposition into national law render assurance diverse, influencing the degree of reliability of the information released.

The last point refers to the possibility that EU member states can define penalties in cases of non-compliance with the national law. Member states had great margins of discretion in defining the penalties to apply in cases of non-compliance. Directive 2014/95/EU does not regulate this aspect. However, the definition of a different penalty in cases of non-compliance could influence the level and quality of information released on environmental and social matters. Possibly, companies may adopt different disclosure behaviours based on the diverse penalties defined by the EU member state in which they operate.

For the abovementioned aspects, Table 4.2 lists the 28 EU member states, with the additional countries of Iceland and Norway, that: (1) transposed the same requirement as it is regulated in the Directive, (2) adapted the requirement to the existing national law, or (3) omitted the requirement.

To define a large undertaking, the majority of member states adopted the same requirement as stipulated in Directive 2014/95/EU, namely as one with an average number of employees exceeding 500 with a total balance sheet exceeding € 20 million or net turnover exceeding € 40 million. However, 11 countries adopted a different definition, specifying lower values for the threshold of the average number of employees (e.g. Denmark, Luxembourg, and Sweden identified the value of 250 employees as the threshold) or of both the balance sheet total and net turnover (e.g. Belgium). Other states defined a large undertaking with reference only to the threshold of the average number of employees over 500 (e.g. Estonia, Portugal, Romania, United Kingdom), or adding to this threshold the

**TABLE 4.2** The transposition of Directive 2014/95/EU into national law

| *Directive 2014/95/EU requirement* | *The same requirement of Directive* | *Requirement adapted to existing national law* | *Requirement omitted into the national law* |
|---|---|---|---|
| ***Definition of large undertaking***<br>- average number of employees exceeding 500<br>- total balance sheet exceeding € 20 million or net turnover exceeding € 40 million | ***19 States***<br>Austria, Bulgaria, Croatia, Cyprus, Finland, France, Germany, Hungary, Ireland, Italy, Latvia, Lithuania, Malta, The Netherland, Norway, Poland, Slovakia, Slovenia, Spain | ***11 States***<br>Belgium, Czech Republic, Denmark, Estonia, Greece, Iceland, Luxembourg, Portugal, Romania, Sweden, United Kingdom | |
| ***Definition of public-interest entity***<br>- company with trading transferable securities on an EU Member State's regulated market<br>- credit institute<br>- insurance undertaking<br>- company designated as a public-interest entity by the EU Member State | ***6 States***<br>Estonia, Finland, Ireland, Malta, Slovenia, United Kingdom | ***24 States***<br>Austria, Belgium, Bulgaria, Croatia, Cyprus, Czech Republic, Denmark, France, Germany, Greece, Hungary, Iceland, Italy, Latvia, Lithuania, Luxembourg, The Netherland, Norway, Poland, Portugal, Romania, Slovakia, Spain, Sweden | |
| ***Thematic aspects***<br>- environment<br>- social and employee matters<br>- respect for human rights<br>- anti-corruption and bribery matters | ***29 States***<br>Austria, Belgium, Bulgaria, Croatia, Cyprus, Czech Republic, Denmark, Estonia, Finland, France, Germany, Greece, Hungary, Iceland, Ireland, Italy, Latvia, Lithuania, Luxembourg, Malta, The Netherland, Norway, Poland, Portugal, Slovakia, Slovenia, Spain, Sweden, United Kingdom | ***1 State***<br>Romania | |

*(Continued)*

**TABLE 4.2** Continued

| *Directive 2014/95/EU requirement* | *The same requirement of Directive* | *Requirement adapted to existing national law* | *Requirement omitted into the national law* |
|---|---|---|---|
| ***Reporting areas***<br>- description of the business model<br>- description of the policies and due diligence<br>- outcomes of the policies<br>- principal risks<br>- non-financial key performance indicators | ***23 States***<br>Austria, Belgium, Bulgaria, Croatia, Cyprus, Czech Republic, Denmark, Estonia, Finland, France, Germany, Hungary, Iceland, Ireland, Italy, Luxembourg, The Netherland, Norway, Poland, Portugal, Romania, Slovakia, United Kingdom | ***7 States***<br>Greece, Latvia, Lithuania, Malta, Slovenia, Spain, Sweden | |
| ***Reporting framework***<br>- national reporting framework<br>- EU-based reporting framework<br>- international reporting framework | ***24 States***<br>Austria, Belgium, Croatia, Cyprus, Czech Republic, Estonia, Finland, France, Germany, Greece, Hungary, Iceland, Ireland, Latvia, Lithuania, Luxembourg, Malta, The Netherland, Norway, Portugal, Romania, Slovenia, Sweden, United Kingdom | ***6 States***<br>Bulgaria, Denmark, Italy, Poland, Slovakia, Spain | |
| ***Disclosure format***<br>- within the management report<br>- separate report available at the same time of the management report, or no later than six months, on the company's website. | ***7 States***<br>Cyprus, Finland, Ireland, Luxembourg, Poland, Portugal, Romania | ***23 States***<br>Austria, Belgium, Bulgaria, Croatia, Czech Republic, Denmark, Estonia, France, Germany, Greece, Hungary, Iceland, Italy, Latvia, Lithuania, Malta, The Netherland, Norway, Slovakia, Slovenia, Spain, Sweden, United Kingdom | |

| | | | |
|---|---|---|---|
| ***Auditor's involvement*** Provide assurance on: - the presence of the non-financial statement - the content of the non-financial statement | ***20 States*** Austria, Belgium, Croatia, Czech Republic, Estonia, Finland, Greece, Hungary, Ireland, Lithuania, Luxembourg, Malta, The Netherland, Norway, Poland, Portugal, Slovakia, Slovenia, Spain, Sweden | ***9 States*** Bulgaria, Cyprus, Denmark, France, Iceland, Italy, Latvia, Romania, United Kingdom | ***1 State*** Germany |
| ***Penalties for non-compliance*** | | ***26 States*** Austria, Belgium, Bulgaria, Croatia, Cyprus, Czech Republic, Finland, France, Germany, Greece, Hungary, Iceland, Ireland, Italy, Latvia, Lithuania, Luxembourg, Malta, Norway, Poland, Portugal, Romania, Slovakia, Slovenia, Sweden, United Kingdom | ***4 States*** Denmark, Estonia, The Netherland, Spain |

*Source:* CSR Europe and GRI (2017)

requirement to have exclusively a net turnover over a specific amount (e.g. the Czech Republic). Greece extended the preparation of the non-financial statement that included a report on environmental and social matters to companies with more than 10 employees and a total balance sheet exceeding € 700.000 or net turnover exceeding € 350.000.

For the definition of a public-interest entity, only six countries adopted the same requirement as in Directive 2014/95/EU. The majority of member states extended the definition of public-interest entities to companies other than listed firms, credit institutions, and insurance undertakings, such as to investment firms (e.g. Hungary), pension funds (e.g. Bulgaria, Croatia, the Czech Republic), state-limited liability companies (e.g. Denmark, Lithuania), or non-listed larger companies (e.g. France).

Regarding reporting features, most member states required companies to release information on the four thematic aspects identified in the Directive (i.e. environmental issues, social and employee matters, respect for human rights, anti-corruption, and bribery matters). Romania added specific topics to each thematic aspect.

Similarly, the majority of member states required companies to release information on the five reporting areas identified in the Directive (description of the business model, description of policies and due diligence, outcomes of the policies, principal risks, and non-financial KPIs). Greece inserted the requirement to release data on the due diligence policy at a separate point from the description of the policies, emphasising this reporting area. The other six countries (Latvia, Lithuania, Malta, Slovenia, Spain, and Sweden) added another point, namely *'an explanation of the sums indicated in the financial statement which are relevant to corporate social responsibility'*, as suggested by Directive 2014/95/EU.

For the reporting framework, the majority of member states stated that companies could rely on an international, national, or EU-based reporting framework to prepare the non-financial statement, allowing great margins for their discretion. Other countries (e.g. Denmark, Spain) added to the previous indication a list of frameworks that could be used, such as the GRI or EMAS, but confirmed companies' flexibility in defining the standard to rely on. Italy and Poland added the possibility of referring to a mixed reporting methodology based on more standards. Finally, Bulgaria required reference to a specific framework identified by the Minister of Finance.

Regarding disclosure format, most member states adapted the Directive requirement. However, reading the various national laws, few differences are evident compared to the Directive requirement to include the non-financial statement in the management report or in a separate report available at the same time as the management report, or no later than six months thereafter, on the company's website. Some countries added the requirement to include the non-financial statement in the annual report (e.g. Greece, Lithuania) or identified different months in which to make available the non-financial statement (e.g. Germany).

Greater variability emerges with respect to auditor involvement. Excepting Germany, which does not require the auditor's verification, 20 member states require the auditor's verification of only the presence of the non-financial statement. Nine states (Bulgaria, Cyprus, Denmark, France, Iceland, Italy, Latvia, Romania, and the United Kingdom) also need the auditor's verification for the content of the non-financial statement.

Finally, concerning penalties for non-compliance, four member states (Denmark, Estonia, the Netherlands, and Spain) did not introduce fines. The other member states specified diverse penalties with reference to other national acts.

In conclusion, the analysis of the transposition of Directive 2014/95/EU into national laws indicates a lack of homogeneity among member states in the identification of companies required to prepare non-financial statements.

Regarding reporting features, although most member states required companies to release information on the four thematic aspects and five reporting areas identified in the Directive, companies have great flexibility in identifying their reporting framework. The option to refer to various reporting frameworks does not exclude the possibility that different companies adopt diverse guidelines, rendering the information released non-comparable (Papa et al., 2022; La Torre et al., 2020).

In addition, the different transpositions into national law of the requirement concerning the auditor's involvement brought about a diverse level of assurance regulated by member states, which reduces the degree of reliability of the information released by companies operating in different countries.

## 4.4 The proposal Corporate Sustainability Reporting Directive

In April 2021, the European Commission issued a proposal for a Corporate Sustainability Reporting Directive (CSRD), which would modify the existing requirements on the environmental and social information to release. This was to overcome critical issues that emerged after the implementation of Directive 2014/95/EU. In the proposal, the European Commission highlighted the inadequacy of Directive 2014/95/EU in satisfying the information needs of various stakeholders (Papa et al., 2022), which emerged during the public consultation by the European Commission to collect stakeholders' views on possible revisions to Directive 2014/95/EU that ended in June 2020. First, most companies do not fall into the scope of the Directive; therefore, they do not have to prepare a non-financial statement despite that stakeholders are interested in their orientation to environmental and social matters and would like to receive information on these topics. According to the European Commission, only around 11,700 large companies and groups are required to prepare a non-financial statement according to existing requirements. In addition, when information is released, it is often non-comparable and difficult for users to find. In fact, companies do not have precise indications of how and what to disclose, or where to report the information. The possibility of referring to different reporting frameworks, flexibility in decisions regarding specific items of information to release and presentation format thereof, and discretion in defining whether to include the non-financial statement in the management report or to prepare a separate report generate confusion among companies. Finally, the decision of some EU member states to exclusively require the assurance of the existence of a non-financial statement, and others' choice to extend that assurance to the content thereof reduces the reliability of the information released by companies operating in different countries.[6]

To overcome these critical issues, the European Commission issued a proposal for the CSRD to boost comparability, reliability, and easy access for stakeholders to environmental and social information, and to ensure sustainability information[7] (the new term) is released by more companies.[8] To achieve this aim, the new directive proposes:

1 Extending the requirement to report sustainability information to other companies, in particular, to all large companies and listed companies (except listed micro-companies)
2 Better specifying the sustainability information to disclose, requiring companies to release it in accordance with mandatory EU sustainability reporting standards
3 Requiring the provision of an assurance of the sustainability information released
4 Requiring companies to disclose the information in a digital and machine-readable format.

Regarding (1), the proposal for a CSRD aims to modify Article 19a of Accounting Directive 2013/34/EU by expanding the scope of the sustainability reporting requirements to all large companies and listed companies (both large and small and medium-sized, except listed micro-companies). Therefore, in the proposal, there is no reference to the threshold for the average number of employees. Consistent with the 'think small first' principle, non-listed small and medium-sized companies and all micro-companies (listed and non-listed) are excluded as it could be too onerous for them to prepare a sustainability report. In addition, to contain the reporting costs for listed small- and medium-sized companies, the proposal states that these companies must prepare a sustainability report as of January 2026.

With this amendment to the Accounting Directive, the European Commission aims to ensure that all companies for whom stakeholders want to receive sustainability information disclose such data. By encouraging a wider diffusion of sustainability information from a greater number of companies, the proposal also aims to boost the allocation of private funds to green investments, as required by the *Sustainability-related Disclosure Regulation* and *Taxonomy Regulation* discussed in the first paragraph of this chapter. In the Impact Assessment accompanying the proposal, the European Commission estimated that the proposed revision in the scope would increase the number of companies that must release sustainability information to approximately 49,000, compared to the 11,600 that must report this information according to the existing requirements.

Regarding (2), the proposal for a CSRD aims to modify Article 19a of Accounting Directive 2013/34/EU by inserting details on the sustainability information companies must release. First, the proposal no longer refers to the four thematic aspects, but only mentions sustainability matters, defined as the sustainability factors laid down in Regulation (EU) 2019/2088 (i.e. environmental issues, social and employee matters, respect for human rights, anti-corruption, and anti-bribery matters). Therefore, the thematic aspects to discuss in the sustainability report have not really changed. Regarding reporting areas, the proposal introduces new information to disclose in addition to the five existing reporting areas. Specifically, the proposal requires companies to release additional information on the strategy pursued, targets defined and progress achieved, function of the board, adverse impacts related to the company value chain, actions to reduce these negative impacts, and intangibles (e.g. intellectual, human, social, and relationship capital). Companies must also describe the process followed to define the information to release using the double materiality perspective.

Another important novelty in the proposal for a CSRD is the introduction of the requirement to disclose both forward-looking and retrospective information, as well as both qualitative and quantitative information. With this requirement, the European Commission highlights the importance of paying attention to both the disclosure quantity and quality, intended in terms of the time orientation (forward-looking or retrospective) and nature (qualitative or quantitative) of the information released.

Furthermore, the proposal for a CSRD requires companies to release sustainability information in accordance with mandatory EU sustainability reporting standards that need to be developed, allowing small- and medium-sized companies to refer to sustainability reporting standards specific to them. The proposal achieves this aim by inserting Articles 19b (Sustainability Reporting Standards) and 19c (Sustainability Reporting Standards for SMEs) in Accounting Directive 2013/34/EU.

According to Article 19b, the European Commission should adopt delegated acts to implement sustainability reporting standards, which should be based on existing standards, frameworks, and rules specifically identified in the article. These sustainability reporting standards shall identify both the sustainability information to release and the structure of its presentation. Article 19b requires the European Commission to adopt the first set of standards by October 2022 to identify the items of information companies must report for all sustainability matters and reporting areas identified. The European Commission should adopt the second set of standards by October 2023 to identify complementary information companies should report for all sustainability matters and reporting areas identified, as well as sector-specific disclosures. In addition, Article 19b identifies the qualitative characteristics the information has to respect, affirming that *'the sustainability reporting standards [...] shall require that the information to be reported is understandable, relevant, representative, verifiable, comparable, and is represented in a faithful manner'*. Finally, Article 19b contains an indicative list of information items that sustainability reporting standards should specify for each thematic aspect. For example, for environmental issues, the proposal for a CSRD specifies the following items of information in this regard:

- Climate change mitigation
- Climate change adaptation
- Water and marine resources
- Resource use and circular economy
- Pollution
- Biodiversity and ecosystems

Article 19c requires the European Commission to adopt delegated acts to implement sustainability reporting standards for small- and medium-sized companies by October 2023.

In the Impact Assessment accompanying the proposal, the European Commission estimated that the proposed revision would increase the number of companies that apply sustainability reporting standards compared to the assessed 20% of companies that fully adopt any sustainability reporting standards. In addition, standardising the information to release would elicit more comparable disclosures.

Regarding the development of sustainability reporting standards, in June 2020, the European Commission mandated the European Financial Reporting Advisory Group (EFRAG) to undertake preparatory work for possible EU sustainability reporting standards. In March 2021, EFRAG published two recommendations. The first is entitled *Proposals for a relevant and dynamic EU sustainability reporting standard-setting* and suggests a roadmap for the development of an inclusive set of EU sustainability reporting standards. The second is entitled *Potential need for changes to the governance and funding of EFRAG* and suggests how to modify EFRAG's governance structure to guarantee the development of EU sustainability reporting standards using a complete and rigorous process. In May 2021, the European Commission asked EFRAG to start technical work to develop draft sustainability reporting standards coherent with the requirements set out in the proposal. In June 2021, EFRAG launched a public consultation and in March 2022, published the *Due Process Procedures for Sustainability Standard-Setting* (DPP), which contains provisions useful for the preparation of draft EU sustainability reporting standards by EFRAG. In April 2022, EFRAG developed exposure drafts on *Draft European Sustainability Reporting Standards*, and launched a public consultation on this exposure draft, setting the deadline as 8 August 2022.

Regarding (3), the proposal for a CSRD requires the assurance of the sustainability information released. Specifically, the proposal aims to amend Article 34 of Accounting Directive 2013/34/EU by inserting the requirement of the auditor to

> *express an opinion based on a limited assurance engagement as regards the compliance of the sustainability reporting with the requirements of this Directive, including the compliance of the sustainability reporting with the reporting standards adopted pursuant to Article 19b, the process carried out by the undertaking to identify the information reported pursuant to those reporting standards.*

In the Impact Assessment accompanying the proposal, the European Commission estimated that the proposed revision would increase the number of companies that assure their sustainability reporting compared to the assessed 30% of companies that currently obtain some form of assurance. In addition, the assurance of the information to release, although limited, would result in more reliable disclosures.

Finally, regarding (4), the proposal for a CSRD requires companies to disclose information in a digital and machine-readable format. Specifically, the proposal aims to amend the Accounting Directive by inserting Article 19d, which requires companies to prepare their *'financial statements and management report in a single electronic reporting format [...] and to mark-up sustainability information as and when specified'*. In the Impact Assessment accompanying the proposal, the European Commission estimated that the proposed revision would ensure more disclosures that are easy to find and use for stakeholders.

In conclusion, when issued, the new CSRD will encourage the release of more comparable, reliable, and easy-to-access sustainability information.

## Notes

1 Since 1973, the Commission of the European Communities implemented different Environmental Action Programmes to define the environmental agenda and Union actions in environmental fields.

2 The EU expressed the need to align the Fourth and Seventh Council Directives to developments in the IAS/IFRS standards several years earlier. Thus, this request was already present in the Communication 'Accounting Harmonisation: A New Strategy vis-à-vis International Harmonisation' issued by the European Commission in 1995.

3 The bold and underline have been inserted by the author.

4 Both the guidelines were issued in 2009. The title of the first guidance is *La relazione sulla gestione art. 2428 codice civile*. The title of the second guidance is *La relazione sulla gestione art. 2428 codice civile. Informativa sull'ambiente e sul personale.*

5 The European Parliament issued both resolutions *Corporate Social Responsibility: Accountable, transparent, and responsible business behaviour and sustainable growth* and *Corporate Social Responsibility: Promoting society's interests and a route to sustainable and inclusive recovery* in February 2013.

6 The European Commission also identified the same critical issues in *the report on the review clauses in Directives 2013/34/EU, 2014/95/EU, and 2013/50/EU* published in 2021. With reference to the review clause in Directive 2014/95/EU, the document reports the answers to the 2020 public consultation, according to which: 1) 84% of users identified the limited comparability of non-financial information as an important problem; 2) 82% of respondents noted that the adoption of a common reporting standard could resolve the problem of a lack of comparability; 3) 73% of respondents identified the limited reliability of non-financial information as an important problem; 4) 70% of respondents would extend the scope of the Directive to all large companies, and 62% to all listed companies.

7 The European Commission introduced the term 'sustainability information' because many stakeholders contended that the term 'non-financial' was inaccurate, as it suggested the information was not financially relevant.

8 When issued, the new directive will amend various existing directives. In particular, it will amend: 1) the Accounting Directive, introducing the concept of sustainability reporting and modifying existing provisions on the environmental and social reporting; 2) Audit Directive and Regulation, inserting the requirement to provide an assurance of the environmental and social information released; and 3) Transparency Directive, requiring the disclosure of environmental and social information to all listed companies independently from the average number of employees.

## References


Accounting Advisory Forum (1995). Environmental issues in financial reporting (Doc. XV/6004/94). Commission of the European Union (December 1995).

Arif, M., Gan, C., & Nadeem, M. (2021). Regulating non-financial reporting: Evidence from European firms' environmental, social and governance disclosures and earnings risk. *Meditari Accountancy Research*, 30(3), 495–523.

Bini, L., & Bellucci, M. (2020). *Integrated sustainability reporting*. Cham: Springer Nature.

Bini, L., Dainelli, F., & Giunta, F. (2017). Is a loosely specified regulatory intervention effective in disciplining management commentary? The case of performance indicator disclosure. *Journal of Management & Governance*, 21(1), 63–91.

Camilleri, M. A. (2015). Environmental, social and governance disclosures in Europe. *Sustainability Accounting, Management and Policy Journal*, 6(2), 224–242.

Criado-Jiménez, I., Fernández-Chulián, M., Larrinaga-González, C., & Husillos-Carqués, F. J. (2008). Compliance with mandatory environmental reporting in financial statements: The case of Spain (2001–2003). *Journal of Business Ethics*, 79(3), 245–262.

CSR Europe and GRI (2017). Member State Implementation of Directive 2014/95/EU. GRI & CSR Europe, Brussels.

De Groen, W. P., Alcidi, C., Simonelli, F., Campmas, A., Di Salvo, M., Musmeci, R.,..., & Tadi, S. (2020). *Study on the non-financial Reporting Directive*. Publications Office of the European Union.

Doni, F., Martini, S. B., Corvino, A., & Mazzoni, M. (2019). Voluntary versus mandatory non-financial disclosure: EU Directive 95/2014 and sustainability reporting practices based on empirical evidence from Italy. *Meditari Accountancy Research*, 28(5), 781–802.

European Commission (1993). "Towards Sustainability" – the European Community Programme of policy and action in relation to the environment and sustainable development (Fifth EC Environmental Action Programme) (COM/92/23, 18.5.1993).

European Commission (1995). Communication From The Commission – Accounting Harmonisation: A New Strategy Vis-A-Vis International Harmonisation (COM/95/508 final, 14.11.1995).

European Commission (2001a). Communication from the Commission to the Council, the European Parliament, the Economic and Social Committee and the Committee of the Regions on the sixth environment action programme of the European Community "Environment 2010: Our future, Our choice" (Sixth Environment Action Programme) (COM/2001/0031 final/24.1.2001).

European Commission (2001b). Commission Recommendation 2001/453/EC on the recognition, measurement and disclosure of environmental issues in the annual accounts and annual reports of companies.

European Commission (2011a). Communication from the Commission to the European Parliament, The Council, the Economic and Social Committee and the Committee of the Regions – Single Market Act. Twelve levers to boost growth and strengthen confidence "Working together to create new growth" (COM/2011/206 final, 13.4.2011).

European Commission (2011b). Communication from the Commission to the European Parliament, The Council, the European Economic and Social Committee and the Committee of the Regions – A renewed EU strategy 2011–14 for Corporate Social Responsibility (COM/2011/681 final, 25.10.2011).

European Commission (2013). Proposal for a Directive of the European Parliament and of the Council amending Council Directives 78/660/EEC and 83/349/EEC as regards disclosure of non-financial and diversity information by certain large companies and groups (COM/2013/207 final, 16.4.2013).

European Commission (2017). Communication from the Commission – Guidelines on non-financial reporting (methodology for reporting non-financial information) (2017/C 215/01, 5.7.2017).

European Commission (2019a). Communication from the Commission – Guidelines on non-financial reporting: Supplement on reporting climate-related information (2019/C 209/01, 20.6.2019).

European Commission (2019b). Communication from the Commission to the European Parliament, the European Council, the Council, the European Economic and Social Committee and the Committee of the Regions — The European Green Deal (COM/2019/640 final, 11.12.2019).

European Commission (2020a). Communication from the Commission to the European Parliament, The Council, The European Economic and Social Committee and the Committee of the Regions – Sustainable Europe Investment Plan: European Green Deal Investment Plan (COM/2020/21 final, 14.1.2020).

European Commission (2020b). Communication from the Commission to the European Parliament, The European Council, the Council, the European Economic and Social Committee and the Committee of the Regions – A New Industrial Strategy for Europe (COM/2020/102 final, 10.3.2020)

European Commission (2020c). Communication from the Commission to the European Parliament, The Council, The European Economic and Social Committee and the Committee Of The Regions – An SME Strategy for a sustainable and digital Europe (COM/2020/103 final, 10.3.2020)

European Commission (2020d). Communication from the Commission to the European Parliament, The Council, The European Economic and Social Committee and the Committee Of The Regions – A new Circular Economy Action Plan For a cleaner and more competitive Europe (COM/2020/98 final, 11.3.2020).

European Commission (2020e). Communication from the Commission to the European Parliament, The Council, the European Economic and Social Committee and the Committee of the Regions – EU Biodiversity Strategy for 2030 Bringing nature back into our lives (COM/2020/380 final, 20.5.2020)

European Commission (2020f). Communication from the Commission to the European Parliament, The Council, the European Economic and Social Committee and the Committee of the Regions – Powering a climate-neutral economy: An EU Strategy for Energy System Integration (COM/2020/299 final, 8.7.2020).

European Commission (2020g). Communication from the Commission to the European Parliament, The Council, the European Economic and Social Committee and the Committee of the Regions – Stepping up Europe's 2030 climate ambition Investing in a climate-neutral future for the benefit of our people (COM/2020/562 final, 17.9.2020).

European Commission (2020h). Communication from the Commission to the European Parliament, The Council, the European Economic and Social Committee and the Committee of the Regions – European Climate Pact (COM/2020/788 final, 9.12.2020).

European Commission (2021a). Commission Staff Working Document Impact Assessment Accompanying the document Proposal for a Directive of the European Parliament and of the Council amending Directive 2013/34/EU, Directive 2004/109/EC, Directive 2006/43/EC and Regulation (EU) No 537/2014, as regards corporate sustainability reporting (SWD/2021/150 final, 21.4.2021).

European Commission (2021b). Proposal for a Directive of the European Parliament and of the Council amending Directive 2013/34/EU, Directive 2004/109/EC, Directive 2006/43/EC and Regulation (EU) No 537/2014, as regards corporate sustainability reporting (COM/2021/189 final, 21.4.2021).

European Commission (2021c). Report from the Commission to the European Parliament, The Council and the European Economic and Social Committee on the review clauses in Directives 2013/34/EU, 2014/95/EU, and 2013/50/EU (COM/2021/199 final, 21.4.2021).

European Commission (2021d). Communication from the Commission to the European Parliament, The Council, The European Economic and Social Committee and the Committee of the Regions – Pathway to a Healthy Planet for All EU Action Plan: "Towards Zero Pollution for Air, Water and Soil" (COM/2021/400 final, 12.5.2021).

European Commission (2021e). Communication from the Commission to the European Parliament, The Council, The European Economic and Social Committee and the Committee Of The Regions – On An Action Plan For The Development Of Organic Production (COM/2021/141 final/2, 19.4.2021).

European Commission (2021f). Communication from the Commission to the European Parliament, The Council, The European Economic and Social Committee and the Committee Of The Regions – on a new approach for a sustainable blue economy in the EU Transforming the EU's Blue Economy for a Sustainable Future (COM/2021/240 final, 17.5.2021).

European Commission (2021g). Communication from the Commission to the European Parliament, The Council, The European Economic and Social Committee and the Committee of the Regions – New EU Forest Strategy for 2030 (COM/2021/572 final, 16.7.2021).

European Commission (2021h). Communication from the Commission to the European Parliament, The Council, the European Economic and Social Committee and the Committee Of The Regions – EU Soil Strategy for 2030. Reaping the benefits of healthy soils for people, food, nature and climate (COM/2021/699 final, 17.11.2021).

European Commission (2022a). Communication from the Commission to the European Parliament, The Council, The European Economic and Social Committee and the Committee Of The Regions – EU Strategy for Sustainable and Circular Textiles (COM/2022/141 final, 30.3.2022).

European Commission (2022b). Communication from the Commission to the European Parliament, The European Council, The Council, The European Economic and Social Committee and the Committee of the Regions – REPowerEU Plan (COM(2022) 230 final, 18.5.2022).

European Parliament (2013a). Resolution on Corporate Social Responsibility: Accountable, transparent and responsible business behaviour and sustainable growth (2012/2098(INI), 6.2.2013).

European Parliament (2013b). Resolution on Corporate Social Responsibility: Promoting society's interests and a route to sustainable and inclusive recovery (2012/2097(INI), 6.2.2013).

European Parliament, Council of the European Union (2003). Directive 2003/51/EC of the European Parliament and of the Council of 18 June 2003 amending Directives 78/660/EEC, 83/349/EEC, 86/635/EEC and 91/674/EEC on the annual and consolidated accounts of certain types of companies, banks and other financial institutions and insurance undertakings.

European Parliament, Council of the European Union (2014). Directive 2014/95/EU of the European Parliament and of the Council of 22 October 2014 amending Directive 2013/34/EU as regards disclosure of non-financial and diversity information by certain large undertakings and groups Text with EEA relevance.

European Parliament, Council of the European Union (2019). Regulation (EU) 2019/2088 of the European Parliament and of the Council of 27 November 2019 on sustainability-related disclosures in the financial services sector.

European Parliament, Council of the European Union (2020). Regulation (EU) 2020/852 of the European Parliament and of the Council of 18 June 2020 on the establishment of a framework to facilitate sustainable investment, and amending Regulation (EU) 2019/2088.

European Parliament, Council of the European Union (2021). Regulation (EU) 2021/783 of the European Parliament and of the Council of 29 April 2021 establishing a Programme for the Environment and Climate Action (LIFE), and repealing Regulation (EU) No 1293/2013.

European Parliament, Council of the European Union (2022a). Decision (EU) 2022/591 of the European Parliament and of the Council of 6 April 2022 on a General Union Environment Action Programme to 2030.

European Parliament, Council of the European Union (2022b). Regulation (EU) 2021/1119 of the European Parliament and of the Council of 30 June 2021 establishing the framework for achieving climate neutrality and amending Regulations (EC) No 401/2009 and (EU) 2018/1999 ('European Climate Law').

European Union (2010). Consolidated version of the Treaty on European Union. http://data.europa.eu/eli/treaty/teu_2010/oj

European Union (2020). Consolidated version of the Treaty on the Functioning of the European. http://data.europa.eu/eli/treaty/tfeu_2016/oj

Fiandrino, S. (2019). *Disclosure of non-financial information. Evolutionary paths and harmonisation to mandatory requirements*. Torino: Giappichelli Editor.

Global Reporting Initiative & United Nations Global Compact (2018). *Integrating the sustainable development goals into corporate reporting: A practical guide.*

Knopf, J., Kahlenborn, W., Hajduk, T., Weiss, D., Feil, M., Fiedler, R., & Klein, J. (2010). Corporate Social Responsibility. National Public Policies in the European Union. European Commission. Directorate-General for Employment, Social Affairs and Inclusion. Unit C2. Manuscript completed in November.

KPMG (2020). The time has come. The KPMG Survey of Sustainability Reporting 2020. https://assets.kpmg/content/dam/kpmg/xx/pdf/2020/11/the-time-has-come.pdf

La Torre, M., Sabelfeld, S., Blomkvist, M., & Dumay, J. (2020). Rebuilding trust: Sustainability and non-financial reporting and the European Union regulation. *Meditari Accountancy Research*, 28(5), 701–725.

La Torre, M., Sabelfeld, S., Blomkvist, M., Tarquinio, L., & Dumay, J. (2018). Harmonising non-financial reporting regulation in Europe: Practical forces and projections for future research. *Meditari Accountancy Research*, 26(4), 598–621.

Lepore, L., Landriani, L., Pisano, S., D'Amore, G., & Pozzoli, S. (2022). Corporate governance in the digital age: The role of social media and board independence in CSR disclosure. Evidence from Italian listed companies. *Journal of Management and Governance*, 1–37.

Muserra, A. L., Papa, M., & Grimaldi, F. (2020). Sustainable development and the European Union Policy on non-financial information: An Italian empirical analysis. *Corporate Social Responsibility and Environmental Management*, 27(1), 22–31.

Papa, M., Carrassi, M., Muserra, A. L., & Wieczorek-Kosmala, M. (2022). The impact of the EU nonfinancial information directive on environmental disclosure: Evidence from Italian environmentally sensitive industries. *Meditari Accountancy Research*, 30(7), 87–120.

Pisano, S., & Alvino, F. (2015). New European Union's requirements and IFRS practice statement "Management Commentary": Does MD&A disclosure quality affect analysts' forecasts? *Journal of Modern Accounting and Auditing*, 11(6), 283–301.

Williamson, N., Stampe-Knippel, A., & Weber, T. (2014). Corporate social responsibility national public policies in the European Union. Compendium, 13.

# 5

# MAIN STANDARDS AND GUIDANCE FOR ENVIRONMENTAL DISCLOSURE

## 5.1 Introduction

In the last few decades, a large number of international standards frameworks have been developed by various parties. From the start, the stated goal has been to improve companies' corporate sustainability and related reporting by developing common and shared practices and language capable of facilitating the comparability of disseminated information, organisational transparency, and accountability. The expansion of political and social struggle movements that marked the 1960s and 1970s, characterised by heated debates on environmental degradation and the need for corporate ethics, appears to have provided the initial push (Gray, 2004, 2003; Gray et al., 1996; Parker, 1986; Puxty, 1986).

The contribution of standard setters has become critical in indicating to organisations the contents and forms of dissemination of the social, environmental, and economic impacts of corporate activities, which has grown in tandem with the growth of interest in sustainability reporting by companies, public opinion, and academia (D'Andrea, 2020).

Several models have been created to assist businesses in reporting environmental and social sustainability (Bartels et al., 2016; Andrew and Cortese, 2011; Reynolds and Yuthas, 2008; Albuquerque et al., 2007; Ransburg and Vagasi, 2007; Kolk, 2004).

In their 2012 paper, Jones and Ratnatun mention six important worldwide standards: the AccountAbility (AA) guidelines, Global Compact principles, Global Reporting Initiative (GRI) guidelines, International Integrated Reporting Council (IIRC) framework, ISO26000 guidelines, and SA8000 guidelines. According to Brown et al. (2009), more than 30 international frameworks for sustainability reporting have been developed by various organisations, including the GRI, AA, IIRC, and Sustainability Accounting Standards Board (SASB).

DOI: 10.4324/9781003245933-6

Numerous studies (Tschopp and Huefner, 2015; Tschopp and Nastanski, 2014; Stubbs and Higgins, 2012; Dumay et al., 2010; Adams and Evans, 2004) showed that the AA1000 (AccountAbility Principles Standards) and GRI are the most commonly used frameworks in the preparation of sustainability reports, and the IIRC conceptual framework is the main framework for drafting integrated reports (Stacchezzini et al., 2016; Thomson, 2015).

Some of these frameworks provide companies with guidelines and policies for responsible corporate strategies and policies, while others establish concepts, norms, practices, metrics, and tools for social, environmental, and economic impact reporting. Some frameworks apply to all companies, whereas others focus on certain industries or a single issue such as greenhouse gas emissions, climate change, or forest damage.

As academics from numerous disciplines became more interested in sustainability reporting, initiatives to categorise worldwide standards frameworks expanded in number. The most appropriate classification for this text is that of the KPMG, United Nations Environment Programme (Unit for Corporate Governance in Africa), and The Global Reporting Initiatives report 'Carrots and Sticks: Global Trends in Sustainability Reporting, Regulation, and Policy' (King et al., 2016). The following classification is used in the report: normative, management, and reporting frameworks. The United Nations Global Compact principles and OECD Guidelines, for example, are classified in the first category, as they provide framework regulations to assist organisations in shaping their sustainability strategy and management approach, and measuring their impacts. Instead, ISO 26000 is a management standard that helps firms understand and define the concept of corporate social responsibility. Finally, the GRI Standards fall into the third category, as they provide firms with sustainable reporting guidelines, information, and measurements.

Given the goal of this study, the next pages of the chapter examine some of the most important frameworks from the third group, namely those classified as reporting frameworks, and analyse their advantages and disadvantages. In particular, Sections 5.2, 5.3, and 5.4 examine the history and distinctive qualities of the GRI Standards, International IIRC Framework, and AA1000, respectively.

## 5.2 The GRI standards

The GRI standards are the most commonly accepted international sustainability reporting guidelines. They are a modular set of interconnected standards that enable companies to publicly report the effects of their operations in a transparent manner to interested parties. GRI was created to assist organisations in being transparent with their stakeholders and taking responsibility for their influence on a sustainable future. Furthermore, the GRI standards play an important role in standardising sustainability reporting. Part of their mission is to create a global standard language for organisations to disclose their impacts. This allows parties to have a more informed conversation and improve their decision-making processes regarding the consequences.

The GRI is a Boston-based non-profit organisation created in 1997. It was a collaboration between the United Nations Environmental Programme and Coalition for Environmentally Responsible Economies (CERES), an American non-governmental organisation.

In 2000, the first version of the GRI Guidelines (G1) was released. It was established with the goal of developing an accounting system that would allow businesses to track their environmental impacts. Subsequently, the focus shifted to social and economic themes. The GRI moved to Amsterdam in 2002 and released the first update of the guidelines (G2) (Figure 5.1).

The guidelines were broadened and refined as the need for GRI reporting and uptake from organisations increased, resulting in G3 (2006) and G4 (2013).

In 2016, the GRI's Global Sustainability Standards Board released the first global standards. They are based on previous guidelines and incorporate all the key principles developed in the past to help every organisation disclose its influence on the environment, economic growth, and society. These standards were created with a flexible structure and clear requirements to create a common language for organisations and stakeholders, and to improve global comparability and the quality of information on these impacts, allowing for greater transparency, accountability, and stakeholder engagement. The GRI standards are still being revised and expanded, with new topic standards on tax and waste coming out in 2019 and 2020, respectively.

With increasing global interest in sustainability reporting, the GRI expanded its network by adding regional offices in Brazil (2007), China (2009), India (2010), the United States (2011), South Africa (2013), Colombia (2014), and Singapore (2019).

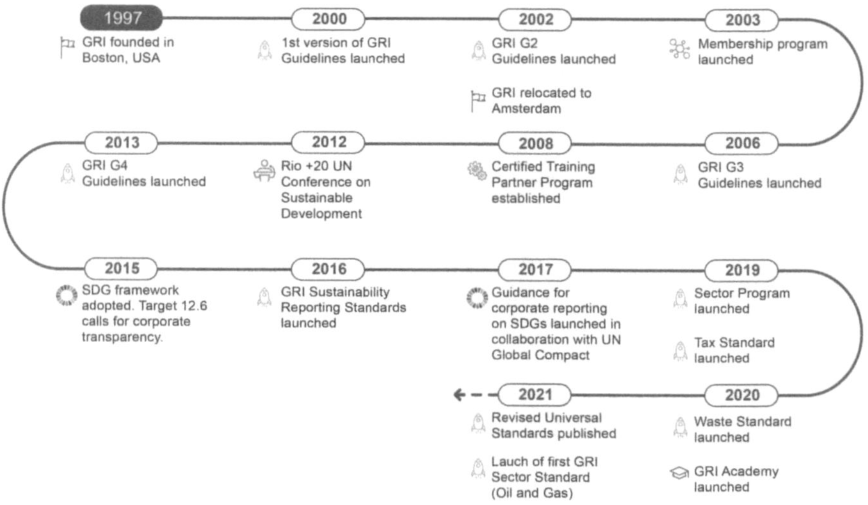


**FIGURE 5.1** History of GRI standards

Disclosures, which might include requirements, recommendations, and guidelines, are included in the actual structure of the GRI standards. The information an organisation must report or instructions it must follow and report in accordance with the GRI standards are listed in the requirements. Recommendations imply that certain information or a specific course of action is recommended but not mandated. The guidelines may contain background information, explanations, and examples to help with comprehension.

The 2021 version of the standards is the most recent. The GRI Standards are divided into four series: one for universal standards (GRI 101 Foundation, GRI 102 General Disclosures, GRI 103 Material Topic) and three for specific (or topic) standards for the three fundamental dimensions of sustainability: economic, environmental, and social sustainability (GRI 200 Economic, GRI 300 Environmental, GRI 400 Social). There are also sector supplements (GRI Sector) that offer sector-specific performance metrics and integrate the Guidelines with interpretations of and recommendations for their application.

Based on the abovementioned classification, the modular structure of the standards is depicted in the figure (Figure 5.2).

The GRI universal standards, which include GRI 101, 102, and 103, apply to all organisations.

GRI 101 (Foundation) outlines the basic concepts for establishing the content and quality of the report. It outlines the requirements for an organisation to report in accordance with the GRI Standards. It also provides fundamental principles of good reporting, such as accuracy, balance, and verifiability. It is feasible to determine the aspects of the company that have major impacts on stakeholders using the GRI 101 principles. It is possible to apply the specific standards (GRI 200, 300 and 400) once the significant implications are recognised.

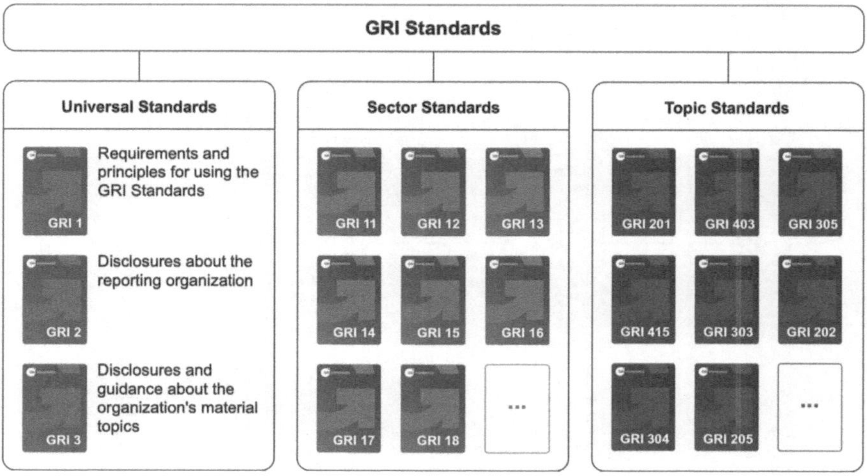


**FIGURE 5.2** Structure of GRI standards

GRI 102 (General Disclosure) is used to report data on the company's context and reporting practices. This comprises details on the company's profile, strategy, ethics, integrity, governance, and how stakeholders can be involved in the reporting process.

GRI 103 (Material Topic), on the other hand, explains how an organisation can identify the topics most relevant to its impacts, i.e. its material topics, and how sector standards are used in this process. It also includes disclosures on the company's material topic list, the process by which the organisation selects its material topics, and how each topic is managed.

Numerous specific standards are included in the GRI 200, 300, and 400 series, which can be used to report a company's economic, environmental, and social impacts. Disclosures for providing information on issues are included in these standards. A few examples are standards for trash, occupational health, and safety. Each standard includes a general overview of the subject as well as specific disclosures about the subject and how an organisation handles its associated affects. An organisation chooses topic standards relevant to the material themes identified and reports on them.

Finally, the sector standards intend to increase the quality, completeness, and consistency of reporting by organisations. Standards will be developed for 40 sectors, starting with those with the highest impacts, such as oil and gas, agriculture, aquaculture, and fishing. The standards identify topics expected to be material for most firms in a given sector and the disclosures that should be made to report on them. When reporting using the GRI Standards, an entity must apply a relevant sector standard if one exists. Each sector standard has two sections: an introduction and a main section. The first provides an overview of the sector's features as well as the activities and business relationships that may underpin its effects. The main section highlights the most likely material subjects in the industry. A sector standard may also include extra disclosures not included in a topic standard, such as when the topic standard's disclosures do not provide enough information regarding an organisation's impacts on the issue.

GRI 101 is the foundation for all organisations that choose to report using the GRI standards. It lays out principles and key concepts, listing the requirements for reporting in accordance with the GRI Standards (Figure 5.3).

First, a company must define its impacts and estimate the importance thereof. The organisation can accomplish this work with the support of sector standards, which outline the features of an industry that underpin its impacts. A corporation must consider the impacts indicated in the sector standards and determine whether they apply to it.

Understanding the context of an organisation is critical in understanding and analysing the magnitude of its impacts. GRI 102 assists this process by defining detailed disclosures for several aspects of an organisation's activities. GRI 103 shows how to identify and evaluate impacts as well as their importance.

Once a company has assessed the significance of its impacts, it must identify its material topics. In other words, the company must decide which impacts to

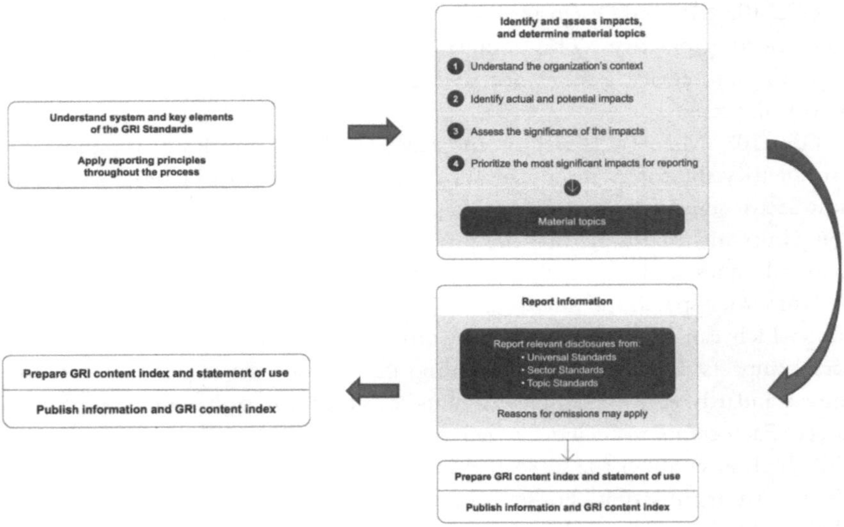


**FIGURE 5.3** Reporting using the GRI standards

report. This work is made easier by grouping the impacts into topics such as water and effluents or child labour. This suggests which topics are most relevant to an organisation's activities.

The company must then choose topic standards that relate to the material topics identified and reported on. Sector standards are also useful during this stage of the material topic selection process. If a relevant sector standard exists, an organisation must use it when reporting in accordance with the GRI Standards.

When a company decides on its material topics, it must collect appropriate data to report specific information on each topic.

If an organisation is unable to comply with some reporting requirements, it may be entitled to omit the information in certain circumstances, provided that a good justification is provided for the omission. There are also recommendations and guidelines that would improve the quality and transparency of a report in addition to the requirements listed under these disclosures.

Organisations can choose between two levels of conformance to the GRI standards for non-financial reports: 'Core' or 'Comprehensive'.

According to the 'Core' choice, the report comprises the bare minimum of data necessary to comprehend the organisation's nature, material aspects, and associated impacts, and how these are managed. The report created with the 'Comprehensive' option adds to the basic information, such as more on the strategy pursued, organisation's ethics and integrity, and its governance. In addition, this report contains more thorough information about the material aspects according to all guidelines provided in the standard specifications. However, organisations can employ a hybrid option such as the 'GRI-referenced' option. This option allows companies to choose which standards or pieces of content they want to use.

The GRI has received much attention from organisations worldwide, and is now considered the most important international framework for sustainability reporting (Federation of European Accountants, 2016). According to a recent KPMG survey, the GRI framework will be used by 67% of the world's top 100 firms (N100) and 73% of the world's 250 largest organisations (G250) by revenue in 2020 based on the Fortune 500 ranking (KPMG, 2020).

The increased need for stakeholders' knowledge regarding non-financial performance and the connected need to standardise corporate reporting practices have pushed legislators to intervene. In the European context, Directive 2014/95/EU (NFRD) represents the most important factor in improving corporate transparency and accountability for social and environmental issues.

This Directive began the process of unifying corporate reporting practices, enhancing information comparability, and thereby addressing stakeholders' interests. The EU Directive mentions several international frameworks and guidelines organisations can use to prepare non-financial reports, such as the Eco-Management and Audit Scheme (EMAS), United Nations (UN) Global Compact Guiding Principles on Business and Human Rights, Organization for Economic Co-operation and Development (OECD) Guidelines for Multinational Enterprises, and International Organization for Standardization (ISO).

The GRI and NFRD are inextricably linked. The GRI recently released a document (*Linking the GRI Standards with the European Directive on Non-financial and Diversity Disclosure*) that demonstrates how to use the GRI Standards to meet the directive's disclosure requirements.

In the context of the GRI Standards, the environmental dimension of sustainability concerns an organisation's impacts on living and non-living natural systems including land, air, water, and ecosystems. The related GRI standards are 301 Materials, 302 Energy, 303 Water and Effluents, 304 Biodiversity, 305 Emissions, 306 Waste, 307 Environmental Compliance, and 308 Supplier Environmental Assessment. The Standards contain disclosures that provide a structured means for an organisation to report information about itself and its environmental impacts. Disclosures can have requirements and include recommendations and guidance.

Regarding GRI 301, the information the standards (requirements) demand is separated into macrogroups. Each macrogroup refers to a collection of similar data. The first group includes 'Materials used by weight or volume' to produce or package an organisation's primary products and services during the reporting period, distinguishing recyclable and non-recyclable materials. The second group includes 'Recycled input materials used', expressed as a percentage. The third group includes 'Reclaimed products and their packaging materials', expressed as a percentage. Data collection methods are also included.

The recommendations included in disclosure 301-1 state that when compiling the specified information, the reporting organisation should include the following material types in the calculation of total materials used: (1) raw materials (i.e. natural resources used for conversion to products or services, such as ores, minerals, and wood); (2) associated process materials (i.e. materials needed for the manufacturing process but that are not part of the final product, such as lubricants for manufacturing machinery); (3) semi-manufactured goods or parts including all forms of materials and components other than raw materials that are part of the final product; and (4) materials for packaging purposes, including paper, cardboard, and plastics. Furthermore, the company should indicate whether each material type was obtained from external suppliers or sourced internally, and whether the data were estimated or derived from direct measurements for each material type. If the data were estimated, the organisation should explain how this was done. Finally, the disclosure 301-1 guidance states that the reported consumption statistics must reflect the content in its original state and should not be subjected to further data manipulation.

GRI 302 (Energy) is similarly structured. The first group of information required by the standard includes the 'Energy consumption within the organization', distinguishing fuel consumption (in joules or multiples) according to its origin from renewable or non-renewable sources. The reporting organisation should specify the type of fuel used. The second group includes the energy used outside the organisation. The third category includes the energy intensity ratio of an organisation's activity. The fourth and fifth relate, respectively, to the indication of the reduction of energy consumed as a direct result of company initiatives, and as the energy needs of the goods and services obtained during the reporting period, the type of energy subject to the reduction and amount of the reduction – expressed in quantitative terms – must be specified and calculation methods and assumptions indicated.

The standards also include advice and recommendations. For example, they advise reporting organisations to use consistent conversion factors for the given data and if practicable, to convert gasoline to joules or multiples using local conversion factors. Furthermore, the standard specifies the context of these data, stating that electricity is the only significant type of energy consumed by some enterprises. However, others may rely on energy sources such as steam or water from a district heating plant or chilled water plant.

Energy can be purchased from external sources or produced by the organisation. Fuel sources could be non-renewable (fuel for combustion in boilers, furnaces, heaters, turbines, flares, incinerators, generators, and vehicles owned or controlled by the organisation) or renewable (biofuels and biomass).

The following table reports requirements related to environmental issues (Table 5.1).[1]

**TABLE 5.1** GRI requirements related to environmental issues

| *Disclosure* | *Requirements*<br>*The reporting organisation shall report the following information* |
|---|---|
| *GRI 301: Materials 2016* | |
| 301-1 Materials used by weight or volume | a Total weight or volume of materials that are used to produce and package the organisation's primary products and services during the reporting period, by:<br>• non-renewable materials used;<br>• renewable materials used. |
| 301-2 Recycled input materials used | a Percentage of recycled input materials used to manufacture the organisation's primary products and services. |
| 301-3 Reclaimed products and their packaging materials | a Percentage of reclaimed products and their packaging materials for each product category.<br>b How the data for this disclosure have been collected. |
| *GRI 302: Energy 2016* | |
| 302-1 Energy consumption within the organisation | a Total fuel consumption within the organisation from non-renewable sources, in joules or multiples, and including fuel types used.<br>b Total fuel consumption within the organisation from renewable sources, in joules or multiples, and including fuel types used.<br>c In joules, watt-hours or multiples, the total:<br>i electricity consumption<br>ii heating consumption<br>iii cooling consumption<br>iv steam consumption<br>d In joules, watt-hours or multiples, the total:<br>i electricity sold<br>ii heating sold<br>iii cooling sold<br>iv steam sold<br>e Total energy consumption within the organisation, in joules or multiples.<br>f Standards, methodologies, assumptions, and/or calculation tools used.<br>g Source of the conversion factors used. |
| 302-2 Energy consumption outside of the organisation | a Energy consumption outside of the organisation, in joules or multiples.<br>b Standards, methodologies, assumptions, and/or calculation tools used.<br>c Source of the conversion factors used. |

(*Continued*)

**TABLE 5.1** Continued

| *Disclosure* | *Requirements*<br>*The reporting organisation shall report the following information* |
|---|---|
| 302-3 Energy intensity | a Energy intensity ratio for the organisation.<br>b Organisation-specific metric (the denominator) chosen to calculate the ratio.<br>c Types of energy included in the intensity ratio; whether fuel, electricity, heating, cooling, steam, or all.<br>d Whether the ratio uses energy consumption within the organisation, outside of it, or both. |
| 302-4 Reduction of energy consumption | a Amount of reductions in energy consumption achieved as a direct result of conservation and efficiency initiatives, in joules or multiples.<br>b Types of energy included in the reductions; whether fuel, electricity, heating, cooling, steam or all.<br>c Basis for calculating reductions in energy consumption, such as base year or baseline, including the rationale for choosing it.<br>d Standards, methodologies, assumptions, and/or calculation tools used. |
| 302-5 Reductions in energy requirements of products and services | a Reductions in energy requirements of sold products and services achieved during the reporting period, in joules or multiples.<br>b Basis for calculating reductions in energy consumption, such as base year or baseline, including the rationale for choosing it.<br>c Standards, methodologies, assumptions, and/or calculation tools used. |
| *GRI 303: Water and Effluents 2018* | |
| 303-1 Interactions with water as a shared resource | a A description of how the organisation interacts with water, including how and where water is withdrawn, consumed, and discharged, and the water-related impacts the organisation has caused or contributed to, or that are directly linked to its operations, products, or services by its business relationships (e.g. impacts caused by runoff).<br>b A description of the approach used to identify water-related impacts, including the scope of assessments, their timeframe, and any tools or methodologies used.<br>c A description of how water-related impacts are addressed, including how the organisation works with stakeholders to steward water as a shared resource, and how it engages with suppliers or customers with significant water-related impacts. |

| | |
|---|---|
| | d An explanation of the process for setting any water-related goals and targets that are part of the organisation's approach to managing water and effluents, and how they relate to public policy and the local context of each area with water stress. |
| 303-2 Management of water discharge-related impacts | a A description of any minimum standards set for the quality of effluent discharge, and how these minimum standards were determined, including:<br>i how standards for facilities operating in locations with no local discharge requirements were determined;<br>ii any internally developed water quality standards or guidelines;<br>iii any sector-specific standards considered;<br>iv whether the profile of the receiving waterbody was considered. |
| 303-3 Water withdrawal | a Total water withdrawal from all areas in megaliters, and a breakdown of this total by the following sources, if applicable:<br>i Surface water;<br>ii Groundwater;<br>iii Seawater;<br>iv Produced water;<br>v Third-party water.<br>b Total water withdrawal from all areas with water stress in megaliters, and a breakdown of this total by the following sources, if applicable:<br>i Surface water;<br>ii ii. Groundwater;<br>iii Seawater;<br>iv Produced water;<br>v Third-party water, and a breakdown of this total by the withdrawal sources listed in i–iv.<br>c A breakdown of total water withdrawal from each of the sources listed in Disclosures 303-3-a and 303-3-b in megaliters by the following categories:<br>i Freshwater (≤1,000 mg/L Total Dissolved Solids);<br>ii Other water (>1,000 mg/L Total Dissolved Solids).<br>d Any contextual information necessary to understand how the data have been compiled, such as any standards, methodologies, and assumptions used. |
| 303-4 Water discharge | a Total water discharge to all areas in megaliters, and a breakdown of this total by the following types of destination, if applicable:<br>i Surface water;<br>ii Groundwater; |

*(Continued)*

**TABLE 5.1** Continued

| *Disclosure* | *Requirements*<br>*The reporting organisation shall report the following information* |
|---|---|
| | iii Seawater;<br>iv Third-party water, and the volume of this total sent for use to other organisations, if applicable.<br>b A breakdown of total water discharge to all areas in megaliters by the following categories:<br>i Freshwater (≤1,000 mg/L Total Dissolved Solids);<br>ii Other water (>1,000 mg/L Total Dissolved Solids).<br>c Total water discharge to all areas with water stress in megaliters, and a breakdown of this total by the following categories:<br>i Freshwater (≤1,000 mg/L Total Dissolved Solids);<br>ii Other water (>1,000 mg/L Total Dissolved Solids).<br>d Priority substances of concern for which discharges are treated, including:<br>i how priority substances of concern were defined, and any international standard, authoritative list or criteria used;<br>ii the approach for setting discharge limits for priority substances of concern;<br>iii the number of incidents of non-compliance with discharge limits.<br>e Any contextual information necessary to understand how the data have been compiled, such as any standards, methodologies, and assumptions used. |
| 303-5 Water consumption | a Total water consumption from all areas in megaliters.<br>b Total water consumption from all areas with water stress in megaliters.<br>c Change in water storage in megaliters, if water storage has been identified as having a significant water-related impact.<br>d Any contextual information necessary to understand how the data have been compiled, such as any standards, methodologies, and assumptions used, including whether the information is calculated, estimated, modelled, or sourced from direct measurements, and the approach taken for this, such as the use of any sector-specific factors. |
| *GRI 304: Biodiversity 2016* | |
| 304-1 Operational sites owned, leased, managed in, or adjacent to, protected areas and areas of high biodiversity value outside protected areas | a For each operational site owned, leased, managed in, or adjacent to, protected areas and areas of high biodiversity value outside protected areas, the following information:<br>i Geographic location;<br>ii Subsurface and underground land that may be owned, leased, or managed by the organisation; |

| | |
|---|---|
| | iii Position in relation to the protected area (in the area, adjacent to, or containing portions of the protected area) or the high biodiversity value area outside protected areas;<br>iv Type of operation (office, manufacturing or production, or extractive);<br>v Size of the operational site in km2 (or another unit, if appropriate);<br>vi Biodiversity value characterised by the attribute of the protected area or area of high biodiversity value outside the protected area (terrestrial, freshwater, or maritime ecosystem);<br>vii Biodiversity value characterised by listing of protected status (such as IUCN Protected Area Management Categories, Ramsar Convention, national legislation). |
| 304-2 Significant impacts of activities, products and services on biodiversity | a Nature of significant direct and indirect impacts on biodiversity with reference to one or more of the following:<br>i Construction or use of manufacturing plants, mines, and transport infrastructure;<br>ii Pollution (introduction of substances that do not naturally occur in the habitat from point and non-point sources);<br>iii Introduction of invasive species, pests, and pathogens;<br>iv Reduction of species;<br>v Habitat conversion;<br>vi Changes in ecological processes outside the natural range of variation (such as salinity or changes in groundwater level).<br>b Significant direct and indirect positive and negative impacts with reference to the following:<br>i Species affected;<br>ii Extent of areas impacted;<br>iii Duration of impacts;<br>iv Reversibility or irreversibility of the impacts. |
| 304-3 Habitats protected or restored The reporting organisation shall report the following information: | a Size and location of all habitat areas protected or restored, and whether the success of the restoration measure was or is approved by independent external professionals.<br>b Whether partnerships exist with third parties to protect or restore habitat areas distinct from where the organisation has overseen and implemented restoration or protection measures.<br>c Status of each area based on its condition at the close of the reporting period.<br>d Standards, methodologies, and assumptions used. |

(*Continued*)

**TABLE 5.1** Continued

| *Disclosure* | *Requirements*<br>*The reporting organisation shall report the following information* |
|---|---|
| 304-4 IUCN Red List species and national conservation list species with habitats in areas affected by operations | a Total number of IUCN Red List species and national conservation list species with habitats in areas affected by the operations of the organisation, by level of extinction risk:<br>a Critically endangered<br>b Endangered<br>c Vulnerable<br>d Near threatened<br>e v. Least concern |
| *GRI 305: Emissions 2016* | |
| 305-1 Direct (Scope 1) GHG emissions | a Gross direct (Scope 1) GHG emissions in metric tons of $CO_2$ equivalent.<br>b Gases included in the calculation; whether $CO_2$, $CH_4$, $N_2$ O, $HFC_s$, $PFC_s$, $SF_6$, $NF_3$, or all.<br>c Biogenic $CO_2$ emissions in metric tons of $CO_2$ equivalent.<br>d Base year for the calculation, if applicable, including:<br>i the rationale for choosing it;<br>ii emissions in the base year;<br>iii the context for any significant changes in emissions that triggered recalculations of base year emissions.<br>e Source of the emission factors and the global warming potential (GWP) rates used, or a reference to the GWP source.<br>f Consolidation approach for emissions; whether equity share, financial control, or operational control.<br>g Standards, methodologies, assumptions, and/or calculation tools used. |
| 305-2 Energy indirect (Scope 2) GHG emissions | a Gross location-based energy indirect (Scope 2) GHG emissions in metric tons of $CO_2$ equivalent.<br>b If applicable, gross market-based energy indirect (Scope 2) GHG emissions in metric tonsof$CO_2$ equivalent.<br>c If available, the gases included in the calculation; whether $CO_2$, $CH_4$, $N_2$ O, HFCs, PFCs, $SF_6$, $NF_3$, or all.<br>d Base year for the calculation, if applicable, including:<br>i the rationale for choosing it;<br>ii emissions in the base year;<br>iii the context for any significant changes in emissions that triggered recalculations of base year emissions. |

| | |
|---|---|
| | e Source of the emission factors and the global warming potential (GWP) rates used, or a reference to the GWP source.<br>f Consolidation approach for emissions; whether equity share, financial control, or operational control.<br>g Standards, methodologies, assumptions, and/or calculation tools used. |
| 305-3 Other indirect (Scope 3) GHG emissions | a Gross other indirect (Scope 3) GHG emissions in metric tons of $CO_2$ equivalent.<br>b If available, the gases included in the calculation; whether $CO_2$, $CH_4$, $N_2$ O, $HFC_s$, $PFC_s$, $SF_6$, $NF_3$, or all.<br>c Biogenic $CO_2$ emissions in metric tons of $CO_2$ equivalent.<br>d Other indirect (Scope 3) GHG emissions categories and activities included in the calculation.<br>e Base year for the calculation, if applicable, including:<br>i the rationale for choosing it;<br>ii emissions in the base year;<br>iii the context for any significant changes in emissions that triggered recalculations of base year emissions.<br>f Source of the emission factors and the global warming potential (GWP) rates used, or a reference to the GWP source.<br>g Standards, methodologies, assumptions, and/or calculation tools used. |
| 305-4 GHG emissions intensity | a GHG emissions intensity ratio for the organisation.<br>b Organisation-specific metric (the denominator) chosen to calculate the ratio.<br>c Types of GHG emissions included in the intensity ratio; whether direct (Scope 1), energy indirect (Scope 2), and/or other indirect (Scope 3).<br>d Gases included in the calculation; whether $CO_2$, $CH_4$, $N_2$ O, $HFC_s$, $PFC_s$, $SF_6$, $NF_3$, or all. |
| 305-5 Reduction of GHG emissions | a GHG emissions reduced as a direct result of reduction initiatives, in metric tons of $CO_2$ equivalent.<br>b Gases included in the calculation; whether $CO_2$, $CH_4$, $N_2$ O, HFCs, PFCs, $SF_6$, $NF_3$, or all.<br>c Base year or baseline, including the rationale for choosing it.<br>d Scopes in which reductions took place; whether direct (Scope 1), energy indirect (Scope 2), and/or other indirect (Scope 3).<br>e Standards, methodologies, assumptions, and/or calculation tools used. |

(*Continued*)

**TABLE 5.1** Continued

| *Disclosure* | *Requirements*<br>*The reporting organisation shall report the following information* |
|---|---|
| 305-6 Emissions of ozone-depleting substances (ODS) | a Production, imports, and exports of ODS in metric tons of CFC-11 (trichlorofluoromethane) equivalent.<br>b Substances included in the calculation.<br>c Source of the emission factors used.<br>d Standards, methodologies, assumptions, and/or calculation tools used. |
| 305-7 Nitrogen oxides (NOx), sulphur oxides (SOx), and other significant air emissions | a Significant air emissions, in kilograms or multiples, for each of the following:<br>a NOx<br>b SOx<br>c Persistent organic pollutants (POP)<br>d Volatile organic compounds (VOC)<br>e Hazardous air pollutants (HAP)<br>f Particulate matter (PM)<br>g Other standard categories of air emissions identified in relevant regulations<br>b Source of the emission factors used.<br>c Standards, methodologies, assumptions, and/or calculation tools used. |
| *GRI 306: Waste 2020* | |
| 306-1 Waste generation and significant waste-related impacts | a For the organisation's significant actual and potential waste-related impacts, a description of:<br>i the inputs, activities, and outputs that lead or could lead to these impacts;<br>ii whether these impacts relate to waste generated in the organisation's own activities or to waste generated upstream or downstream in its value chain. |
| 306-2 Management of significant waste-related impacts | a Actions, including circularity measures, taken to prevent waste generation in the organisation's own activities and upstream and downstream in its value chain, and to manage significant impacts from waste generated.<br>b If the waste generated by the organisation in its own activities is managed by a third party, a description of the processes used to determine whether the third party manages the waste in line with contractual or legislative obligations.<br>c The processes used to collect and monitor waste-related data. |
| 306-3 Waste generated | a Total weight of waste generated in metric tons, and a breakdown of this total by composition of the waste.<br>b Contextual information necessary to understand the data and how the data has been compiled. |

| | | |
|---|---|---|
| 306-4 Waste diverted from disposal | a | Total weight of waste diverted from disposal in metric tons, and a breakdown of this total by composition of the waste. |
| | b | Total weight of hazardous waste diverted from disposal in metric tons, and a breakdown of this total by the following recovery operations:<br>i Preparation for reuse;<br>ii Recycling;<br>iii Other recovery operations. |
| | c | Total weight of non-hazardous waste diverted from disposal in metric tons, and a breakdown of this total by the following recovery operations:<br>i Preparation for reuse;<br>ii Recycling;<br>iii Other recovery operations. |
| | d | For each recovery operation listed in Disclosures 306-4-b and 306-4-c, a breakdown of the total weight in metric tons of hazardous waste and of non-hazardous waste diverted from disposal:<br>i onsite;<br>ii offsite. |
| | e | Contextual information necessary to understand the data and how the data has been compiled. |
| 306-5 Waste directed to disposal | a | Total weight of waste directed to disposal in metric tons, and a breakdown of this total by composition of the waste. |
| | b | Total weight of hazardous waste directed to disposal in metric tons, and a breakdown of this total by the following disposal operations:<br>i Incineration (with energy recovery);<br>ii Incineration (without energy recovery);<br>iii Landfilling;<br>iv Other disposal operations. |
| | c | Total weight of non-hazardous waste directed to disposal in metric tons, and a breakdown of this total by the following disposal operations:<br>i Incineration (with energy recovery);<br>ii Incineration (without energy recovery);<br>iii Landfilling;<br>iv Other disposal operations. |
| | d | For each disposal operation listed in Disclosures 306-5-b and 306-5-c, a breakdown of the total weight in metric tons of hazardous waste and of non-hazardous waste directed to disposal:<br>i onsite;<br>ii offsite. |
| | e | Contextual information necessary to understand the data and how the data has been compiled. |

(*Continued*)

**TABLE 5.1** Continued

| *Disclosure* | *Requirements*<br>*The reporting organisation shall report the following information* |
|---|---|
| *GRI 307: Environmental Compliance 2016* | |
| 307-1 Non-compliance with environmental laws and regulations | a Significant fines and non-monetary sanctions for non-compliance with environmental laws and/or regulations in terms of:<br>i total monetary value of significant fines;<br>ii total number of non-monetary sanctions;<br>iii cases brought through dispute resolution mechanisms.<br>b If the organisation has not identified any non-compliance with environmental laws and/or regulations, a brief statement of thisfact is sufficient. |
| *GRI 308: Supplier Environmental Assessment 2016* | |
| 308-1 New suppliers that were screened using environmental criteria | a Percentage of new suppliers that were screened using environmental criteria. |
| 308-2 Negative environmental impacts in the supply chain and actions taken | a Number of suppliers assessed for environmental impacts.<br>b Number of suppliers identified as having significant actual and potential negative environmental impacts.<br>c Significant actual and potential negative environmental impacts identified in the supply chain.<br>d Percentage of suppliers identified as having significant actual and potential negative environmental impacts with which improvements were agreed upon as a result of assessment.<br>e Percentage of suppliers identified as having significant actual and potential negative environmental impacts with which relationships were terminated as a result of assessment, and why. |

## 5.3 The International IR Framework

Integrated Reporting (IR) is an accounting method capable of combining financial and narrative information from an annual report with non-financial and narrative information from a sustainability report (Eccles and Krzus, 2010). In this regard, it is the most recent progression in organisations' external accountability (Cheng et al., 2014; Busco et al., 2013; D'Este et al., 2013). Integrated reports are sometimes understood as the evolution of financial reporting (Baron, 2014; King and Roberts, 2013). However, they are sometimes intended as the latest development of sustainability reporting. Consequently, the Integrated Reporting

Framework serves as a link between the various business reporting models previously stated (Pozzoli, 2018; Silvestri and Veltri, 2016).

Integrated Reporting has a lengthy history commencing in 1994 with the publication of the first King Code of Corporate Governance Principles in South Africa (King I). The Code, named after the former South African Supreme Court Justice Mervyn King, was distinguished by its stakeholder-inclusive vision of the corporation's scope (Gleeson-White, 2014). The connection between the King Code and Integrated Reporting is indirect, as the King Code did not mandate sustainability reporting, but did require disclosure of executive and non-executive directors' remuneration, established guidelines for effective auditing, and encouraged companies to adopt a code of ethics (Eccles and Krzus, 2014).

The King II report followed in 2002, addressing sustainability more directly. It was inspired by the Johannesburg Earth Summit and contained new elements specific to sustainability (Eccles and Krzus, 2014). This new report was based on the GRI and Triple Bottom Line reporting frameworks (Gleeson-White, 2014). In response to many financial scandals (e.g. Enron and WorldCom), the New York Stock Exchange embraced certain King II principles and incorporated them into the Sarbanes-Oxley Act (Gleeson-White, 2014).

In 2009, the King Report on Governance for South Africa was revised for the third time (King III) to include a set of principles for the implementation of integrated reporting. In February 2010, these principles were incorporated into the listing criteria of the Johannesburg Stock Exchange. The report promotes IR as a complete and integrated picture of an organisation's financial and sustainability performance.

Sir Michael Peat of the Prince of Wales' Accounting for Sustainability Project (A4S), an English non-profit organisation, Paul Druckman of the GRI, and Mervyn King met in 2009 to discuss sustainability reporting. According to Elkington (2009), this meeting was notable because it was the first time two prominent sustainability reporting bodies, A4S and GRI, met to promote uniformity in sustainability reporting. Consequently, the 'International Integrated Reporting Committee' (IIRC) was formed in 2010.

The IIRC is an international organisation formed to define principles and criteria for integrated reporting, thereby supporting organisations with their financial, social, environmental, and governance reporting procedures. Since its inception, numerous regulatory organisations, companies, investors, standard-setters, institutions, individual professionals, and NGOs have joined the IIRC.

The IIRC's institutional mission is to raise public awareness of integrated reporting, identify priority sectors in which additional technical and scientific work appears necessary, evaluate whether sector standards should be adopted voluntarily or mandatorily, and prepare its own reporting standard suitable for 'regulating' a process that integrates in a transparent, consistent, and comprehensive manner, the collection, analysis, and communication of both financial and non-financial information.

The IIRC has created its principles and content with an approach receptive to the contributions of the sector's leading international organisations. In reality, the IIRC has not imposed restrictions or detrimental incompatibility. The IIRC wants its IR Framework to be consistent with the reporting principles produced by other organisations such as the International Financial Reporting Standards (IFRS) and GRI Standards.

As mentioned, in December 2009, the A4S organised a meeting with investors, companies, organisations in the accounting profession, representatives of the United Nations, and standard setters (International Accounting Standards Board (IASB) and Financial Accounting Standards Board (FASB)) to establish an international body to develop a generally accepted Integrated Reporting Framework. A4S and GRI had the most significant roles in this endeavour.

The IIRC was formally constituted in August 2010.

Several multinational corporations, large consulting and auditing firms, independent entities, and national and worldwide institutes of the accounting profession joined the committee, including the International Federation of Accountants (IFAC).

In November 2011, following an organisational and governance reorganisation, the committee changed its name to the 'International Integrated Reporting Council'.

In September 2011, the IIRC presented the first draft of its Framework for public consultation in the form of a Discussion Paper titled 'Towards Integrated Reporting: Communicating Value in the 21st Century'. In 2011, the IIRC organised its work around three main directions ('content', 'governance', and 'stakeholder engagement and communication').

The IR Pilot Program, a project pushed by the IIRC to test the 2011 Discussion Paper and integrated reporting processes in the reporting of 80 big enterprises participating in the program, was launched in October (for Italy, Atlantia, Enel, Eni, Generali, Terna, Snam, etc.). The results of the test on the 2012 reports provided the initial evidence required for both the revision of the framework outlined in the 2011 Discussion Paper and establishment of operational guidelines and tools.

Moreover, the results of the Pilot Program made it evident that the model must be revised through a three-year sharing process: a) compilation and dissemination of working documents based on the 2011/2012 Pilot Program; b) elaboration of the exposure draft of the IR Framework in 2012, then published in November under the title 'IR Working Draft of Prototype Framework'; and c) publication of the Standard in 2013.

In 2012, the Framework of the 2011 Discussion Paper was revised based on the responses to a public consultation (more than 200 organisations) and outcomes of the Pilot Program trials. In addition, the IIRC conducted a series of ongoing

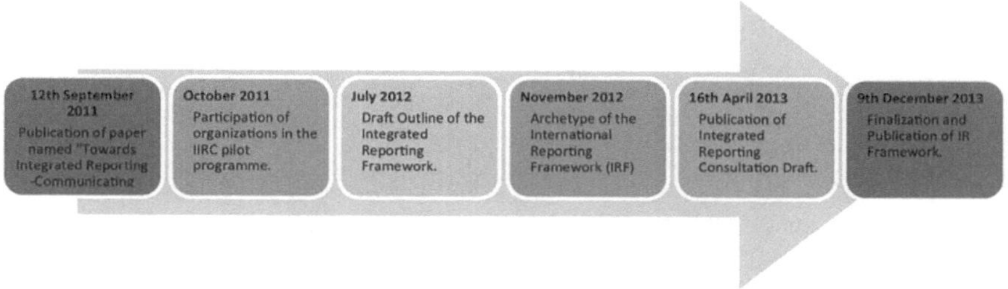


**FIGURE 5.4** History and development of IR framework

consultation activities including territorial and international round tables with representatives and experts from the financial community, governments, and other stakeholders to verify their expectations regarding integrated reporting and obtain technical contributions for the development and adoption of a framework.

The IR Draft Framework was released on 16 April 2013 followed by a three-month public consultation. The International IR Framework 1.0 went public on 9 December after feedback supplied by Pilot Program businesses and international operators was gathered and analysed (Figure 5.4).

As noted, IR Framework 1.0 is intended to strengthen the link between the financial, social, and environmental components of corporate performance that contribute to the creation of value via an organisation's business model and operational strategies.

For this purpose, the framework depicts how an organisation interacts with its external environment and the resources (types of 'capital') employed to create short-, medium-, and long-term value.

Business models and strategies are the primary means by which inputs are converted into results and outputs that can generate value over time. In practice, company production activity employs a series of capital (financial capital, manufactured capital, human capital, intellectual capital, natural capital, and social capital) to transform them into a specific economic process for the production of goods and services. This process occurs within the framework of legislative regulations and corporate values, and an organisational system based on governance procedures, risk management, and policies aimed at stakeholders. These generate outcomes in the short, medium, and long term (contributions to public administration, distribution of the added value generated, increase in the know-how of management processes, and results in terms of the environmental impact of production dynamics) (Figure 5.5).

The IR Framework is based on general principles. Its main innovation is that it contributes to the 'standardisation' of a process and not a report, considering the goal of spreading the application of the standards not only among large organisation, but also among SMEs, and thus among a universe

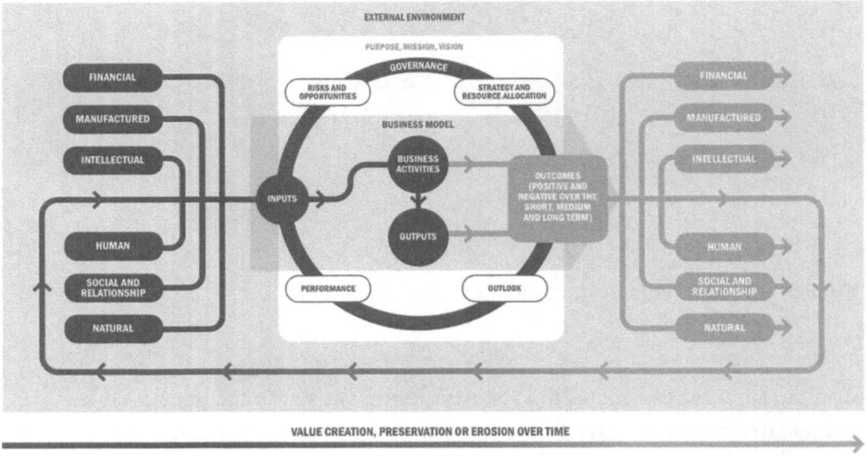


**FIGURE 5.5** The process through which value is created, preserved or eroded

of companies operating in vastly different dimensional, territorial, social, and cultural contexts.

The Framework drives companies along the value chain disclosure process via the 'guiding principles' and 'content elements', the two main pillars through which the IR Framework guides the preparation of integrated reports. The seven 'guiding principles' highlight the preparation and presentation of an integrated report, providing information on the content of the report and how to present it. An integrated report should be characterised by a a) strategic focus and future orientation, b) connectivity of information, c) stakeholder relationships, d) materiality, e) conciseness, f) reliability and completeness, and g) consistency and comparability. Therefore, the IR Framework is principle-based guidance. It does not indicate a list of key performance indicators to disclose, leaving the company broad margins for manoeuvre. However, this is the reason for the many differences often found between reports prepared based on the IR Framework. On the other hand, the 'content elements' follow the value creation process; thus, the integrated report should be related to and contain information about the eight 'content elements' modelled in the form of questions to be answered: a) organisational overview and external environment, b) governance, c) business model, d) risks and opportunities, e) strategy and resource allocation, f) performance, g) outlook, and h) basis of preparation and presentation. In doing so, it considers the general reporting guidelines included in Chapter 5 of the Framework, which pertains to several 'content elements': disclosure of material matters; disclosures concerning capitals; short-, medium-, and long-term time frames; and aggregation and disaggregation.

The following table reports the 'guiding principles' and 'content elements' that guide the preparation of the integrated reports. These are related to environmental, social, and financial issues (Table 5.2).[2]

**TABLE 5.2** "Guiding Principles" and the "Content Elements" of International IR Framework

| | |
|---|---|
| Guiding Principles | The seven Guiding Principles underpin the preparation and presentation of an integrated report, informing the content of the report and how information is presented.<br>These Guiding Principles are applied individually and collectively to prepare and present an integrated report; accordingly, judgement is needed in applying them, particularly when there is an apparent tension between them (e.g. between conciseness and completeness). |
| **3A Strategic focus and future orientation** | |
| 3.3 | An integrated report should provide insight into the organisation's strategy, and how it relates to the organisation's ability to create value in the short, medium and long term and to its use of and effects on the capitals. |
| … | … |
| **3B Connectivity of information** | |
| 3.6 | An integrated report should show a holistic picture of the combination, interrelatedness and dependencies between the factors that affect the organisation's ability to create value over time. |
| … | … |
| **3C Stakeholder relationship** | |
| 3.10 | An integrated report should provide insight into the nature and quality of the organisation's relationships with its key stakeholders, including how and to what extent the organisation understands, takes into account and responds to their legitimate needs and interests |
| … | … |
| **3D Materiality** | |
| 3.17 | An integrated report should disclose information about matters that substantively affect the organisation's ability to create value over the short, medium and long term. |
| … | |
| **3E Conciseness** | |
| 3.36 | An integrated report should be concise. |
| … | … |
| **3F Reliability and completeness** | |
| 3.39 | An integrated report should include all material matters, both positive and negative, in a balanced way and without material error. |
| … | … |
| **3G Consistency and comparability** | |
| 3.54 | The information in an integrated report should be presented:<br>• On a basis that is consistent over time<br>• In a way that enables comparison with other organisations to the extent it<br>• is material to the organisation's own ability to create value over time. |

*(Continued)*

**TABLE 5.2** Continued

| | |
|---|---|
| Content Elements | An integrated report includes eight Content Elements, posed in the form of questions to be answered.<br>In doing so, it takes into account the general reporting guidance in Chapter 5.<br>The Content Elements are fundamentally linked to each other and are not mutually exclusive. The order of the Content Elements as listed here is not the only way they could be sequenced; accordingly, the Content Elements are not intended to serve as a standard structure for an integrated report with information about them appearing in a set sequence or as isolated, standalone sections. Rather, information in an integrated report is presented in a way that makes the connections between the Content Elements apparent. (See Section 3B).<br>The content of an organisation's integrated report will depend on the individual circumstances of the organisation.<br>The Content Elements are therefore stated in the form of questions rather than as checklists of specific disclosures. Accordingly, judgement needs to be exercised in applying the Guiding Principles to determine what information is reported, as well as how it is reported, as discussed below. |
| **4A Organisational overview and external environment** | |
| 4.4 | An integrated report should answer the question: What does the organisation do and what are the circumstances under which it operates? |
| … | … |
| **4B Governance** | |
| 4.8 | An integrated report should answer the question: How does the organisation's governance structure support its ability to create value in the short, medium and long term? |
| … | … |
| **4C Business model** | |
| 4.10 | An integrated report should answer the question: What is the organisation's business model? |
| … | … |
| **4D Risks and opportunities** | |
| 4.24 | An integrated report should answer the question: What are the specific risks and opportunities that affect the organisation's ability to create value over the short, medium and long term, and how is the organisation dealing with them? |
| … | … |
| **4E Strategy and resource allocation** | |
| 4.28 | An integrated report should answer the question: Where does the organisation want to go and how does it intend to get there? |
| … | … |

**4F Performance**

4.31 An integrated report should answer the question: To what extent has the organisation achieved its strategic objectives for the period and what are its outcomes in terms of effects on the capitals?

... ...

**4G Outlook**

4.35 An integrated report should answer the question: What challenges and uncertainties is the organisation likely to encounter in pursuing its strategy, and what are the potential implications for its business model and future performance?

... ...

**4H Basis of preparation and presentation**

4.41 An integrated report should answer the question: How does the organisation determine what matters to include in the integrated report and how are such matters quantified or evaluated?

... ...

## 5.4 The AA1000 AccountAbility principles

The AA1000 Accountability Principles were released by the Institute of Social and Ethical AccountAbility (ISEA) in 1999. The ISEA, known informally as AccountAbility, is a global consulting institute headquartered in the United Kingdom founded in 1996 as an international membership organisation dedicated to enhancing the social responsibility and ethical conduct of for-profit and non-profit organisations.

One primary objective of the ISEA is to promote best practices in social and ethical accounting, auditing, and reporting (SEAAR); develop standards; provide certification procedures; and consequently establish a professional qualification in the sector. The institute provides information and training in SEAAR, providing a place for members to share their knowledge and experiences, and thereby promoting convergence in sustainability practices and standards. Companies and consultancies, non-profit organisations, academic institutions, business schools, and the accountancy profession are members of the ISEA.

Since 1995, AccountAbility has assisted businesses, non-profit organisations, and governments in integrating ethical, environmental, social, and governance accountability into their operations.

Organisations, corporations, and governments use AccountAbility's AA1000 standards to guide their approach to sustainability strategy, governance, and operations, and to demonstrate leadership and performance in accountability, responsibility, and sustainability.

The AA1000 series of standards include the following:

- AA1000 AccountAbility Principles for developing, analysing, and implementing sustainability initiatives (AA1000AP, 2018)
- AA1000 Stakeholder Engagement Standard for creating and conducting inclusive stakeholder engagement practices related to sustainability (AA1000SES, 2015)
- AA1000 Assurance Standard for assuring credibility in reporting on progress towards sustainability goals (AA1000AS v3)

The AA1000 Framework Standard was officially launched in 1999 to improve the quality of specialised accountability standards and act as a stand-alone system for directing, monitoring, and communicating social and ethical accountability and performance.

The standard AA1000 AccountAbility Principles (AA1000AP -2018) was produced through a multi-stakeholder process managed by a working group of experts from various stakeholder organisations, locations, and subject areas. Using sustainability market trends and pertinent international guidelines, frameworks, and standards, the working group assisted a core AccountAbility team in the production of applicable principle-based guidance for organisations. The establishment of the principle was a collaborative effort. In fact, the draft materials were made available for public comment via an Internet platform at the beginning of 2017 and then amended accordingly. The working group approved the final document, which was then submitted to the AccountAbility Standards Board, which approved its publication in April 2018. As of 1 January 2019, organisations may use the AA1000AP for reports released. To promote the widest possible application of the standard's principles, it was agreed in the 2018 edition that the standard would take the form of an overall framework and guiding system for principles-based sustainability management and reporting. Now, in its true form, it is an internationally recognised, principles-based framework and guidance organisations can use to identify, prioritise, and respond to sustainability concerns to enhance their long-term performance.

In 2003, the first edition of the AA1000 Assurance Standard was released. It was created to ensure the integrity and quality of sustainability performance and reporting, and was the first sustainability assurance standard in the world. In 2008, the second edition of the AA1000 Assurance Standard was published, with improvements and upgrades focusing on engagement for sustainability assurance.

The third edition of the AA1000 Assurance Standard has undergone iterative research and review processes to optimise its relevance, usability, and applicability for successful sustainability assurance, whether employed as a standalone or complementary instrument. As demand for non-financial assurance has increased, sustainability assurance mechanisms have entered the market. AA1000AS was developed through a broad-based, multi-stakeholder process. Following a period of preliminary study, working group consultations led to the development of a draft standard for public review. In June and July 2019, a large panel of experts representing various stakeholders were consulted worldwide. The draft was reviewed and amended in response to pertinent comments received during the public review period. The AccountAbility AA1000 Steering Committee reviewed the final document and submitted it to the AccountAbility Standards Board, which approved its publication in August 2020.

The AA1000 Stakeholder Engagement Standard was published in 2005 to support organisations' achievement of the principle of inclusivity.

It provides direction on how to plan and implement stakeholder involvement.

In 2015, considering feedback from the first version and a critical expert review following a broad-based multi-stakeholder process, the AA1000SES exposure draft released in 2011 was edited, refined, validated, and published as the final A1000 Stakeholder Engagement Standard (AA1000SES, 2015) (Figure 5.6).

The 2018 AA1000AP consists of three sections. The introduction describes the objectives, scope, and benefits of the standard, and defines its possible users. This section also describes how all types of organisations might apply the AccountAbility principles for accountability and sustainability guidance. The second section addresses each of the four principles (inclusivity, materiality, responsiveness, and impact) separately, including formulations of the principle, relevant definitions, a thorough explanation, and criteria required to support its implementation and assurance. The third section examines the interrelationships between the principles and order in which an organisation may implement them.

Originally, the standard AA1000 AccountAbility Principles were intended to include three principles: inclusivity, materiality, and responsiveness. Subsequently, a fourth principle, impact, was added, and the definitions, explanations, and criteria connected to the three original principles were revised to reflect the evolution of sustainability since the first publication of the guidelines.

The principle of impact refers to the necessity for organisations to monitor, assess, and account for how their actions influence their ecosystems as a whole.

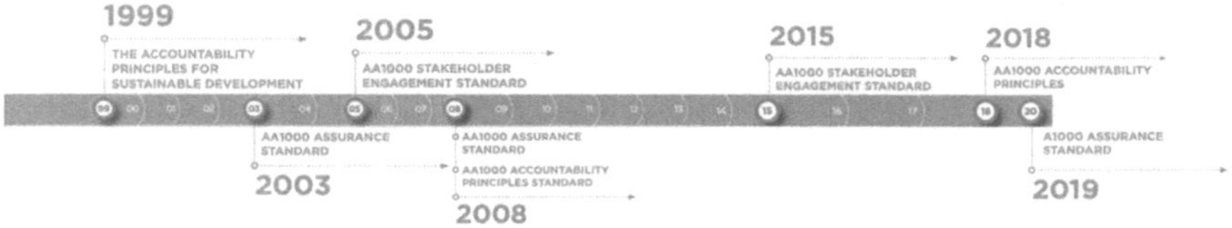


**FIGURE 5.6** History and development of AA1000 standards

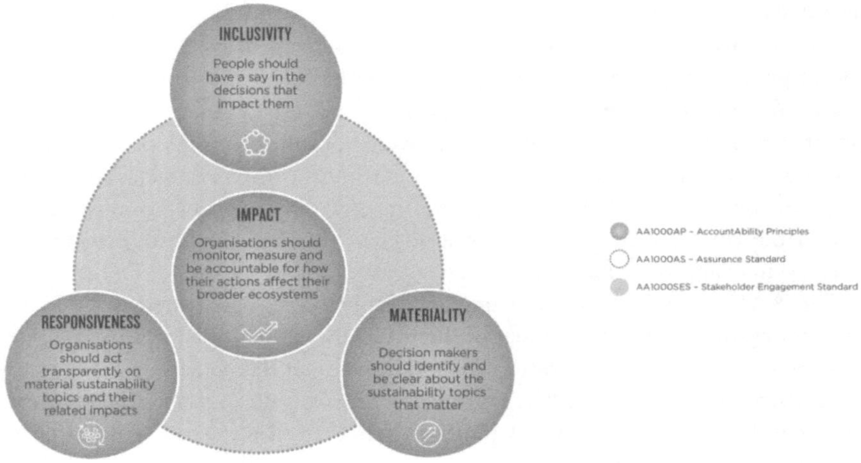


**FIGURE 5.7** AA1000 AccountAbility Principles

This is crucial because it promotes interaction among other principles. According to the principle of inclusion, an organisation should be accountable to its stakeholders, comprehend their needs, and offer solutions to meet these demands. The foundation of the materiality and responsiveness principles is inclusivity. Materiality refers to the identification of key topics that impact stakeholders, whereas responsiveness refers to the need for an organisation's timely response to material sustainability issues and their impacts, including the formulation and implementation of appropriate strategies, policies, objectives, and improvements in the governance structure and processes, and in management and reporting practices (Figure 5.7).

The AA1000 AccountAbility Principles standard establishes a link between national laws, local standards, and guidelines. In fact, the standards state that any of the AccountAbility Principles stated in the document may have alternative definitions in national standards, local legislation, and mandatory financial or regulatory disclosures. If the definitions are not complementary, the predominant definition used by the organisation to achieve the related requirement should be indicated in the disclosure along with any variations that occur (AA1000 AccountAbility Principles, 2018).

The following table outlines the 'key definitions', 'explanations' (or 'discussions'), and 'criteria' associated with each principle. Similar to the International IR Framework, the AA1000 principles lack specific provisions for environmental sustainability. All principles refer to social, economic, and environmental sustainability without distinction (Table 5.3).[3]

**TABLE 5.3** "Principles" of AA1000 Accountability

| *Principles* | |
|---|---|
| **Inclusivity** | |
| Principle | People should have a say in the decisions that impact them |
| Key definition | Inclusivity is actively identifying stakeholders and enabling their participation in establishing an organisation's material sustainability topics and developing a strategic response to them. An inclusive organisation accepts its accountability to those on whom it has an impact and to those who have an impact on it. |
| Explanations (or discussion) | **Identifying external and internal stakeholders**<br>Stakeholders are those individuals, groups of individuals and/or organisations that affect and/or could be affected by an organisation's activities, products or services and associated performance.<br>Organisations generally have many stakeholders, each with distinct types and levels of involvement, and often with diverse and sometimes conflicting interests and concerns.<br>Inclusivity of these stakeholders means allowing full and balanced involvement in the organisation's varied decision-making processes related to sustainability, resulting in strategies, plans, actions and outcomes that address material topics and impacts in an accountable manner.<br>Inclusivity is the commitment of an organisation to be accountable to its stakeholders and to enable their participation. It also involves internal collaboration at all levels of an organisation, across governance, strategy, management and operations, to achieve continual improvement.<br>The outputs of stakeholder engagement and stakeholder responses, including formalised action plans, should inform an organisation's strategy, governance and operational management.<br>**Implementing engagement**<br>To begin the engagement process, an organisation should develop a comprehensive understanding of:<br>• who its stakeholders are;<br>• their needs and concerns; and<br>• the impact (where impact represents a significant influence) of its strategies and operations on them.<br>The AA1000 Stakeholder Engagement Standard (AA1000SES) establishes the benchmark for high-quality engagement and is recommended as a useful starting point for organisations committed to achieving Inclusivity. |
| Required adherence criteria | The following action items are designed to guide organisations in both applying the Principle of Inclusivity and monitoring their progress in its application. Fulfilment of the criteria leads to adherence to the Principle. These criteria are also used by assurance providers to assess an organisation's enactment of the Principle. |

(*Continued*)

**TABLE 5.3** Continued

| *Principles* | |
|---|---|
| | **Commitment, integration & capacity building**<br>1 Formalise a commitment from the highest governing body of the organisation to be accountable to stakeholders.<br>2 Integrate stakeholder engagement processes into governance, strategy and relevant decision-making processes across the full organisation, seeking senior management, cross-functional and cross-geographical involvement as appropriate.<br>3 Establish the scope and objectives of stakeholder participation.<br>4 Integrate stakeholder engagement and responses into relevant policies, operational procedures and systems, for example, by performing risk analyses, materiality assessments, and setting and monitoring meaningful objectives.<br>5 Ensure that the necessary competencies and resources are allocated and available for stakeholder engagement.<br>**Engagement strategy & process development**<br>6 Identify and understand stakeholders, including their capacity to engage and their views and expectations, and address potential stakeholder and engagement risks.<br>7 Develop formal strategies for ongoing engagement and communication with stakeholders.<br>**Performance measurement & stakeholder communications**<br>8 Set relevant metrics to measure engagement effectiveness, outcomes and impact.<br>9 Use outputs of engagement to facilitate understanding, learning and improvement of the organisation.<br>10 Communicate with stakeholders in an appropriate, transparent and timely manner, as per the organisation's established boundaries of disclosure. |
| **Materiality** | |
| Principle | Decision makers should identify and be clear about the sustainability topics that matter. |
| Key definition | Materiality relates to identifying and prioritising the most relevant sustainability topics, taking into account the effect each topic has on an organisation and its stakeholders. A material topic is a topic that will substantively influence and impact the assessments, decisions, actions and performance of an organisation and/or its stakeholders in the short, medium and/or long term. |
| Explanations (or discussion) | **Determining materiality**<br>The term materiality has been defined in the context of financial reporting. However, its meaning now includes the disclosure of sustainability topics. |

AccountAbility prioritises a principles-based process of materiality, one that should be used in conjunction with a rules-based process of materiality relevant to the organisation and its regulatory environment.

To make informed decisions and take calculated actions, an organisation and its stakeholders need to identify the topics that are material to the sustainability performance of the organisation.

Determining which topics are material requires a materiality determination process, which evaluates both the actual and likely impacts of an organisation's strategy, governance and activities, including:

- the identification and fair representation of topics relative to an organisation's sector, industry, geography, business model and structure;
- the development of clear, balanced and replicable assessment criteria; and
- an assessment approach that is integrated into organisational processes.

**Collecting and analysing inputs**

The materiality determination process should consider and analyse comprehensive and balanced information. An organisation needs input from all relevant sources and stakeholders, including both internal and external sources, covering an appropriate time period.

Such inputs include a broad range of information beyond financial information and drivers, including stakeholder profiles, stakeholder concerns and suggestions, societal and peer-based norms, sustainability context, macroeconomic and geopolitical factors, and appropriate policy, reporting, and regulatory frameworks.

Analysis of the collected information needs to include consideration of sustainability drivers, which may include financial impacts and should account for the needs, interests, and priorities of the organisation and its stakeholders.

**Undertaking the assessment**

The materiality determination or assessment process should be undertaken regularly and aligned with the organisation's processes for strategy development, decision-making, risk and compliance management, operational management and reporting. It should also be documented and disclosed to stakeholders.

An effective materiality assessment provides an organisation with a comprehensive understanding of its sustainability context, which topics are material or not, and to whom these topics are material and why.

An organisation's material topics will evolve over time as topics mature, drivers fluctuate, and understanding improves based on additional stakeholder input.

**Considering likely as well as actual impacts**

Given this continuous evolution, evaluating both the actual and likely impacts of an organisation's strategy, governance and activities are all the more important. Regularly assessing the evolution of likely impacts will support the accuracy, relevance, and effectiveness of an organisation's overall materiality determination process over time.

(*Continued*)

**TABLE 5.3** Continued

| *Principles* | |
|---|---|
| Required adherence criteria | The following action items are designed to guide organisations in both applying the Principle of Materiality and monitoring their progress in its application. Fulfilment of the criteria leads to adherence to the Principle. These criteria are also used by assurance providers to assess an organisation's enactment of the Principle.<br>**Commitment, integration & capacity building**<br>1 Establish an organisation-wide, robust, and systematic materiality determination process under the governance of senior management.<br>2 Ensure integration of the assessment process across the organisation.<br>3 Provide the necessary competencies and resources to apply the results of the materiality assessment process.<br>**Materiality determination**<br>4 Set consistent and clear boundaries, as well as a purpose, time period and scope, for the materiality assessment.<br>5 Identify and fairly represent topics from a wide range of sources.<br>6 Evaluate the relevance of identified material sustainability topics based on suitable and explicit criteria.<br>7 Determine the significance, likelihood, and present and expected future impact of identified material sustainability topics, using appropriate criteria and thresholds.<br>8 Take into account the evolving sustainability, macroeconomic, geopolitical, and regulatory contexts and maturity of topics and concerns.<br>9 Include a means of addressing conflicts or dilemmas arising from diverging or conflicting expectations regarding material topics.<br>**Communication**<br>10 Create and disclose a comprehensive and balanced understanding and prioritisation of material sustainability topics for the organisation and its stakeholders. |
| **Responsiveness** | |
| Principle | Organisations should act transparently on material sustainability topics and their related impacts. |
| Key definition | Responsiveness is an organisation's timely and relevant reaction to material sustainability topics and their related impacts. Responsiveness is realised through decisions, actions and performance, as well as communication with stakeholders. |
| Explanations (or discussion) | **Acting on material topics**<br>Responsiveness comprises when and how an organisation responds to material sustainability topics and their related impacts on its external and internal stakeholders. An effective response is aligned with the organisation's objectives and integrated into its strategy, taking into account identified material topics and their related impacts. |

Responses may include establishing policies, objectives and targets; enhancing governance structures; developing or advancing management systems and processes; developing or implementing action plans; engaging stakeholders; measuring and monitoring sustainability performance and impacts; reporting; issuing communications; and/or achieving assurance.

**Prioritising responses**

Since responses will compete for available resources within an organisation, they, like material topics, should be prioritised and addressed in a timely manner.

Response prioritisation should align with:

- organisational strategies and operations;
- outcomes of materiality and impact assessments;
- stakeholder interests and/or legitimacy;
- availability of resources;
- internal management and reporting schedules and timelines; and
- regulatory reporting requirements.

**Determining scope**

How an organisation responds to a material topic should depend on the nature, impact, and prioritisation of the topic as well as the maturity of the organisation's strategy, positioning, objectives, policies, systems and processes.

Resources are adequate when they allow an organisation to achieve its stated commitments within a stated time period and to communicate its responses. Organisations should put in place the necessary competencies, capacities and processes to achieve the responses to which they commit.

A responsive organisation should respond to its material sustainability topics, related impacts, and stakeholders in a comprehensive, accurate, timely, accessible and balanced manner. Whilst stakeholders may provide input in the development of responses, an organisation's responses may not be consistent with the views of all stakeholders.

Required adherence criteria

The following action items are designed to guide organisations in both applying the Principle of Responsiveness and monitoring their progress in its application. Fulfilment of the criteria leads to adherence to the Principle. These criteria are also used by assurance providers to assess an organisation's enactment of the Principle.

**Commitment, integration & capacity building**

1 Under the governance of senior management, implement a process for developing responses related to material topics and communicating them to stakeholders that is applied across the organisation.
2 Integrate this process into the organisation, including through relevant organisational processes, such as risk management, compliance, and strategy development.
3 Provide the necessary competencies and resources to respond appropriately to material topics, using a range of response types.

*(Continued)*

**TABLE 5.3** Continued

| *Principles* | |
|---|---|
| | **Response strategy development**<br>4 Implement a process for developing responses and communicating with stakeholders that is continuous.<br>5 Consider the relationship between the maturity, impact, and prioritisation of a topic and the appropriateness of the response.<br>6 Validate proposed responses with internal and, when appropriate, external stakeholders, and assure feasibility to deliver reasonable and viable responses.<br>**Response implementation & ongoing communication**<br>7 Respond in a way that addresses the needs, concerns, and expectations of stakeholders.<br>8 Report to stakeholders in a comprehensive, accurate, timely, accessible, and balanced way, using suitable reporting principles, frameworks, and guidelines that support comparability of information. |
| **Impact** | |
| Principle | Organisations should monitor, measure and be accountable for how their actions affect their broader ecosystems. |
| Key definition | Impact is the effect of behaviour, performance and/or outcomes, on the part of individuals or an organisation, on the economy, the environment, society, stakeholders or the organisation itself.<br>Material topics have potential direct and indirect impacts – which may be positive or negative, intended or unintended, expected or realised, and short, medium or long term. |
| Explanations (or discussion) | **Appreciating impact**<br>Acknowledging, understanding, measuring, managing, and evaluating impact leads to more effective decision-making and results-based management within an organisation.<br>Impact is the result of an organisation's plans and activities.<br>Evaluating the actual and likely impacts of an organisation's material topics requires an effective management process that includes:<br>• a defined strategic intent;<br>• accompanying goals, baselines and boundaries;<br>• relevant, complete and accurate data/information; and<br>• appropriate resources and competencies.<br>**Measuring impact**<br>Impact can encompass a range of environmental, social and governance topics and can be measured on a local, regional, or global level.<br>The monitoring, measurement and evaluation of impact may be qualitative, quantitative or monetised in nature. It can also focus on an immediate or a longer-term time period, depending on the sustainability context. |

The processes of monitoring, measuring, and evaluating impact should consider science, ethics, laws, regulations, and context-based metrics.

In measuring an identified impact, organisations should consider all sources that may also contribute to the impact, to reduce the possibility of attributing the impact incorrectly. Further, a structured analysis of the probability of impacts should be included.

**Informing engagement and compensation practices**

Identified impacts should be incorporated into both stakeholder engagement and the periodic materiality assessment process to inform organisational governance, strategy, goal-setting, and operations, thus enabling more informed decision-making and greater responsiveness.

Linking short- and long-term management remuneration to organisational impact through the performance management system is an effective method of integrating impact into decision making. Impact should inform relevant people management, work accountability and compensation practices within an organisation.

**Disclosing impact**

Impact should be measured and disclosed in the most balanced and effective way possible, indicating both realised and unrealised goals and taking into account the target audience and objective of the disclosure.

Required adherence criteria

The following action items are designed to guide organisations in both applying the Principle of Impact and monitoring their progress in its application. Fulfilment of the criteria leads to adherence with the Principle. These criteria are also used by assurance providers to assess an organisation's enactment of the Principle.

**Commitment, integration & capacity building**

1 Perform robust processes to understand, measure, evaluate, and manage the organisation's impacts that are applied across the organisation under the governance of senior management.
2 Ensure these processes are documented and integrated into the organisation.
3 Provide the necessary competencies and resources to understand, measure, evaluate, and manage the organisation's impacts.
4 Integrate identified impacts into key management processes, for example, the materiality assessment process and organisational strategy, governance, goal-setting and operations.

**Impact identification & metrics development**

5 Set consistent and clear boundaries, as well as a purpose, time period and scope, for impact assessment.
6 Establish processes to understand, measure, evaluate and manage impacts that are credible, clear and understandable as well as replicable, defensible and can be subject to external assurance.

*(Continued)*

**TABLE 5.3** Continued

| *Principles* | |
|---|---|
| | 7 Include a means of capturing and measuring actual as well as potential impacts, such as direct and indirect, intended and unintended, and positive and negative impacts.<br>8 Identify and fairly represent impacts from a wide range of sources, such as activities, policies, programmes, decisions, and products and services, as well as any related performance. Furthermore, the sustainability context of each impact should be clearly understood.<br>9 Present impacts as a qualitative, quantitative or monetised measurement. |
| | **Impact assessment & disclosure**<br>10 Create and disclose a comprehensive and balanced understanding of the measurement and evaluation of the organisation's impacts on stakeholders and on the organisation itself. |

## 5.5 Similarities and differences, and strengths and weaknesses of reporting frameworks

Researchers studying sustainability standards in recent years have elucidated the strengths, weaknesses, advantages, and disadvantages of various frameworks, albeit without reaching consensus (Fiandrino, 2019). Several organisations such as the GRI, AccountAbility (AA), IIRC, SASB, United Nations Global Compact (UNGC), OECD, and European Federation of Financial Analysts have developed more than 30 international frameworks for sustainability reporting. Some provide compliance disclosure frameworks and standards through comprehensive instrumental procedures for non-financial reporting (e.g. GRI, SASB, EFFAS, and ISO 26000). Others provide more flexible reporting frameworks and structures through principles-based approaches (e.g. IIRC, AA, OECD, and FEE). Some are oriented towards the views of various stakeholders (e.g. GRI, AA, ISO, and FEE), and others are primarily geared towards financial stakeholders (e.g. IIRC, SASB, and EFFAS).

There are several distinctions between the various frameworks and some parallels. Standard setters continuously vie for a leadership position in the field of sustainability disclosure standards (La Torre et al., 2018). The main variations tend to revolve around materiality criteria and impact the type of information to include in a non-financial statement.

This situation, alongside the fact that companies are substantially free to choose the preferred framework, makes it complex to achieve the objectives of improving the comparability of non-financial information and enhancing the accountability of companies.

Next, we analyse the differences and similarities between the three reporting frameworks discussed in the preceding pages of this chapter. Our goal is to clarify the benefits and drawbacks that can result from a company's decision to operate under one of the aforementioned frameworks.

de Colle et al. (2014) identify several advantages and disadvantages. They highlight the advantages of operationalising CSR, uncertainty avoidance, and assistance for CSR adoption. In addition, the facilitation of stakeholder interaction, promotion of continuous improvement, and enhancement of business reputation are derived from these benefits. The implementation of a framework for CSR disclosure may result in disadvantages such as the introduction of additional expenditures, a fixation on compliance, and the over- or under-communication of data (Fiandrino, 2019).

The purpose of the three frameworks examined earlier is to improve the sustainability performance of enterprises and non-profit organisations by codifying their behaviour and standardising, as far as possible, the disclosure they use to engage with stakeholders.

Although the three frameworks share a similar objective, they are distinguished by their distinct approaches. While the GRI standards are characterised by a standards-based approach, the International IR Framework and AccountAbility's AA1000 are principles-based.

The IR Framework is a principle-based guideline for an integrated type of reporting in which the links between a company's strategy, business model, governance, and performance demonstrate how it creates long-term value (IIRC, 2013). As a framework based on principles, the IR Framework offers only general principles and content pieces, which organisations may interpret differently (Flower, 2015). In fact, it does not provide a list of key performance indicators that must be disclosed, providing the company with significant room for manoeuvre. This is why there are so many variances between reports that use the IR Framework as a foundation for their creation. Similarly, AccountAbility's AA1000 standards are frameworks based on the principles organisations, businesses, and governments use to direct their approach to sustainability. To assist the widest possible use of the standard's principles, it has taken the shape of an overall framework and guiding system for principles-based sustainability management and reporting. In its true form, it is a principle-based framework and guidelines for identifying, prioritising, and responding to sustainability concerns to enhance long-term performance.

In contrast to the GRI principles, the IR Framework and AccountAbility's AA1000 standards lack defined rules and metrics for consistently framing non-financial information, which is at the expense of comparability and comprehensiveness.

Another important distinction relates to the orientation of the framework and selection of the stakeholder to whom sustainability communication is directed. While the GRI standards and AccountAbility's AA1000 standards are explicitly designed for all organisations – profit and non-profit, public and private – and focus on all stakeholders, the International IR Framework is explicitly designed for large companies and focuses on investors, i.e. the providers of risk capital.

As indicated earlier, the GRI standards are a modular set of interconnected standards that permit various types of organisations to publicly report on the impacts of their operations in a transparent manner. The GRI standards advocate a multi-stakeholder approach and play a crucial role in sustainability reporting standardisation. Thus, their objective is to create a global standard language for organisations to use when reporting their impacts. This facilitates informed discourse between all stakeholders and informs their decision-making processes pertaining to impacts.

Similarly, AccountAbility's AA1000 standards are frameworks based on principles that all types of organisations, businesses, and governments can use to guide their approach to sustainability strategy, governance, operations, and disclosure. As stated in AA1000AP (2018), organisations of various sizes and types can use the AccountAbility principles to connect with all types of stakeholders.

Unlike the two preceding frameworks, the IR Framework focuses primarily on an organisation's equity providers. Actually, the framework's definition of 'integrated reporting' explicitly states that it represents a process that aims to promote a more efficient approach to the corporate report by enhancing the quality of information transmitted to capital suppliers, thereby enabling them to allocate capital more effectively and efficiently.

This definition also suggests that the framework is largely, if not exclusively, intended for large enterprises, i.e. those with a significant need to contact potential investors. Typically, the financial structure of small- and medium-sized businesses is extremely stable over time; hence, discussion with possible investors is theoretical.

Prior studies on why organisations choose particular frameworks demonstrate that companies select multi-stakeholder-oriented frameworks such as the GRI Guidelines to increase their credibility (Buhr et al., 2014). In their pursuit of legitimacy, businesses are also influenced by institutional factors and want to adhere to the most widespread reporting methods in a certain industry. To achieve a competitive advantage, it can be advantageous to mimic the strategies of one's competitors and to be viewed as sustainable (Buhr et al., 2014). Thus, the decision to embrace a given framework is also influenced by the degree of institutionalisation in a particular setting or industry. Consequently, some businesses are likely to adopt the same framework based on perceived legitimacy or institutional pressures (Bebbington et al., 2012).

This may be the primary reason the GRI standards, one of the earliest and most institutionalised sustainability frameworks, are also the most prevalent.

The explicit provision of financial and non-financial information complementarity is another important aspect in the comparison and contrast of the similarities and differences between the three analysed frameworks. This complementarity is explicitly stated in the IR Framework, but less so in the other two frameworks.

The greater clarity of the IR framework in ensuring that financial and non-financial information are produced in a complementary manner by companies likely stems from the framework's explicit design for integrated reporting, whereas the other two frameworks focus on sustainability reporting, despite that scholars addressing the topic and sometimes the standard setter itself suggest the integration of sustainability reporting.

## Notes

1 Due to space constraints, no recommendations or guidance are provided; instead, please refer to the GRI Standards for more information.
2 Not all the contents of the Framework are reported because of space requirements. Thus, please refer to the International IR Framework for further information.
3 Not all contents of the Principles are reported because of space requirements. Thus, please refer to the AA1000 AccountAbility Principles (2018) for more information.

## References


Adams, C. A., & Evans, R. (2004). Accountability, completeness, credibility and the audit expectations gap. *Journal of Corporate Citizenship*, (14), 97–115.

Albuquerque, P., Bronnenberg, B. J., & Corbett, C. J. (2007). A spatiotemporal analysis of the global diffusion of ISO 9000 and ISO 14000 certification. *Management science*, 53(3), 451–468.

Andrew, J., & Cortese, C. (2011, September). Accounting for climate change and the self-regulation of carbon disclosures. *Accounting Forum*, 35(3), 130–138. No longer published by Elsevier.

Baron, R. (2014). The evolution of corporate reporting for integrated performance. *Background Paper for the 30th Round Table on Sustainable Development*, 25, 1–35.

Bartels, W., Fogelberg, T., Hoballah, A., & van der Lugt, C. T. (2016). *Carrots & Sticks: Global trends in sustainability reporting regulation and policy*. Amsterdam, The Netherlands: GRI.

Bebbington, J., Kirk, E. A., & Larrinaga, C. (2012). The production of normativity: A comparison of reporting regimes in Spain and the UK. *Accounting, Organizations and Society*, 37(2), 78–94.

Buhr, N., Gray, R., & Milne, M. J. (2014). Histories, rationales, voluntary standards and future prospects for sustainability reporting: CSR, GRI, IIRC and beyond. In J. Bebbington, J. Unerman, and B. O'Dwyer, (Eds.), *Sustainability accounting and accountability* (pp. 51–71). London: Routledge.

Busco, C., Frigo, M. L., Riccaboni, A., & Quattrone, P. (2013). *Integrated reporting. Concepts and cases that redefine corporate accountability*. Cham: Springer International Publishing.

Brown, H. S., de Jong, M., & Levy, D. L. (2009), Building institutions based on information disclosure: Lessons from GRI's sustainability reporting. *Journal of Cleaner Production*, 17(6), 571–580.

Cheng, B., Ioannou, I., & Serafeim, G. (2014). Corporate social responsibility and access to finance. *Strategic Management Journal*, 35(1), 1–23.

D'Andrea, A. (2020). *Il principio di materialità dell'informativa non finanziaria*. Torino: Giappichelli Editore.

De Colle, S., Henriques, A., & Sarasvathy, S. (2014). The paradox of corporate social responsibility standards. *Journal of Business Ethics*, 125(2), 177–191.

D'Este, C. E., Sharman, C., Dutta, R., Morshed, A., Lethbridge, J., Terhorst, A., & Howell, B. (2013). Sustainability, scalability, and sensor discovery with cloud robotics. In *Australasian conference on robotics and automation* (pp. 250–258).

Dumay, J., Guthrie, J., & Farneti, F. (2010). GRI sustainability reporting guidelines for public and third sector organizations: A critical review. *Public Management Review*, 12(4), 531–548.

Eccles, R. G., & Krzus, M. P. (2010). *One report: Integrated reporting for a sustainable strategy*. Hoboken, NJ: John Wiley & Sons.

Eccles, R. G., & Krzus, M. P. (2014). *The integrated reporting movement: Meaning, momentum, motives, and materiality*. Hoboken, NJ: John Wiley & Sons.

Elkington, J. (2009), The Holy Grail of Integrated Reporting. Available at http://www.sustainability.com/blog/the-holy-grail-of-integrated-reporting#.VUFE05Me4ZN.

Federation of European Accountants (FEE) (2016). EU Directive on disclosure of non-financial and diversity information: Achieving Good Quality and Consistent Reporting, FEE, Brussels.

Fiandrino, S. (2019). Disclosure of non-financial information. In *Evolutionary paths and harmonisation to mandatory requirements* (pp. 1–162). Torino: Giappichelli Editore.

Flower, J. (2015). The international integrated reporting council: A story of failure. *Critical Perspectives on Accounting*, 27, 1–17.

Gleeson-White, J. (2014). *Six Capitals: The revolution capitalism has to have--or can accountants save the planet?* Crows Nest: Allen & Unwin.

Gray, R. H. (2003). *Social and environmental accounting and reporting: From ridicule to revolution? From hope to hubris?* United Kingdom: University of Glasgow.

Gray, R. (2004). Why is social accounting so difficult?–Part I. *Social and Environmental Accountability Journal*, 24(1), 12–17.

Gray, R., Owen, D., & Adams, C. (1996). *Accounting & accountability: Changes and challenges in corporate social and environmental reporting*. Hoboken, NJ: Prentice hall.

Jones, S., & Ratnatunga, J. (2012). Contemporary issues in sustainability accounting, assurance and reporting. Bingley: Emerald Group Publishing Limited, p. 142.

King A., Bartels, W., Fogelberg, T., Hoballah, A., & van der Lugt, C. T. (2016). *Carrots & Sticks: Global trends in sustainability reporting regulation and policy*. Amsterdam, The Netherlands: GRI.

King, M., & Roberts, L. (2013). *Integrate. Doing business in the 21 century*. Cape Town: Juta e Co, Ltd.

Kolk, A. (2004). A decade of sustainability reporting: Developments and significance. *International Journal of Environment and Sustainable Development*, 3(1), 51–64.

KPMG (2020). The time has come. The KPMG Survey of Sustainability Reporting 2020. KPMG IMPACT

La Torre, M., Sabelfeld, S., Blomkvist, M., Tarquinio, L., & Dumay, J. (2018). Harmonising non-financial reporting regulation in Europe: Practical forces and projections for future research. *Meditari Accountancy Research*.

Lepore, L., Landriani, L., Pisano, S., D'Amore, G., & Pozzoli, S. (2022). Corporate governance in the digital age: The role of social media and board independence in CSR disclosure. Evidence from Italian listed companies. *Journal of Management and Governance*. https://doi.org/10.1007/s10997-021-09617-2.

Parker, L. D. (1986). Polemical themes in social accounting: A scenario for standard setting. *Advances in Public Interest Accounting*, 1, 67–93.

Pozzoli, M. (2018). *Integrated reporting: principi generali e prassi applicative* (Vol. 8). Torino: Giappichelli Editore.

Puxty, A. G. (1986). Social accounting as immanent legitimation: A critique of a technicist ideology. *Advances in Public Interest Accounting*, 1(6), 95–111.

Ransburg, B., & Vágási, M. (2007). Concepts and standards for the corporate internalization of sustainable development. *Periodica Polytechnica Social and Management Sciences*, 15(2), 43–51.

Reynolds, M., & Yuthas, K. (2008). Moral discourse and corporate social responsibility reporting. *Journal of Business Ethics*, 78(1), 47–64.
Silvestri A., & Veltri, S. (2016). Evaluating the Integrated Report quality. In SIDREA, L. Marchi, R. Lombardi, L. Anselmi (Eds.), *il governo aziendale tra tradizione e innovazione* (pp. 71–90 e pp. 91–108). Milano: Franco Angeli.
Stacchezzini, R., Melloni, G., & Lai, A. (2016). Sustainability management and reporting: The role of integrated reporting for communicating corporate sustainability management. *Journal of Cleaner Production*, 136, 102–110.
Stubbs, W., & Higgins, C. (2012). *Sustainability and integrated reporting: A study of the inhibitors and enablers of integrated reporting*. Sydney, N. S. W: Institute of Chartered Accountants in Australia.
Thomson, I. (2015). 'But does sustainability need capitalism or an integrated report' a commentary on 'The International Integrated Reporting Council: A story of failure' by Flower, J. *Critical Perspectives on Accounting*, 27, 18–22.
Tschopp, D., & Huefner, R. J. (2015). Comparing the evolution of CSR reporting to that of financial reporting. *Journal of Business Ethics*, 127(3), 565–577.
Tschopp, D., & Nastanski, M. (2014). The harmonization and convergence of corporate social responsibility reporting standards. *Journal of Business Ethics*, 125(1), 147–162.
Zinenko, A., Rovira, M. R., & Montiel, I. (2015). The fit of the social responsibility standard ISO 26000 within other CSR instruments. *Sustainability Accounting, Management and Policy Journal*, 6(4), 498–526.

# 6

# EMPIRICAL ANALYSIS OF THE DETERMINANTS OF THE ENVIRONMENTAL DISCLOSURES RELEASED BY EUROPEAN LISTED COMPANIES

## 6.1 Aim, research model, and hypotheses development

This chapter analyses the evolution of sustainability reporting practices in EU countries over the past few decades and investigates the relationship between environmental disclosure and board characteristics such as board independence and gender diversity, as well as other corporate governance mechanisms.

A sustainability disclosure strategy is crucial for corporate governance and credibility, and defining it is among the board's responsibilities (Lim and Greenwood, 2017; Garcia-Sanchez et al., 2014; Schultz et al., 2013).

Companies release environmental disclosure to minimise information asymmetry and conflict of interest between competing parties, legitimise their actions, and influence stakeholder opinions (Odriozola and Baraibar-Diez, 2017; Martnez-Fernández et al., 2016). According to agency theory, voluntary disclosure is one of the most important mechanisms for monitoring the behaviour of corporate management or the largest shareholders (Ho and Wong, 2001; Frankforter et al., 2000) and for reducing the likelihood of conflict (Ho and Wong, 2001; Frankforter et al., 2000). Moreover, legitimacy theory (Suchman, 1995) asserts that corporations earn legitimacy through various behaviours such as corporate transparency to important stakeholders (Ashforth and Gibbs, 1990). Through environmental disclosure, businesses demonstrate that they adhere to the terms of their social contracts (Garcia-Sanchez et al., 2014).

In this scenario, directors are required to disclose information on sustainability to demonstrate that their organisations comply with the rules and act ethically, thus enhancing their reputation. However, the success of directors as a mechanism to encourage environmental disclosure is contingent on their degree of independence. In reality, when board members are involved in the management of a company, collusion with controlling shareholders or top management

DOI: 10.4324/9781003245933-7

becomes more likely (Fama and Jensen, 1983), resulting in a loss of effectiveness. To mitigate these risks, companies typically include on their boards of directors professionals who have no ties to the firm's owners or executives. According to resource dependence theory (Pfeffer and Salancik, 1978), independent directors can readily incorporate the interests of different stakeholders into their decision-making processes, thereby promoting sustainable business practices.

Agency theory suggests that a greater proportion of independent directors results in more effective board monitoring of executives and controlling shareholders (Zattoni and Cuomo, 2010; Hillman and Dalziel, 2003; Fama, 1980). Independent directors' reputational concerns may push them to act in the best interests of all stakeholders, not just shareholders (Armstrong et al., 2010; Lim et al., 2007; Fama and Jensen, 1983). Consequently, independent directors encourage corporations to become more accessible to external investors by making their disclosures more complete and precise (Chau and Grey, 2010; Ho and Wong, 2001; Forker, 1992). Indeed, independent directors are likely to be interested in demonstrating that the company's conduct is appropriate in order to enhance their own reputation (Fich and Shivdasani, 2007; Zahra and Stanton, 1988). In general, status, credibility, employment prospects, and networking are the principal benefits of directorships for independent directors (Lorsch and Maciver, 1989; Fama and Jensen, 1983).

Based on these arguments, several scholars (e.g. Ali et al., 2017) have used agency theory and legitimacy theory and found a positive influence of independent directors on the degree of corporate disclosure, particularly sustainability disclosure. For instance, Cerbioni and Parbonetti (2007) showed that the proportion of independent directors is one of the most influential governance-related variables in determining the level of intellectual capital disclosure for a sample of European companies. Donnelly and Mulcahy (2008) found that enterprises in Ireland with more independent boards of directors provide more information than those with less independent boards. Similarly, Cuadrado-Ballesteros et al. (2015) emphasise empirical evidence supporting the usefulness of board independence as an incentive mechanism for CSR disclosure for a sample of globally listed businesses from 2003 to 2009. Several other studies have also reported similar results (e.g. Yunus et al., 2020; Fernàndez-Gago et al., 2018; Jaggi et al., 2018; Pavlopoulos et al., 2017; Garcia-Sanchez et al., 2014; Cheng and Courtnenay, 2006). Based on these arguments, we propose the following hypothesis:

**Hypothesis 1:** Board independence positively affects the level of environmental disclosure.

Over the last two decades, corporate governance studies have focused with increasing attention the issue of gender diversity on boards of directors. According to previous research, female administrators play a significant role in enhancing the efficacy of the board, raising the quality of financial information, and supporting sound business practices (Pucheta-Martnez et al., 2020; Rogelberg and Rumery,

1996). In the context of sustainability, agency theory suggests that a female leadership style favours the disclosure of CSR concerns, as women in top roles are more sensitive than men (Kim, 2013). Nielsen and Huse (2010) and Matsa and Miller (2013) also indicated that women are more attentive and receptive to stakeholder concerns, particularly regarding social and environmental issues.

Psychological, social, and cognitive approaches also assert that female administrators have an impact on corporate governance and key company choices. An earlier study (Levi et al., 2014; Man and Wong, 2013) demonstrated that women administrators are more risk-averse, cautious, and careful in their decision-making processes about crucial topics. These characteristics indicate that they possess greater social and ethical skills than male directors, resulting in the adoption of more responsible behaviours and are capable of aligning both manager and shareholder interests in the adoption of salient corporate decisions such as CSR disclosure.

From a stakeholder theory standpoint, the external environment might perceive that corporations are devoted to CSR concerns when they include female board members, signalling a tangible orientation of the company towards the expectations and interests of stakeholders (Ibrahim and Angelidis, 1994). Moreover, this perspective argues that women administrators promote CSR reporting because they are more open-minded than men are, thereby guaranteeing the support of stakeholders' interests and ensuring that businesses become more environmentally and socially engaged (Larrieta-Rubn de Celis et al., 2017; Hillman et al., 2002).

In this regard, Rao et al. (2012) noted that diverse boards boost CSR reporting. Various studies found a positive correlation between gender diversity on boards of directors and environmental, social, and governance disclosure (Tamini and Sebastianelli, 2017; Lone et al., 2016; Fernandez-Feijoo et al., 2014, 2012; Ntim and Soobaroyen, 2013; Barako and Brown, 2008). Therefore, the literature highlights that, in combination with other characteristics of female directors' leadership style, their attitude and sensitivity can influence the board to become more engaged in the social and environmental issues, which female directors are more oriented towards. This leads to an increase in CSR disclosure and consequently, we propose the following hypothesis:

**Hypothesis 2:** Board gender diversity positively affects the level of environmental disclosure.

Birindelli et al. (2018) observed that in recent years, an increasing number of corporations have created a subcommittee inside the board of directors to address sustainability concerns.

Several guidelines and corporate governance regulations acknowledge the importance of a CSR committee in handling social responsibility problems from the viewpoints of risks, strategic possibilities, and commitments to stakeholders. However, the formation of a CSR committee is implicit in most regulations and includes other board committees (Baraibar-Diez and Odriozola, 2019). For instance, in a comment to the article on the creation and operation of board committees, Italy's corporate governance code proposes that listed companies establish a committee dedicated to the oversight of sustainability concerns.

In general, a CSR committee's objectives are to create, execute, and evaluate sustainability policies and activities (Liao et al., 2015). Concerning sustainability disclosure, the CSR committee must oversee the validity of the organisation's sustainability reporting policies (Michelon and Parbonetti, 2012).

Fuente et al. (2017) confirmed that the dissemination of knowledge on sustainability concerns is the CSR committee's primary objective. Therefore, the inclusion of a CSR committee is considered an effective method for enhancing CSR disclosure (Garcia-Sánchez et al., 2019a). In other words, the presence of a CSR committee serves as an indicator of the board's commitment to sustainability (Hussain et al., 2018). The establishment of a CSR committee is a response to stakeholder theory, based on its capacity to satisfy stakeholder requirements (Baraibar-Diez and Odriozola, 2019; Salvioni and Gennari, 2019). However, the formation of a CSR committee may also be the result of a coercive procedure that compels a business to follow the same practices as other businesses exposed to the same set of institutional restrictions (Hawley, 1968). Thus, firms may implement CSR committee to imitate other firms without addressing stakeholder interests. In this case, the adoption of a CSR committee is consistent with the assertions of institutional theory that the operating setting of organisations influences their behaviour (Campbell, 2007; Roe, 1991).

Numerous scholars have examined the link between the presence of a CSR committee and the disclosure of sustainability concerns, hypothesising a positive association between these factors. Several studies have found a significant positive relationship between CSR committee and sustainability disclosures (Pucheta-Martnez and Gallego-Alvarez, 2019; Cucari et al., 2018; Mahmood et al., 2018; Fuente et al., 2017) and environmental disclosures (Cucari et al., 2018; Liao et al., 2015). Considering these facts, we propose the following hypothesis:

**Hypothesis 3:** The presence of a CSR/sustainability committee positively affects the level of environmental disclosure.

According to institutional theory, companies' behaviours are affected by the institutions in the context in which they operate (Campbell, 2007; Roe, 1991). In this manner, corporations perform environmental audits in response to external demand or to comply with new non-financial disclosure laws, rules, guidelines, and standards. Firms are increasingly required to comply with laws and standards that mandate third-party verification of the given information to ensure its reliability. For example, GRI guidelines emphasise the significance of sustainability reporting assurance for enhancing stakeholder recognition, confidence, and credibility. Thus, firms' use of external audits for CSR disclosure is a response to public criticism over the lack of reliability and accuracy of environmental information (Baalouch et al., 2019; Braam et al., 2016). Companies suffer coercive isomorphism and opt to conform to regulations and norms imposed by external forces. Deeper consideration shows that the use of external assurance services for environmental disclosure can be connected to both normative and mimetic isomorphism (DiMaggio and Powell, 1983). The former is the result of professionalisation and occurs when corporations opt to do what members of a profession consider correct, whereas the latter stems from the decision to imitate other businesses. In this view, firms implement the assurance of environmental disclosure behaviour to function similarly to other businesses.

By signalling the legitimacy of their corporate environmental reporting practice via external assurance, corporations impact stakeholder views of their responsibility, thus enhancing stakeholder confidence and company reputation (Braam et al., 2016).

Several authors have explored the link between external assurance and environmental disclosure, hypothesising a positive relationship between these factors. Some studies discovered a positive relationship; for example, Moroney et al. (2012) found that companies with assurances have higher ratings for voluntary environmental disclosure than those without. Similarly, Braam et al. (2016) reveal a positive and statistically significant relationship between external verification and the accuracy and reliability of environmental information presented in corporate environmental reports.

Consequently, based on these factors, we expand earlier research by investigating the function of external assurance in raising the degree of environmental disclosure, proposing the following hypothesis:

**Hypothesis 4:** External assurance of CSR sustainability reports positively affects the level of environmental disclosure.

Globally, the GRI is the most extensively used CSR reporting framework. It provides detailed guidance for various sustainability measures pertaining to social, environmental, and economic performance.

The GRI has gained widespread recognition among business in recent decades and is considered the most consistent reporting methodology (Boiral, 2015). Today, it serves as the standard for measuring, monitoring, and reporting CSR data (Savitz and Weber, 2006). Consequently, several businesses have adopted GRI standards to enhance their sustainability reporting.

Similar to the implementation of external assurance and the formation of CSR committee, the adoption of GRI standards by businesses may be interpreted in light of institutional theory, namely, the mimetic, normative, and coercive isomorphism of DiMaggio and Powell (1983).

Some studies that examine the influence of GRI standards on enhancing enterprises' sustainability reports have revealed a substantial positive association between environmental information levels and the implementation of GRI standards. For instance, Galani et al. (2012) highlight such a conclusion for top Greek enterprises. Similarly, Leal et al. (2019) noted that enterprises that publish their reports in accordance with the GRI standard tend to disclose more information on greenhouse gas emissions. These results corroborate Hahn and Lulfs'

(2014) argument that the adoption of GRI guidelines plays a relevant role in pressing companies to release environmental and emissions information.

Based on these considerations, we hypothesise as follows:

**Hypothesis 5:** Adoption of GRI standards positively affects the level of environmental disclosure.

Figure 6.1 illustrates the research model derived from the prior hypotheses.

Although several studies have found a positive relationship between board independence and CSR or sustainability disclosures, some scholars have also found a negative relationship between these variables. According to Gul and Leung (2004), an increase in outside directors diminishes Hong Kong corporations' voluntary disclosures. Eng and Mak (2003) discovered similar outcomes in Singaporean enterprises. Similarly, Barako et al. (2006) discovered that the proportion of non-executive directors on the board is significantly and negatively related to the level of voluntary disclosure among Kenyan enterprises. Similar to Eng and Mak (2003), Gul and Leung (2004) defend their results by stating that enhanced monitoring by independent outside directors results in lower disclosure when a substitution effect exists between the two mechanisms. Tejedo-Romero et al. (2017) corroborated the same findings for Spanish enterprises, demonstrating that external independent directors have a detrimental influence on intellectual capital disclosure due to a replacement effect. However, several other studies failed to find a significant relationship. Bueno et al. (2018), for instance, found that board independence is not statistically related to the sustainability disclosure of Brazilian listed firms, similar to the findings of Michelon and Parbonetti (2012) and Amran et al. (2014) for US and European companies and firms from 12 Asian nations, respectively. Other researchers have reached comparable conclusions (e.g. Miras-Rodrguez et al., 2020; Michelon et al., 2015; Prado-Lorenzo and

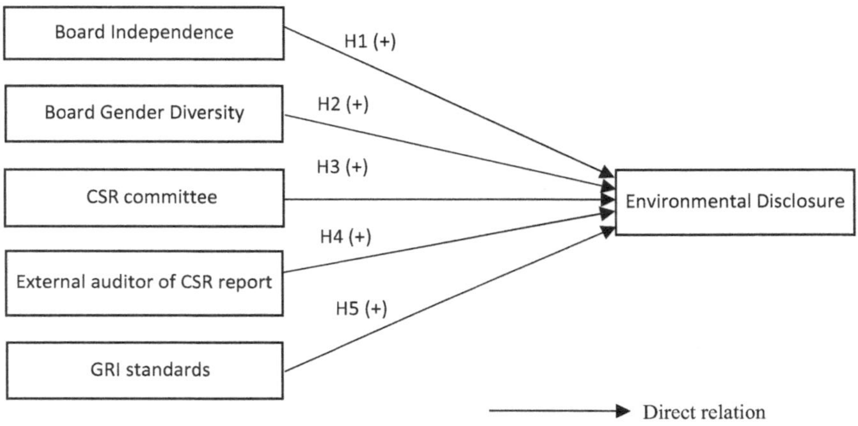


**FIGURE 6.1** Research model
*Source*: Author's elaboration

Garcia-Sánchez, 2010; Prado-Lorenzo et al., 2009; Wan-Hussin, 2009; Leung and Horwitz, 2004; Haniffa and Cooke, 2002).

These empirical findings may differ for various reasons. For instance, it could be important to consider whether board independence and other corporate governance systems interact meaningfully. From an empirical standpoint, inconsistent findings by researchers implies that various corporate governance mechanisms may interact in different ways. To comprehend the interconnectedness of various corporate governance mechanisms, Aguinis et al. (2011) and Jain and Jamali (2016) recommended using a multilevel approach. Thus, to more clearly understand the results of previous studies and provide larger managerial and policymaking implications independent of the historical period's circumstances and the setting under study, empirical research must consider moderating variables in the examined connection (Dalton and Dalton, 2011). By examining if and how the existence of a CSR committee, the adoption of GRI standards, and the assurance of a CSR report moderate the links between environmental disclosure and board independence and gender diversity, this study advances the field of research in this area.

To test the existence of the above-mentioned moderating roles, we propose hypotheses $H_6$, $H_7$, and $H_8$.

**Hypothesis 6:** The positive relationship between board independence and level of environmental disclosure is positively moderated by the presence of a CSR committee.

**Hypothesis 7:** The positive relationship between board independence and the level of environmental disclosure is positively moderated by the presence of an external auditor in CSR reports.

**Hypothesis 8:** The positive relationship between board independence and level of environmental disclosure is positively moderated by the adoption of GRI standards.

Although most studies examining the relationship between board gender diversity and CSR disclosure highlight the existence of a positive relationship (i.e. Tamini and Sebastianelli, 2017; Lone et al., 2016; Fernandez-Feijoo et al., 2014, 2012; Ntim and Soobaroyen, 2013; Barako and Brown, 2008), some studies contradict these findings. In contrast to earlier theoretical claims, Khan (2010) and Mallin et al. (2013) found no significant association between the proportion of women on the board and CSR reporting. Prado-Lorenzo et al. (2009) discovered that diversity has a detrimental effect on transparency in CSR reporting. Similarly, Amran et al. (2014) found no statistically significant association between the proportion of women on the board of directors and the level of sustainability reporting. Likewise, Giannarakis et al. (2014) reported that the presence of women on the board is not significantly related to the degree of CSR disclosure.

As stated above, these empirical results may be divergent for various reasons such as the existence of relevant interactions between board gender diversity and other corporate governance mechanisms. Therefore, it may be worth investigating whether board gender diversity acts as a complementary or alternative mechanism to the adoption of GRI standards, the presence of a CSR committee, or the presence of an external audit body for sustainability reporting.

To test the existence of these moderating roles, we propose the following hypotheses:

**Hypothesis 9:** The positive relationship between board gender diversity and level of environmental disclosure is positively moderated by the presence of a CSR committee.

**Hypothesis 10:** The positive relationship between board gender diversity and the level of environmental disclosure is positively moderated by the presence of an external auditor in CSR reports.

**Hypothesis 11:** The positive relationship between board gender diversity and level of environmental disclosure is positively moderated by the adoption of GRI standards.

The basic idea that supports these hypotheses is that, in affecting the environmental disclosure board independence, board gender diversity, and other corporate governance mechanisms, such as CSR committee, GRI standards, and assurance of sustainability reports, act as complementary mechanisms. In other words, if the company has a CSR committee within the board, has adopted the GRI standard, or has an external audit board that assures environmental disclosure, the tendency and effectiveness of independent and female directors to stimulate a higher level of environmental disclosure could increase.

Many board characteristics and other corporate governance mechanisms, such as board independence, gender diversity, board size, role duality, and the presence of a CSR committee, have been included in empirical models in the literature to examine the relationships between each board characteristic and CSR disclosure. However, to the best of our knowledge, few studies have analysed how different board characteristics and other corporate governance mechanisms interact with each other in affecting environmental disclosure. In this research, we attempt to fill this gap by examining how the inclusion of a CSR committee, GRI standards, and assurance, together with board independence and gender diversity, affect environmental disclosure. The objective is to determine whether these board features affect a company's environmental disclosure as substitutes or complements.

The hypothesised interactions are showed in the following graph (Figure 6.2):

## 6.2 Method

### *6.2.1 Sample selection and data source*

We gathered data from the Refinitiv Eikon DataStream.[1] Our initial balanced sample was composed of 5,588 listed firms from the 27 European Union

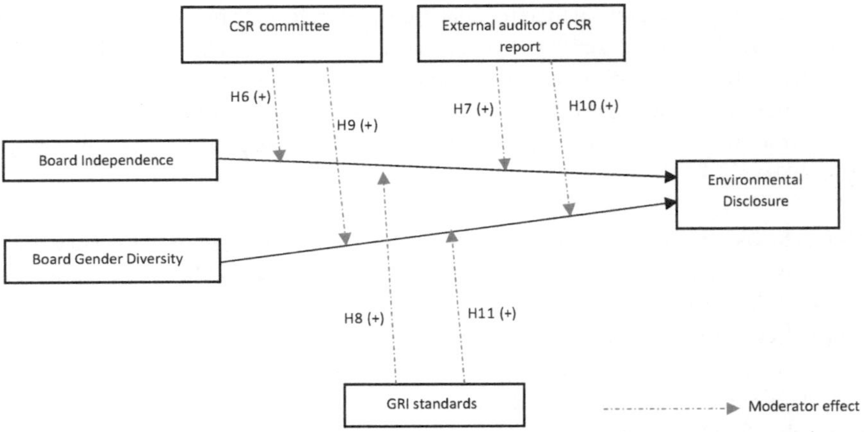


**FIGURE 6.2** Hypothesised interactions
*Source*: Author's elaboration

countries operating in all industries, except the finance and insurance sectors, for the 2002–2021 period (111,760 firm-year observations). Thereafter, we eliminated companies that had not published a CSR report during the investigated period and obtained a sample of 1050 companies and 21,000 firm-year observations (see Panels A and B in Table 6.1).

We used Sample I to analyse the evolution of environmental disclosure during the investigated period across 27 EU countries. To this end, we use the information available in the Thomson Reuters Eikon database. These data are used to create the *EnvDisc* index, which is an unweighted sum of different environmental elements measuring the firm's level of environmental disclosure and awarding a score of 1 when the company discloses environmental information, and 0 otherwise (Gallego-Álvarez and Ortas, 2017; Du et al., 2010; Kolk and Pinkse, 2010; Chen and Bouvain, 2009). As a result, *EnvDisc* is a multifaceted concept that addresses all actions taken and revealed by companies in the environmental domain (Rupp and Mallory, 2015; Lee et al., 2012; Mio, 2009; Carroll, 1979). The 63 items considered to define the value of *EnvDisc* belonged to three different categories: 19 items for emission, 25 for innovation, and 19 for resource use. A company's dedication to and success in decreasing environmental emissions during the production and operating processes are indicated by the emissions items. The ability of a business to lower costs and environmental responsibilities while generating new economic prospects through innovative technologies, environment-friendly practices, or ecological goods is referred to as innovation. The ability of a business to use less energy, water, or other resources while looking for more effective ways to enhance supply chain management is shown in the last category, which is related to resource usage. These 63 items are listed in Table 6.2.

**TABLE 6.1** Sample I

| *Panel A. Sample I by geographic zone* | | | | | *Panel B. Sample I by industries* | | | | |
|---|---|---|---|---|---|---|---|---|---|
| | *Country of headquarter* | *n. of firms* | *n. of obs* | *% of obs* | | *Sector* | *n. of firms* | *n. of obs* | *% of obs* |
| 1 | Austria | 31 | 620 | 2.95% | 1 | Accommodation & Food Services | 12 | 240 | 1.14% |
| 2 | Belgium | 42 | 840 | 4.00% | 2 | Admin. & Supp., Waste Manag. & Remed. Services | 29 | 580 | 2.76% |
| 3 | Bulgaria | 0 | 0 | 0% | 3 | Agriculture, Forestry, Fishing and Hunting | 6 | 120 | 0.57% |
| 4 | Cyprus | 7 | 140 | 0.67% | 4 | Arts, Entertainment, & Recreation | 9 | 180 | 0.86% |
| 5 | Croatia | 0 | 0 | 0% | 5 | Construction | 61 | 1,220 | 5.81% |
| 6 | Czech Republic | 2 | 40 | 0.19% | 6 | Educational Services | 1 | 20 | 0.10% |
| 7 | Denmark | 52 | 1,040 | 4.95% | 7 | Health Care & Social Assistance | 11 | 220 | 1.05% |
| 8 | Estonia | 0 | 0 | 0% | 8 | Information | 98 | 1,960 | 9.33% |
| 9 | Finland | 65 | 1,300 | 6.19% | 9 | Manufacturing | 475 | 9,500 | 45.24% |
| 10 | France | 133 | 2,660 | 12.67% | 10 | Mining, Quarrying, Oil & Gas Extraction | 24 | 480 | 2.29% |
| 11 | Germany | 206 | 4,120 | 19.62% | 11 | Other Services (except Public Administration) | 5 | 100 | 0.48% |
| 12 | Greece | 20 | 400 | 1.90% | 12 | Professional, Scientific, & Technical Services | 83 | 1,660 | 7.90% |
| 13 | Hungary | 3 | 60 | 0.29% | 13 | Real Estate, Rental & Leasing | 69 | 1,380 | 6.57% |
| 14 | Ireland | 35 | 700 | 3.33% | 14 | Retail Trade | 49 | 980 | 4.67% |
| 15 | Italy | 76 | 1,520 | 7.24% | 15 | Transportation & Warehousing | 45 | 900 | 4.29% |
| 16 | Latvia | 0 | 0 | 0% | 16 | Utilities | 44 | 880 | 4.19% |
| 17 | Lithuania | 0 | 0 | 0% | 17 | Wholesale Trade | 29 | 580 | 2.76% |
| 18 | Luxembourg | 30 | 600 | 2.86% | | Tot. | 1,050 | 21,000 | 100.00% |

(*Continued*)

**TABLE 6.1** Continued

| *Panel A. Sample I by geographic zone* | | | | | *Panel B. Sample I by industries* | | | |
|---|---|---|---|---|---|---|---|---|
| | *Country of headquarter* | *n. of firms* | *n. of obs* | *% of obs* | *Sector* | *n. of firms* | *n. of obs* | *% of obs* |
| 19 | Malta | 5 | 100 | 0.48% | | | | |
| 20 | Netherlands | 50 | 1,000 | 4.76% | | | | |
| 21 | Poland | 28 | 560 | 2.67% | | | | |
| 22 | Portugal | 13 | 260 | 1.24% | | | | |
| 23 | Romania | 1 | 20 | 0.10% | | | | |
| 24 | Slovakia | 0 | 0 | 0% | | | | |
| 25 | Slovenia | 1 | 20 | 0.10% | | | | |
| 26 | Spain | 61 | 1,220 | 5.81% | | | | |
| 27 | Sweden | 189 | 3,780 | 18.00% | | | | |
| | Tot. | 1,050 | 21,000 | 100.00% | | | | |

**TABLE 6.2** Description of environmental disclosure items

| *Environmental disclosure* | | |
|---|---|---|
| *Emissions category* | *Innovation category* | *Resource use category* |
| *Title* | *Title* | *Title* |
| *Description* | *Description* | *Description* |
| *Policy Emissions*<br>Does the company have a policy to improve emission reduction?<br>– in scope are the various forms of emissions to land, air or water from the company's core activities<br>– processes, mechanisms or programs in place as to what the company is doing to reduce emissions in its operations<br>– system or a set of formal, documented processes for controlling emissions and driving continuous improvement | *Eco-Design Products*<br>Does the company report on specific products which are designed for reuse, recycling or the reduction of environmental impacts?<br>– products that have been specifically designed with the goal of being recycled, reused or which are disposed of without negatively impacting the environment<br>– there must be some discussion of environmental concerns during the product design | *Environment Management Team*<br>Does the company have an environmental management team?<br>– in scope are any team that performs the functions dedicated to environmental issues<br>–- an individual or team at any level composed of employees, even if the name of the team is different performing implementation of the environmental strategy<br>– it is important to understand that the members of the team include employees of the company, who are operational on a day to day basis and are not the board committees (directors) |
| *Environmental Expenditures Investments*<br>Does the company report on its environmental expenditures or does the company report to make proactive environmental investments to reduce future risks or increase future opportunities? | *Environmental Products*<br>Does the company report on at least one product line or service that is designed to have positive effects on the environment or which is environmentally labelled and marketed?<br>– in focus are the products and services that have positive environmental effects, or marketed as which solve environment problems | *Environment Management Training*<br>Does the company train its employees on environmental issues?<br>– employee environmental (resource reduction & emission reduction) related training provided by the company or external trainers<br>– in focus include the code of conduct training encompasses environmental aspects |

*(Continued)*

**TABLE 6.2** Continued

| *Environmental disclosure* | | |
|---|---|---|
| *Emissions category* | *Innovation category* | *Resource use category* |
| *Title* | *Title* | *Title* |
| *Description* | *Description* | *Description* |
| *VOC or Particulate Matter Emissions Reduction* | *Noise Reduction* | *Policy Water Efficiency* |
| Does the company report on initiatives to reduce, substitute, or phase out volatile organic compounds (VOC) or particulate matter less than ten microns in diameter (PM10)? | Does the company develop new products that are marketed as reducing noise emissions?<br>– products that have been specifically designed to reduce noise emissions or marketed as emitting less noise<br>– in scope include also those companies which are retailing such products which are emitting less noise | Does the company have a policy to improve its water efficiency?<br>– in scope are the various forms of processes/ mechanisms/procedures to improve water use in operation efficiently<br>– system or a set of formal documented processes for efficient use of water and driving continuous improvement |
| *Targets Emissions* | *Hybrid Vehicles* | *Policy Energy Efficiency* |
| Has the company set targets or objectives to be achieved on emission reduction?<br>- in scope are the short-term or long-term reduction target to be achieved on emissions to land, air or water from business operations | Is the company developing hybrid vehicles? | Does the company have a policy to improve its energy efficiency?<br>– in scope are the various forms of processes/ mechanisms/procedures to improve energy use in operation efficiently<br>– system or a set of formal documented processes for efficient use of energy and driving continuous improvement |

| | | |
|---|---|---|
| *Biodiversity Impact Reduction* | *Environmental Assets Under Mgt* | *Policy Sustainable Packaging* |
| Does the company report on its impact on biodiversity or on activities to reduce its impact on the native ecosystems and species, as well as the biodiversity of protected and sensitive areas? | Does the company report on assets under management which employ environmental screening criteria or environmental factors in the investment selection process? | Does the company have a policy to improve its use of sustainable packaging?<br>– description of processes /procedures used as sustainable packaging or to reduce the use of packaging for products by the company<br>– information on environmentally friendly (resource and energy efficient) packaging<br>– green packaging, returnable containers, biodegradable packaging |
| *NOx and SOx Emissions Reduction* | *Equator Principles* | *Policy Environmental Supply Chain* |
| Does the company report on initiatives to reduce, reuse, recycle, substitute, or phase out SOx (sulphur oxides) or NOx (nitrogen oxides) emissions?<br>– any new project undertaken or initiated to reduce NOx (nitrogen oxide) & SOx (sulphur oxide) emissions<br>– general legal compliance is not qualified data<br><br>– inline with the legal compliance or government imosed processes to reduce SOx (sulfur oxides) or NOx (nitrogen oxides) which are well described are qualified<br>– we follow greenhouse gas (GHG) protocol for all our emission classifications by type | Is the company a signatory of the Equator Principles (commitment to manage environmental issues in project financing)?<br>- in focus are the companies who have adopted the equator principles which ensures that the projects being financed meet environmental standards | Does the company have a policy to include its supply chain in the company's efforts to lessen its overall environmental impact?<br>– legal compliance data on the supply chain to reduce environmental impact is in scope<br>– data on collaboration with suppliers towards reducing their environmental impacts<br>– data on the reduction of environmental impacts at the suppliers operations |

(*Continued*)

**TABLE 6.2** Continued

| *Environmental disclosure* | | |
|---|---|---|
| *Emissions category* | *Innovation category* | *Resource use category* |
| *Title* | *Title* | *Title* |
| *Description* | *Description* | *Description* |
| *VOC Emissions Reduction* | *Environmental Project Financing* | *Environmental Materials Sourcing* |
| Does the company report on initiatives to reduce, substitute, or phase out volatile organic compounds (VOC)?<br>– processes, mechanisms or programs in place as to what the company is doing to reduce or phase out volatile organic compounds in its operations<br>– any new project undertaken to reduce voc emissions<br>– general legal compliance is not qualified data<br>– inline with the legal compliance or government imosed processes to reduce VOC which are well described are qualified | Does the company claim to evaluate projects on the basis of environmental or biodiversity risks as well?<br>– relevant to the financial sector and focus is on project financing data<br>– evaluating projects based on environmental and biodiversity risks prior to providing funding to its customers | Does the company claim to use environmental criteria (e.g. life cycle assessment) to source or eliminate materials? |
| *Particulate Matter Emissions Reduction* | *Nuclear* | *Toxic Chemicals Reduction* |
| Does the company report on initiatives to reduce, substitute, or phase out particulate matter less than ten microns in diameter (PM10)?<br>– initiatives which the company has put in place to reduce, substitute, or phase out particulate matter less than ten microns in diameter (PM10) | Does the company construct nuclear reactors, produce nuclear energy or is active in another way in the nuclear energy industry?<br>– relevant to the utilities and industrial sector | Does the company report on initiatives to reduce, reuse, substitute, or phase out toxic chemicals or substances?<br>– in scope, the data includes chemicals, toxic materials, hazardous, PBT (persistent bio-accumulative toxic) and PVC (polyvinyl chloride) |

| | | |
|---|---|---|
| – any new project undertaken focusing on reduction of particulate matter emissions<br>– dust, fugitive dust and soot are also considered as particulate matter | – data on a company holding a stake in any particular company involved in nuclear<br>– in scope are the companies involved in the consulting or planning or construction of nuclear facilities or nuclear reactors, extraction/use of uranium or nuclear mining | |
| *Waste Reduction Initiatives* | *Labelled Wood* | *Renewable Energy Use* |
| Does the company report on initiatives to recycle, reduce, reuse, substitute, treat, or phase out total waste?<br>– initiatives to reduce any type of waste generated by reporting organisation<br>– partnership with waste management companies to treat waste generated<br>– does not include the data on waste management companies, which collect & recycle the waste for their customers | Does the company claim to produce, source or distribute wood or forest products that are labelled (e.g. Forest Stewardship Council (FSC))?<br>– relevant to paper industries, publishing companies, wood producers<br>– produces or distributes products that are certified sustainable forest products | Does the company make use of renewable energy?<br>– renewable energy produced/purchased for its own use only<br>– waste that is converted to energy and is used by the company for their own use |
| *e-Waste Reduction* | *Organic Products Initiatives* | *Green Buildings* |
| Does the company report on initiatives to recycle, reduce, reuse, substitute, treat, or phase out e-waste?<br>– any initiatives which the company has put in place to reduce e-waste<br>– e-waste is used as a generic term embracing all types of waste containing electrically powered components | Does the company report or show initiatives to produce or promote organic food or other products?<br>– relevant for companies in food industries, agricultural produce, and chemicals (organic fertilisers), textile & apparels (which use biodegradable materials including organic fibres) | Does the company report about environmentally friendly or green sites or offices?<br>– office/green site where the company engages in some operations<br>– LEED/BREEAM certifications for its own building |

(*Continued*)

**TABLE 6.2** Continued

| *Environmental disclosure* | | |
|---|---|---|
| *Emissions category* | *Innovation category* | *Resource use category* |
| *Title* | *Title* | *Title* |
| *Description* | *Description* | *Description* |
| – e-waste may contain hazardous materials which require special handling and recycling methods<br>– includes all products covered under WEEE (waste electrical and electronic equipment) regulations like<br>fluorescent tubes, sodium lamps, computers, mobiles, telephones, fax machines, copiers, printers, washing machines, dryers, refrigerators, air-conditioners, televisions, VCR/DVD/CD players, Wi-Fi sets, radios, drills, electric saws, sewing machines, batteries, toner cartridges | – in scope data also include on the companies that are involved in promoting organic food in their retail chain | – major refurbishments to improve the environmental aspects of sites/buildings/offices<br>– the building has to be operational at least at the end of the fiscal year<br>– if building is under construction then grade as 'false' |
| *Emissions Trading* | *Take-back and Recycling Initiatives* | *Environmental Supply Chain Management* |
| Does the company report on its participation in any emissions trading initiative?<br>– emissions trading (cap and trade) is a market-based approach used to control pollution by providing economic incentives for achieving reductions in the emissions of pollutants | Does the company reports about take-back procedures and recycling programs to reduce the potential risks of products entering the environment?<br>– take back or recycle the company's own product at the end of use | Does the company use environmental criteria (ISO 14000, energy consumption, etc.) in the selection process of its suppliers or sourcing partners?<br>– data can also be on existing suppliers who were selected using some environmental criteria |

| | | |
|---|---|---|
| – if a company claims to participate in an emission trading scheme in the future we grade as false | – waste management company collecting various products and recycling is not in the scope<br>– a product recall is not considered as qualified data | |
| *Environmental Restoration Initiatives*<br>Does the company report or provide information on company-generated initiatives to restore the environment?<br>– any initiatives to restore the environment like restoration, rehabilitation, clean up and remediation activities<br>– company's own operation disturbing the environment and restoring the same later is not qualified as restoration initiatives | *Product Environmental Responsible Use*<br>Does the company report about product features and applications or services that will promote responsible, efficient, cost-effective and environmentally preferable use?<br>- a product or service that reduces the negative impact (less emission, pollution, noise, etc.) on the environment | *Env Supply Chain Partnership Termination*<br>Does the company report or show to be ready to end a partnership with a sourcing partner, if environmental criteria are not met? |
| *Staff Transportation Impact Reduction*<br>Does the company report on initiatives to reduce the environmental impact of transportation used for its staff?<br>- when the company encourages its staff to use alternate options like carpooling, telephone, video and web conferencing, encouraging employees to use public transport, cycle-to-work scheme, purchase of environmentally friendlier vehicles or eco-friendly cars for staff and thereby reducing the environmental impact | *GMO Products*<br>Does the company produce or distribute genetically modified organisms (GMO) or seeds?<br>– relevant to agriculture, food products, consumer products, non-cyclical consumer goods & services sector<br>- production of genetically modified seeds, data on green biotech or bio-engineering related information<br>- some examples on agricultural GMO produce are Bt cotton, Bt brinjal | *Land Environmental Impact Reduction*<br>Does the company report on initiatives to reduce the environmental impact on land owned, leased, or managed for production activities or extractive use?<br>- relevant to companies involved in agriculture, mining & oil and gas<br>- in scope are the information on remediation, reclamation or remediation of disturbed land by operations |

(*Continued*)

**TABLE 6.2** Continued

| *Environmental disclosure* | | |
|---|---|---|
| *Emissions category* | *Innovation category* | *Resource use category* |
| *Title* | *Title* | *Title* |
| *Description* | *Description* | *Description* |
| *Environmental Partnerships* | *Agrochemical Products* | *Environmental Supply Chain Monitoring* |
| Does the company report on partnerships or initiatives with specialised NGOs, industry organisations, governmental or supra-governmental organisations, which are focused on improving environmental issues? | Does the company produce or distribute agrochemicals like pesticides, fungicides, or herbicides?<br>– this is sector specific data measure for chemical companies producing agrochemicals like insecticides, pesticides, herbicides and fungicides which are specifically produced for agricultural purposes<br>– modern synthetic fertilisers which are composed mainly of nitrogen, phosphorous, and potassium compounds with secondary nutrients added are also in scope | Does the company conduct surveys of the environmental performance of its suppliers?<br>– any evidence that the company monitors its suppliers on environmental issues through surveys, audits, supplier site visits, and questionnaire |
| *ISO 14000 or EMS* | *Agrochemical 5 % Revenue* | *Resource Reduction Policy* |
| Does the company claim to have an ISO 14000 or EMS certification?<br>– any of the individual site that has the ISO-14001 certification is qualified information<br>– merely stating adherence to ISO 14000 or following ISO 14000 policies does not qualify, certification is required | Are the revenues generated by the company from agrochemicals like pesticides, fungicides, or herbicides 5% or more of company sales?<br>– this is sector specific data measure for chemical companies producing agrochemicals like insecticides, pesticides, herbicides, and fungicides which are specifically produced for agricultural purposes | Does the company have a policy for reducing the use of natural resources or to lessen the environmental impact of its supply chain? |

| | | |
|---|---|---|
| | – agrochemical revenue 5% or more of company sales<br>– agrochemical revenue/total revenue*100 ('true' if agrochemical revenue is >5%, answer 'false' if it is less<br>– modern synthetic fertilisers which are composed mainly of nitrogen, phosphorous, and potassium compounds with secondary nutrients added are also in scope | |
| *Environmental Investments Initiatives* | *Animal Testing* | *Resource Reduction Targets* |
| Does the company report on making proactive environmental investments or expenditures to reduce future risks or increase future opportunities?<br>– investment made in the current fiscal year so as to reduce future risks and increase future opportunities related to the environment<br>– investments made in new technologies to increase future opportunities<br>– treatment of emissions (e.g. expenditures for filters, agents), installation of cleaner technologies | Is the company directly or indirectly involved in animal testing?<br>– applicable to pharmaceutical, healthcare sector, cosmetics<br>– in scope are the data on cases where the company is testing its products on animals or if it is sourcing raw materials which are tested on animals<br>– if a company claims to be gradually reducing or replacing the number of animal tests we consider the data positively and grade it as true<br>– if company claims to perform animal tests solely in cases where this is required by law it is concluded as true | Does the company set specific objectives to be achieved on resource efficiency? |

*(Continued)*

**TABLE 6.2** Continued

| *Environmental disclosure* | | |
|---|---|---|
| *Emissions category* | *Innovation category* | *Resource use category* |
| *Title* | *Title* | *Title* |
| *Description* | *Description* | *Description* |
| *Policy Nuclear Safety* | *Animal Testing Cosmetics* | *Environmental Controversies* |
| Does the company have policy in place for nuclear safety and emergency preparedness to minimise the impact of nuclear disasters in and around nuclear plants?<br>– related to 'electric utility' sector<br>– nuclear safety methods can be for internal and external safety<br>– general business continuity and employee training is not considered | Is the company directly or indirectly involved in animal testing for cosmetics?<br>– relevant for the non-cyclical consumer goods & service sector<br>– conduct animal testing for cosmetics when mandated by law is considered positively as 'true'<br>- in scope are the data on cases where the company is testing cosmetics on animals or if it is sourcing raw materials which are tested on animals | Is the company under the spotlight of the media because of a controversy linked to the environmental impact of its operations on natural resources or local communities? |
| *Climate Change Commercial Risks Opportunities* | *Animal Testing Reduction* | *Targets Water Efficiency* |
| Is the company aware that climate change can represent commercial risks and/or opportunities?<br>– development of new products/services to overcome the threats of climate change to the existing business model of the company | Has the company established a program or an initiative to reduce, phase out, or substitute for animal testing?<br>– initiatives by the company to reduce, phase out or substitute animal testing, 3Rs (refine, reduce, replace) | Has the company set targets or objectives to be achieved on water efficiency?<br>– in scope, are the short-term or long-term reduction target to be achieved on efficiently using the water at business operations |

| | | |
|---|---|---|
| – some companies take climate change as a business opportunity and develop new products/services | – relevant to pharmaceutical, chemical, cosmetic and food producing companies<br>– if the company mentions about using alternatives to animal testing then we conclude it as reduction initiative | |
| *Internal Carbon Pricing*<br>Does the company have an internal price on carbon? | *Renewable/Clean Energy Products*<br>Does the company develop products or technologies for use in the clean, renewable energy (such as wind, solar, hydro and geo-thermal and biomass power)?<br>– in scope, we also include data on the financing of renewable energy projects<br>– if a utility company is deriving at least 25% of the power produced or revenue from clean technologies or energy<br>*Water Technologies*<br>Does the company develop products or technologies that are used for water treatment, purification or that improve water use efficiency?<br>– in scope are the products or services addressing water purification or greater water conservation or efficiency<br>– also includes companies providing technologies/software to detect water leaks | *Targets Energy Efficiency*<br>Has the company set targets or objectives to be achieved on energy efficiency?<br>– in scope, are the short-term or long-term reduction target to be achieved on efficiently using the energy from business operations |

(*Continued*)

**TABLE 6.2** Continued

| *Environmental disclosure* | | |
|---|---|---|
| *Emissions category* | *Innovation category* | *Resource use category* |
| *Title* | *Title* | *Title* |
| *Description* | *Description* | *Description* |
| | *Sustainable Building Products* | |
| | Does the company develop products and services that improve the energy efficiency of buildings?<br>– in focus are products and services that the company offer to improve the energy efficiency of buildings<br>– also on companies that provide smart metering services to improve the energy efficiency of buildings | |
| | *Equator Principles or Env Project Financing* | |
| | Is the company a signatory of the Equator Principles (commitment to manage environmental issues in project financing) or does it claim to evaluate projects on the basis of environmental or biodiversity risks as well? | |

*Product Impact Minimisation*

Does the company reports about take-back procedures and recycling programmes to reduce the potential risks of products entering the environment or does the company report about product features or services that will promote responsible and environmentally preferable use?

*Real Estate Sustainability Certifications*

Does the company claim to lease, rent or market buildings that are certified by BREEAM, LEED or any other nationally recognised real estate certification?

- applies to construction, hospitality and real estate companies only
- pre-certification are also qualified positively
- BREEAM (building research establishment environmental assessment method)
- LEED (leadership in energy and environmental design)
- the certified green building no matter the level of certification are qualified

*Fossil Fuel Divestment Policy*

Does the financial company have a public commitment to divest from fossil fuel?

The following graphs show the evolution of the cumulative *EnvDisc* of firms in EU countries during the period 2002–2021. France, Germany, and Sweden showed a stronger evolution of *EnvDisc*, followed by Italy, Spain, Finland, and the Netherlands. In each of these countries, the level of *EnvDisc* grew significantly around 2017–2018, in correspondence with the issue of Non-Financial Reporting Directive 2014/95/EU (Figure 6.3).

The following figures and tables show the mean values for 2021 for both *EnvDisc* level and its components *(Resources Use, Emission and Innovation)* for firms across the countries. It shows the state of the art of environmental disclosure across EU countries (Figure 6.4).

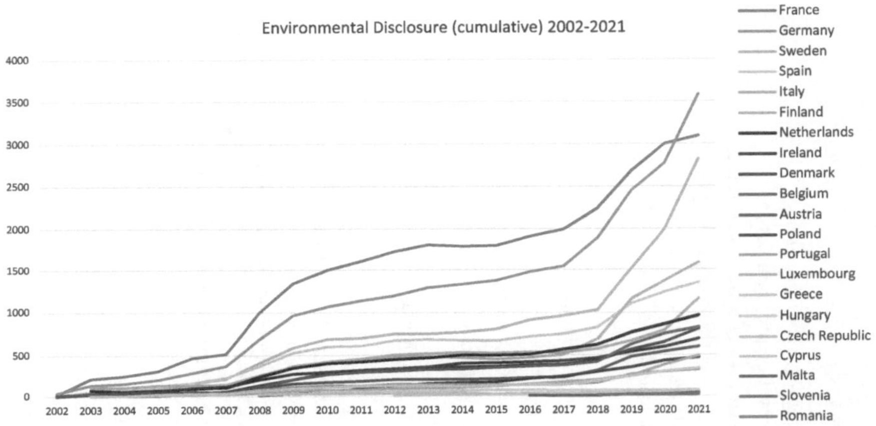


**FIGURE 6.3** Cumulative *EnvDisc* in EU countries 2002–2021

**FIGURE 6.4** *EnvDisc* mean values 2021

Companies from Romania, Portugal, France, Hungary, Spain, Italy, and the Czech Republic had mean values higher than 20 for *EnvDisc*. Companies from Ireland, Belgium, the Netherlands, Austria, Finland, Greece, Germany, Poland, Luxembourg, Slovenia, and Denmark have values between 15 and 20. Companies from Sweden, Cyprus, and Malta close the list with values of less than 15. These values must be interpreted in light of the number of companies in each country present in the sample investigated using these descriptive statistics. In this sense, for example, Sweden's value is 14.93, the third lowest value in the ranking, but must still be considered good, because it is an average value of 189 companies. Conversely, Romania's apparently good value of 30, the highest in the sample, must be interpreted considering that only one Romanian company publishes information on environmental disclosure in 2021.

In more general terms, the number of companies from each country in the sample must be interpreted as an indicator of the diffusion of environmental disclosure practices in EU countries. Indeed, when firms that had not issued a CSR report in the period under investigation are removed from the initial sample, the countries with the highest number of firms in the final sample must be considered as the most attentive and most committed with reference to the theme of environmental disclosure.

The figures and tables illustrated below show similar classifications which, however, make specific reference to the three components of environmental disclosure: *resource use*, *emission*, and *innovation*. They clearly indicate, among other things, that French companies are characterised by high levels of communication in all three sub-categories of environmental disclosure. All three values were higher than the European average values of the three subcategories. In contrast, German companies communicate much more about innovation than about the use of resources and emissions. In fact, the values of the disclosure on innovation are higher than the European average value, while the values relating to resource use and emissions are lower than the European average value (Figures 6.5–6.7).

The following figures highlight the evolution of environmental disclosure through its main categories for EU countries, showing the mean values for the 2002 and 2021 *EnvDisc* information categories for all companies. As the two figures show, in 2002, the information disclosed almost exclusively regarding resource use and emissions, while in 2021, companies disclose information about environmental innovation. Today, the dominant disclosure is regarding resource use (49%), followed by emissions (36%), and environmental innovation (15%) (Figure 6.8).

Following the descriptive analysis of the environmental disclosure phenomenon, we excluded from Sample I the firm-year observations of firms without corporate governance and financial data useful to test our hypotheses. The final unbalanced sample used for our regression analysis, Sample II, was composed of 592 listed firms (3,392 observations) from 17 industries and 19 different countries for the 2003–2021 period (see Panels A and B in Table 6.3).

**FIGURE 6.5** *Resources Use* mean values 2021

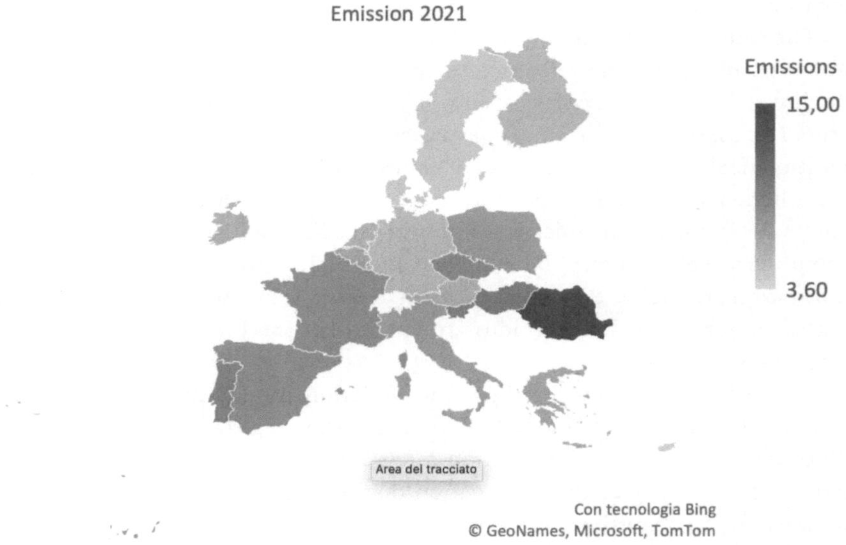


**FIGURE 6.6** *Emission* mean values 2021

Most observations in Sample II concern French companies (682), followed by German (533), Swedish (480), Spanish (294), Italian (290), Finnish (268), Dutch (239), and Belgian companies (127), and so on.

The companies in the sample operate mainly in the manufacturing sector (47.9%), followed by the information sector (10.1%), utilities (6.9%), construction

**FIGURE 6.7** *Innovation* mean values 2021

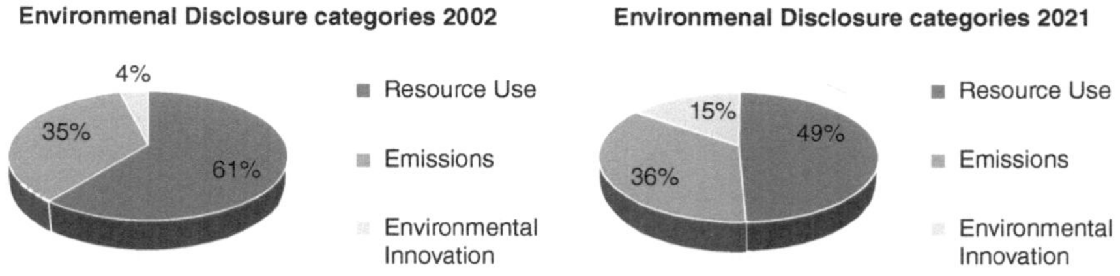


**FIGURE 6.8** Evolution of environmental disclosure through its main categories

(6.8%), transportation and warehousing (5.3%), real estate and rental and leasing (5.3%), and so on.

## *6.2.2 Dependent, independent, moderating and control variables*

The dependent, independent, moderating, and control variables are listed in Table 6.4 along with details on how they were measured and the data source.

### *6.2.2.1 Dependent variable*

*EnvDisc*, our dependent variable, is a multidimensional construct that considers all activities conducted and disclosed by businesses in the environmental sector (Rupp and Mallory, 2015; Lee et al., 2012; Mio, 2009; Carroll, 1979). It was put into practice by utilising 63 environmental issues that companies may or may not report. These items belong to three different categories: 19 items for emissions, 25 for innovation, and 19 for resource use (see Table 6.2). The *EnvDisc* index is an unweighted sum of the environmental items that measure the firm's level of environmental disclosure and assigns, for each item, a value of 1 when the company does present information on that environmental aspect, and 0 otherwise (Gallego-Álvarez and Ortas, 2017; Du et al., 2010; Kolk and Pinkse, 2010; Chen and Bouvain, 2009). Our strategy adhered to the methodology employed in earlier research to evaluate corporate social responsibility disclosure (e.g. Marano et al., 2017; Hawn and Ioannou, 2016).

#### *6.2.2.2 Independent variables*

To analyse the effects of corporate governance on the environmental disclosure of EU companies, we use several independent variables related to the characteristics and composition of the board of directors. The independent variables used are: *BoInd*, which is the percentage of all independent directors appointed on the board as reported by the company; *BoGenDiv,* that is, the percentage of females on the board; *CSRSustComm,* a dummy that takes a value of 1 if the company has a CSR committee and 0 otherwise; *Ass,* that is, assurance, a dummy assuming a value of 1 if the company has an external auditor for its CSR sustainability report and 0 otherwise; *GRI*, that is a dummy variable that takes the value of 1 if the company's CSR report is published in accordance with the GRI guidelines and 0 otherwise.

#### *6.2.2.3 Moderating variables*

To evaluate the combined effects of the most important board attributes (*BoInd* and *BoGenDiv*) with other corporate governance mechanisms (*CSRSustComm, GRI* and *Ass*), we included in our regression models several interaction terms obtained by multiplying *BoInd* and *BoGenDiv* with other CG mechanisms such as *CSRSustComm*, *GRI*, and *Ass*.

The interaction terms *BoIndCSRSustComm*, *BoIndGRI*, and *BoIndAss* are used to test the joint effect of board independence with the presence of a CSR sustainability committee, utilisation of the GRI standard, and presence of an external auditor of the CSR sustainability report. The interaction terms *BoGenDivCSRSustComm*, *BoGenDivGRI*, and *BoGenDivAss* are used to test the combined effect of board gender diversity and the presence of a CSR sustainability committee, the utilisation of the GRI standard, and the presence of an external auditor of the sustainability report.

#### *6.2.2.4 Control variables*

The current analysis uses a collection of firm-specific characteristics to control for the analysed relationships to prevent biased results and resolve any potential endogeneity issues related to the omitted variables. In particular, we inserted

**TABLE 6.3** Sample II

| Panel A. Sample by geographic zone | | | | | Panel B. sample by industries | | | | |
|---|---|---|---|---|---|---|---|---|---|
| | *Country of headquarter* | *n. of firms* | *n. of obs* | *% of obs* | *Sector* | | *n. of firms* | *n. of obs* | % of obs |
| 1 | Austria | 19 | 90 | 2,65% | 1 | Accommodation & Food Services | 7 | 50 | 1,47% |
| 2 | Belgium | 27 | 127 | 3,74% | 2 | Admin. & Supp., Waste Manag. & Remed. Services | 16 | 67 | 1,98% |
| 3 | Bulgaria | 0 | 0 | 0% | 3 | Agriculture, Forestry, Fishing & Hunting | 3 | 5 | 0,15% |
| 4 | Cyprus | 2 | 10 | 0,29% | 4 | Arts, Entertainment, & Recreation | 6 | 21 | 0,62% |
| 5 | Croatia | 0 | 0 | 0% | 5 | Construction | 37 | 231 | 6,81% |
| 6 | Czech Republic | 2 | 4 | 0,12% | 6 | Educational Services | 1 | 2 | 0,06% |
| 7 | Denmark | 16 | 81 | 2,39% | 7 | Health Care and Social Assistance | 4 | 8 | 0,24% |
| 8 | Estonia | 0 | 0 | 0% | 8 | Information | 55 | 344 | 10,14% |
| 9 | Finland | 42 | 268 | 7,90% | 9 | Manufacturing | 277 | 1627 | 47,97% |
| 10 | France | 87 | 682 | 20,11% | 10 | Mining, Quarrying, Oil & Gas Extraction | 10 | 66 | 1,95% |
| 11 | Germany | 110 | 533 | 15,71% | 11 | Other Services (except Public Administration) | 3 | 7 | 0,21% |
| 12 | Greece | 5 | 36 | 1,06% | 12 | Professional, Scientific, & Technical Services | 27 | 140 | 4,13% |
| 13 | Hungary | 2 | 20 | 0,59% | 13 | Real Estate, Rental & Leasing | 44 | 180 | 5,31% |
| 14 | Ireland | 16 | 108 | 3,18% | 14 | Retail Trade | 27 | 150 | 4,42% |
| 15 | Italy | 60 | 290 | 8,55% | 15 | Transportation & Warehousing | 29 | 180 | 5,31% |
| 16 | Latvia | 0 | 0 | 0% | 16 | Utilities | 30 | 236 | 6,96% |
| 17 | Lithuania | 0 | 0 | 0% | 17 | Wholesale Trade | 16 | 78 | 2,30% |
| 18 | Luxembourg | 5 | 32 | 0,94% | | Tot. | 592 | 3,392 | 100,00% |

*(Continued)*

**TABLE 6.3** Continued

| *Panel A. Sample by geographic zone* | | | | | *Panel B. sample by industries* | | | |
|---|---|---|---|---|---|---|---|---|
| | *Country of headquarter* | *n. of firms* | *n. of obs* | *% of obs* | *Sector* | *n. of firms* | *n. of obs* | % of obs |
| 19 | Malta | 1 | 4 | 0,12% | | | | |
| 20 | Netherlands | 29 | 239 | 7,05% | | | | |
| 21 | Poland | 7 | 21 | 0,62% | | | | |
| 22 | Portugal | 13 | 73 | 2,15% | | | | |
| 23 | Romania | 0 | 0 | 0% | | | | |
| 24 | Slovakia | 0 | 0 | 0% | | | | |
| 25 | Slovenia | 0 | 0 | 0% | | | | |
| 26 | Spain | 46 | 294 | 8,67% | | | | |
| 27 | Sweden | 103 | 480 | 14,15% | | | | |
| | Tot. | 592 | 3,392 | 100,00% | | | | |

**TABLE 6.4** Description of variables and measurement

| *Variable* | *Description* | *Measurement* | *Source* |
|---|---|---|---|
| Dependent variable | | | |
| EnvDisc | Environmental Disclosure | Index obtained by the unweighted sum of various environmental items, assigning value 1 when the company does present information on that environmental aspect and 0 otherwise (Gallego-Álvarez & Ortas, 2017; Du et al., 2010; Kolk and Pinkse, 2010; Chen and Bouvain, 2009) | Eikon |
| Independent variables | | | |
| ***Board attributes*** | | | |
| BoInd | Board independence | The ratio between independent directors and the total number of boards directors | Eikon |
| BoGenDiv | Board Gender Diversity | Percentage of female on the board | Eikon |
| ***Other CG mechanisms*** | | | |
| CSRSustComm | CSR Sustainability Committee | Dummy variable equal to 1 if there is a CSR committee or team and 0 otherwise | Eikon |
| Ass | Assurance | Dummy variable assuming value of 1 if the company has an external auditor of its CSR/Sustainability report | Eikon |
| GRI | GRI standards | Dummy variable that take the value of 1 if the company's CSR report is published in accordance with the GRI guidelines | Eikon |
| Interaction terms | | | |
| BoInd*CSR SustCom | Interaction term | Two ways interaction term obtained by multiplying the BoInd and CSRsustCom | Eikon |
| BoInd*GRI | Interaction term | Two ways interaction term obtained by multiplying the BoInd and GRI | Eikon |
| BoInd*Ass | Interaction term | Two ways interaction term obtained by multiplying the BoInd and Ass | Eikon |
| BoGenDiv* CSRSustCom | Interaction term | Two ways interaction term obtained by multiplying the BoGenDiv and CSRSustCom | Eikon |
| BoGenDiv*GRI | Interaction term | Two ways interaction term obtained by multiplying the BoGenDiv and GRI | Eikon |

*(Continued)*

**TABLE 6.4** Continued

| *Variable* | *Description* | *Measurement* | *Source* |
|---|---|---|---|
| BoGenDiv*Ass | Interaction term | Two ways interaction term obtained by multiplying the BoGenDiv and Ass | Eikon |
| Control variables | | | |
| BoSize | Board Size | The total number of board members at the end of the fiscal year | Eikon |
| BoMeetings | Board Meetings | Number of board meetings during the year | Eikon |
| RoleDual | Ceo Chairman Duality | Dummy variable equal to 1 if the Ceo simultaneously chair the board or has the chairman of the board been the Ceo of the company | Eikon |
| BoMemAff | Board Member Affiliations | Average number of other corporate affiliations for the board member | Eikon |
| BoTenur | Average Board Tenure | Average number of years each board member has been on the board | Eikon |
| FirmSize | Firm Size | Natural logarithm of total assets | Eikon |
| Lev | Leverage | Long-term debt divided by total assets | Eikon |
| ROA | Return On Asset | Return On Assets | Eikon |
| EnvSensSect | Environmental Sensitive Sector | Dummy variable equal to 1 if the company operates in an environmental sensitive industry, 0 otherwise | Eikon |

*BoSize*, that is, the total number of board members at the end of the fiscal year; *BoMeetings,* that is, the number of board meetings during the year; *RoleDual,* a dummy variable that equals to 1 if the CEO simultaneously chairs the board or the chairman of the board has been the CEO of the company; *BoMemAff,* the average number of other corporate affiliations for the board member; *BoTenur,* the average number of years each board member has been on the board; *FirmSize,* the natural logarithm of total assets; *Lev,* the long-term debt divided by total assets; *ROA*, the return on total assets. Finally, we include the *EnvSensSect* dummy variable in the robustness analysis to distinguish between environmentally sensitive and non-sensitive companies.

### 6.2.3 Regression analysis

To test our hypotheses, we created the following regression model based on panel data-dependence approaches:

$$\begin{aligned} EnvDisc = {} & \alpha + \beta_1 BoInd + \beta_2 BoGenDiv + \beta_3 RoleDual + \beta_4 BoSize \\ & + \beta_5 BoMeet + \beta_6 BoMemAff + \beta_7 BoTenur + \beta_8 CSRSustComm \\ & + \beta_9 GRI + \beta_{10} Ass + \beta_{11} FirmSize + \beta_{12} Lev + \beta_{13} ROA + \varepsilon \end{aligned} \tag{1}$$

$$EnvDisc = \alpha + \beta_1 BoInd + \beta_2 BoGenDiv + \beta_3 BoInd \star CSRSustComm + \beta_4 RoleDual + \beta_5 BoSize + \beta_6 BoMeet + \beta_7 BoMemAff + \beta_8 BoTenur + \beta_9 CSRSustComm + \beta_{10} GRI + \beta_{11} Ass + \beta_{12} FirmSize + \beta_{13} Lev + \beta_{14} ROA + \varepsilon \tag{2}$$

$$EnvDisc = \alpha + \beta_1 BoInd + \beta_2 BoGenDiv + \beta_3 BoInd \star Ass + \beta_4 RoleDual + \beta_5 BoSize + \beta_6 BoMeet + \beta_7 BoMemAff + \beta_8 BoTenur + \beta_9 CSRSustComm + \beta_{10} GRI + \beta_{11} Ass + \beta_{12} FirmSize + \beta_{13} Lev + \beta_{14} ROA + \varepsilon \tag{3}$$

$$EnvDisc = \alpha + \beta_1 BoInd + \beta_2 BoGenDiv + \beta_3 BoInd \star GRI + \beta_4 RoleDual + \beta_5 BoSize + \beta_6 BoMeet + \beta_7 BoMemAff + \beta_8 BoTenur + \beta_9 CSRSustComm + \beta_{10} GRI + \beta_{11} Ass + \beta_{12} FirmSize + \beta_{13} Lev + \beta_{14} ROA + \varepsilon \tag{4}$$

$$EnvDisc = \alpha + \beta_1 BoInd + \beta_2 BoGenDiv + \beta_3 BoGenDiv \star CSRSustComm + \beta_4 RoleDual + \beta_5 BoSize + \beta_6 BoMeet + \beta_7 BoMemAff + \beta_8 BoTenur + \beta_9 CSRSustComm + \beta_{10} GRI + \beta_{11} Ass + \beta_{12} FirmSize + \beta_{13} Lev + \beta_{14} ROA + \varepsilon \tag{5}$$

$$EnvDisc = \alpha + \beta_1 BoInd + \beta_2 BoGenDiv + \beta_3 BoGenDiv \star Ass + \beta_4 RoleDual + \beta_5 BoSize + \beta_6 BoMeet + \beta_7 BoMemAff + \beta_8 BoTenur + \beta_9 CSRSustComm + \beta_{10} GRI + \beta_{11} Ass + \beta_{12} FirmSize + \beta_{13} Lev + \beta_{14} ROA + \varepsilon \tag{6}$$

$$EnvDisc = \alpha + \beta_1 BoInd + \beta_2 BoGenDiv + \beta_3 BoGenDiv \star GRI + \beta_4 RoleDual + \beta_5 BoSize + \beta_6 BoMeet + \beta_7 BoMemAff + \beta_8 BoTenur + \beta_9 CSRSustComm + \beta_{10} GRI + \beta_{11} Ass + \beta_{12} FirmSize + \beta_{13} Lev + \beta_{14} ROA + \varepsilon \tag{7}$$

Regression models for panel data enhance the econometric specifications. Examining observations from several successive years for the same sample of companies facilitates the evaluation of business behaviour across time. According to Fuente et al. (2017), Martnez-Ferrero et al. (2016), and Petersen (2009), panel data enables the capture of unobserved heterogeneity and undetected differences among company behaviours and traits that may be connected with the explanatory variables.

We will be able to control for the effects of environmental disclosure procedures over various time periods thanks to the study of the temporal dimension of the data, which will also provide an analysis with some dynamism while enhancing consistency and explanatory power.

## 6.3 Results

### *6.3.1 Descriptive statistics*

Table 6.5 shows the descriptive statistics of the variables.

**TABLE 6.5** Descriptive statistics

| *Variables* | *n. obs* | *mean* | *sd* | *min* | *max* |
|---|---|---|---|---|---|
| EnvDisc | 3,392 | 23.25 | 7.742 | 1 | 42 |
| ResUse | 3,392 | 11.14 | 3.52 | 0 | 18 |
| Emiss | 3,392 | 8.44 | 3.51 | 0 | 17 |
| EnvInnov | 3,392 | 3.67 | 2.4 | 0 | 12 |
| BoInd | 3,392 | 58.15 | 25.36 | 0 | 100 |
| BoGenDiv | 3,392 | 26.45 | 13.97 | 0 | 75 |
| CSRSustCom | 3,392 | 0.846 | 0.361 | 0 | 1 |
| GRI | 3,392 | 0.973 | 0.163 | 0 | 1 |
| Ass | 3,392 | 0.847 | 0.360 | 0 | 1 |
| RoleDual | 3,392 | 0.301 | 0.459 | 0 | 1 |
| BoSize | 3,392 | 12.03 | 4.200 | 2 | 27 |
| BoMeet | 3,392 | 9.854 | 4.914 | 2 | 100 |
| BoTenur | 3,392 | 6.418 | 2.688 | 0.288 | 23.17 |
| BoMemAff | 3,392 | 1.001 | 0.829 | 0 | 8 |
| FirmSize | 3,392 | 22.83 | 1.459 | 17.76 | 26.93 |
| ROA | 3,392 | 0.0419 | 0.0599 | -0.354 | 0.603 |
| Lev | 3,392 | 0.376 | 1.671 | 0 | 76.88 |
| Number of firms | 592 | | | | |

The skewness and kurtosis of the environmental disclosure data used were both acceptable. The assumption of normality was validated through visual inspection and normality testing.

*EnvDisc* has minimum and maximum values of 1 and 42, respectively, with an average value of 23.25. In other words, the sampled companies presented an average of 23 indicators. The large difference between the minimum and maximum values and the standard deviation of 7.74 point suggests a variety of EnvDisc-related behaviours among businesses. The fact that there are companies that only disclose one metric suggests that some still view environmental disclosure as only a legal requirement. In other words, environmental transparency did not play a strategic role.

Analysis of various types of environmental data shows that businesses focus more on resource use and emissions and less on environmental advances.

The independent variable *BoInd* varies widely between businesses, ranging from 0% to 100%, with an average of 58.15%. Similarly, *BoGenDiv* varies greatly between businesses, ranging from 0% to 75%, with an average of 26.45%, which indicates that a comparatively small number of female directors have been appointed to boards.

A CSR committee is present in 84% of companies. The GRI standards are adopted by 97% of businesses, and 84% have an external auditor reviewing their CSR sustainability reports.

In terms of control variables, the average CEO duality value is 30.1%. The minimum and maximum values of *BoSize* are 2 and 27, respectively, whereas the average value is 12.03. The average BoMeet amounts to 9.85 a year.

The average number of years each board member has been on the board (*BoTenur*) is 6.4, and the value ranges from 0.28 and 23.1. The average number of other corporate affiliations with board members (*BoMemAff*) is 1.

The average firm size, Lev, and ROA are 22.83, 0.376, and 0.042, respectively.

Tables 6.6 and 6.7 show the descriptive statistics of the main variables for each country.

The correlations between the variables were evaluated before performing a regression analysis to detect collinearity; the results are displayed in Table 6.8. *BoInd* was negatively correlated with *EnvDisc*, whereas *BoGenDiv* was positively correlated with *EnvDisc*. No correlation was statistically significant. Conversely, some variables exhibited several correlations. *CSRSustCom*, *GRI* and *Ass* were positively and significantly correlated with *EnvDisc*. Both *BoSize* and *FirmSize* were positively and significantly correlated with *EnvDisc*. *BoSize* was negatively correlated with *BoInd*. *FirmSize* was positively and significantly correlated with *BoSize*.

We also provide the variance inflation factors (VIF), which gauge how much each explanatory variable is interpreted in light of the other explanatory variables, taking into account the numerous correlations between variables. There is no multicollinearity in the multiple regression models, as shown by the fact that VIF statistics for all independent variables are less than 3 (Hair et al., 1998).

## 6.3.2 Regression results

### 6.3.2.1 Direct effects

The outcomes of the regression analyses obtained using Stata software are shown in Table 6.9. We used a panel regression with a time fixed effects model to test our hypotheses. We also propose a fixed effect model, a random effects model, and a pooled ordinary least squares method, but the time fixed effects specification is supported by the Breush–Pagan, Hausman, and Chow F-tests. We verified that time-fixed effects are needed in this case using the testparm command in Stata.

Model 1 in Table 6.9 tests hypotheses $H_1$ to $H_5$, whereas Table 6.10 shows the results for hypotheses $H_6$ to $H_{10}$.

Model 1 outlines the findings from the estimation of equation (1), which sheds light on the direct relationship between each corporate governance mechanism and environmental disclosure.

The explanatory strength of the regression is highlighted by the R2 of Model 1 (54.1%), which is consistent with the R2 obtained by earlier studies on the factors influencing environmental disclosure that considered the same control variables as the current study.

The results of Model 1 do not confirm $H_1$ and show a negative and insignificant association between board independence and *EnvDisc*. Our results for $H_1$ are consistent with the results of several other studies that find no statistically significant relationship between board independence and CSR disclosure. For example, Bueno et al. (2018) highlighted that board independence does not present statistical significance for the sustainability disclosure of Brazilian listed firms. Similarly, Michelon and Parbonetti (2012) did not find statistically significant results for the same relationship in US and European companies. Amran et al. (2014) also confirm that there are no significant results for firms in 12 countries in the Asia-Pacific region. Similarly, Prado-Lorenzo and Garcia-Sanchez (2010) found no significant results regarding the effect of board independence on the dissemination of information on the greenhouse gases of firms from 28 countries. Other scholars have likewise highlighted analogous findings (e.g. Wan-Hussin, 2009; Leung and Horwitz, 2004; Haniffa and Cooke, 2002).

These results support $H_2$ and show that *BoGenDiv* positively affects *EnvDisc*. The coefficient of *BoGenDiv* is positive and statistically significant ($\beta$=0.0309, $p<0.01$). This finding confirms that women are more inclined towards equity and social and environmental issues (Ellwood and Garcia-Lacalle, 2015; Jaffee and Hyde, 2000; Ibrahim and Angelidis, 1995). Women on boards have a substantial impact on sustainability initiatives and disclosures, as found by Barako and Brown (2008), Post et al. (2011), Fernandez-Feijoo et al. (2012), Ntim and Soobaroyen (2013), Friaz-Aceituno et al. (2013), Boulouta (2013), Fernandez-Feijoo et al. (2014), Harjoto et al. (2015), Lone et al. (2016), Tamini and Sebastianelli (2017), and Bueno et al. (2018). Our findings are consistent with research showing that women are more socially conscious than men, which enhances the effectiveness of board decision making, particularly when it comes to matters of social responsibility (Ibrahim and Angelidis, 1995).

Concerning *CSRSustComm,* the results in Model 1 in Table 6.9 confirm $H_3$, indicating a positive relationship between the presence of a CSR sustainability committee and *EnvDisc*. More specifically, the coefficient of *CSRSustComm* is statistically significant at better than the 1% level to explain variations in *EnvDisc* ($\beta$=2.049, $p<0.01$). Our findings are consistent with other research that find that CSR committee and sustainability or environmental disclosure are positively associated (Pucheta-Martínez and Gallego-Álvarez, 2019; Cucari et al., 2018; Mahmood et al., 2018; Fuente et al., 2017; Konadu, 2017; Liao et al., 2015). Accordingly, in recent years, several guidance and corporate governance codes have increasingly suggested that firms create such committee, and an increasing number of companies have established them within the board of directors to manage sustainability issues (Birindelli et al., 2018).

Regarding external assurance of environmental disclosure, our results confirm $H_4$, showing a positive association between *Ass* and *EnvDisc*. The coefficient of *Ass* is statistically significant at better than the 1% level to explain variations in *EnvDisc* ($\beta = 1.159$, $p < 0.01$). Our findings are consistent with research that has

**TABLE 6.6** Descriptive statistics for each country (I)

| *Country* | *Variable* | *Obs* | *Mean* | *Std. Dev.* | *Min* | *Max* | *Country* | *Variable* | *Obs* | *Mean* | *Std. Dev.* | *Min* | *Max* |
|---|---|---|---|---|---|---|---|---|---|---|---|---|---|
| Austria | EnvDisc | 90 | 20,83 | 5,33 | 3,00 | 31,00 | Finland | EnvDisc | 268 | 23,22 | 6,33 | 3,00 | 35,00 |
| | – ResourceUse | 90 | 10,03 | 2,96 | 2,00 | 15,00 | | – ResourceUse | 268 | 11,16 | 3,26 | 0,00 | 17,00 |
| | – Emissions | 90 | 7,92 | 3,12 | 1,00 | 14,00 | | – Emissions | 268 | 8,04 | 3,16 | 1,00 | 15,00 |
| | – EnvInnov | 90 | 2,88 | 1,56 | 0,00 | 5,00 | | – EnvInnov | 268 | 4,02 | 1,85 | 0,00 | 8,00 |
| | BoInd | 90 | 66,85 | 24,12 | 0,00 | 100,00 | | BoInd | 268 | 84,23 | 16,89 | 10,34 | 100,00 |
| | BoGenDiv | 90 | 20,65 | 12,04 | 0,00 | 46,67 | | BoGenDiv | 268 | 29,06 | 11,62 | 0,00 | 57,14 |
| | CSRSustComm | 90 | 0,77 | 0,43 | 0,00 | 1,00 | | CSRSustComm | 268 | 0,78 | 0,42 | 0,00 | 1,00 |
| | GRI | 90 | 0,99 | 0,11 | 0,00 | 1,00 | | GRI | 268 | 0,97 | 0,17 | 0,00 | 1,00 |
| | Ass | 90 | 0,89 | 0,32 | 0,00 | 1,00 | | Ass | 268 | 0,81 | 0,39 | 0,00 | 1,00 |
| Belgium | EnvDisc | 127 | 20,64 | 7,37 | 1,00 | 39,00 | France | EnvDisc | 682 | 25,84 | 7,13 | 5,00 | 41,00 |
| | – ResourceUse | 127 | 9,97 | 3,55 | 0,00 | 16,00 | | – ResourceUse | 682 | 12,20 | 3,14 | 2,00 | 18,00 |
| | – Emissions | 127 | 7,18 | 2,98 | 0,00 | 15,00 | | – Emissions | 682 | 9,67 | 2,95 | 1,00 | 17,00 |
| | – EnvInnov | 127 | 3,49 | 2,43 | 0,00 | 9,00 | | – EnvInnov | 682 | 3,98 | 2,45 | 0,00 | 10,00 |
| | BoInd | 127 | 51,10 | 17,33 | 7,14 | 88,89 | | BoInd | 682 | 52,21 | 19,11 | 8,33 | 100,00 |
| | BoGenDiv | 127 | 25,05 | 13,66 | 0,00 | 53,33 | | BoGenDiv | 682 | 33,00 | 14,30 | 0,00 | 64,29 |
| | CSRSustComm | 127 | 0,78 | 0,42 | 0,00 | 1,00 | | CSRSustComm | 682 | 0,93 | 0,26 | 0,00 | 1,00 |
| | GRI | 127 | 0,96 | 0,20 | 0,00 | 1,00 | | GRI | 682 | 0,96 | 0,19 | 0,00 | 1,00 |
| | Ass | 127 | 0,76 | 0,43 | 0,00 | 1,00 | | Ass | 682 | 0,93 | 0,26 | 0,00 | 1,00 |
| Cyprus | EnvDisc | 10 | 17,70 | 9,48 | 5,00 | 28,00 | Germany | EnvDisc | 533 | 24,32 | 9,12 | 1,00 | 42,00 |
| | – ResourceUse | 10 | 10,00 | 5,03 | 3,00 | 15,00 | | – ResourceUse | 533 | 11,59 | 3,88 | 0,00 | 18,00 |
| | – Emissions | 10 | 7,70 | 4,52 | 2,00 | 13,00 | | – Emissions | 533 | 8,33 | 3,82 | 0,00 | 16,00 |
| | – EnvInnov | 10 | 0,00 | 0,00 | 0,00 | 0,00 | | – EnvInnov | 533 | 4,39 | 2,85 | 0,00 | 12,00 |
| | BoInd | 10 | 50,78 | 17,85 | 26,67 | 72,73 | | BoInd | 533 | 50,51 | 34,22 | 0,00 | 100,00 |
| | BoGenDiv | 10 | 20,67 | 8,05 | 11,11 | 33,33 | | BoGenDiv | 533 | 24,95 | 12,07 | 0,00 | 57,14 |
| | CSRSustComm | 10 | 0,80 | 0,42 | 0,00 | 1,00 | | CSRSustComm | 533 | 0,86 | 0,35 | 0,00 | 1,00 |
| | GRI | 10 | 1,00 | 0,00 | 1,00 | 1,00 | | GRI | 533 | 0,97 | 0,17 | 0,00 | 1,00 |
| | Ass | 10 | 0,60 | 0,52 | 0,00 | 1,00 | | Ass | 533 | 0,79 | 0,41 | 0,00 | 1,00 |

*(Continued)*

**TABLE 6.6** Continued

| *Country* | *Variable* | *Obs* | *Mean* | *Std. Dev.* | *Min* | *Max* | *Country* | *Variable* | *Obs* | *Mean* | *Std. Dev.* | *Min* | *Max* |
|---|---|---|---|---|---|---|---|---|---|---|---|---|---|
| Czech | EnvDisc | 4 | 24,00 | 10,03 | 9,00 | 30,00 | Greece | EnvDisc | 36 | 23,39 | 4,71 | 11,00 | 32,00 |
| Republic | – ResourceUse | 4 | 9,50 | 3,70 | 4,00 | 12,00 | | – ResourceUse | 36 | 10,03 | 1,90 | 6,00 | 13,00 |
| | – Emissions | 4 | 11,00 | 5,42 | 3,00 | 15,00 | | – Emissions | 36 | 11,31 | 3,92 | 3,00 | 17,00 |
| | – EnvInnov | 4 | 3,50 | 1,00 | 2,00 | 4,00 | | – EnvInnov | 36 | 2,06 | 1,96 | 0,00 | 6,00 |
| | BoInd | 4 | 0,00 | 0,00 | 0,00 | 0,00 | | BoInd | 36 | 31,23 | 17,36 | 0,00 | 60,00 |
| | BoGenDiv | 4 | 11,11 | 3,93 | 8,33 | 16,67 | | BoGenDiv | 36 | 6,57 | 7,37 | 0,00 | 25,00 |
| | CSRSustComm | 4 | 1,00 | 0,00 | 1,00 | 1,00 | | CSRSustComm | 36 | 0,97 | 0,17 | 0,00 | 1,00 |
| | GRI | 4 | 0,75 | 0,50 | 0,00 | 1,00 | | GRI | 36 | 1,00 | 0,00 | 1,00 | 1,00 |
| | Ass | 4 | 1,00 | 0,00 | 1,00 | 1,00 | | Ass | 36 | 0,81 | 0,40 | 0,00 | 1,00 |
| Denmark | EnvDisc | 81 | 21,60 | 5,33 | 3,00 | 30,00 | Hungary | EnvDisc | 20 | 27,40 | 3,70 | 22,00 | 33,00 |
| | – ResourceUse | 81 | 11,74 | 2,77 | 3,00 | 17,00 | | – ResourceUse | 20 | 11,15 | 2,13 | 7,00 | 15,00 |
| | – Emissions | 81 | 6,59 | 2,16 | 0,00 | 10,00 | | – Emissions | 20 | 12,70 | 2,32 | 9,00 | 15,00 |
| | – EnvInnov | 81 | 3,27 | 2,03 | 0,00 | 7,00 | | – EnvInnov | 20 | 3,55 | 0,51 | 3,00 | 4,00 |
| | BoInd | 81 | 46,52 | 16,97 | 13,33 | 100,00 | | BoInd | 20 | 48,50 | 15,09 | 22,73 | 69,57 |
| | BoGenDiv | 81 | 22,04 | 9,60 | 0,00 | 42,86 | | BoGenDiv | 20 | 9,38 | 5,16 | 0,00 | 18,18 |
| | CSRSustComm | 81 | 0,93 | 0,26 | 0,00 | 1,00 | | CSRSustComm | 20 | 1,00 | 0,00 | 1,00 | 1,00 |
| | GRI | 81 | 0,93 | 0,26 | 0,00 | 1,00 | | GRI | 20 | 1,00 | 0,00 | 1,00 | 1,00 |
| | Ass | 81 | 0,85 | 0,36 | 0,00 | 1,00 | | Ass | 20 | 1,00 | 0,00 | 1,00 | 1,00 |

**TABLE 6.7** Descriptive statistics for each country (II)

| *Country* | *Variable* | *Obs* | *Mean* | *Std. Dev.* | *Min* | *Max* | *Country* | *Variable* | *Obs* | *Mean* | *Std. Dev.* | *Min* | *Max* |
|---|---|---|---|---|---|---|---|---|---|---|---|---|---|
| Ireland | EnvDisc | 108 | 25,58 | 7,72 | 7,00 | 39,00 | Poland | EnvDisc | 21 | 19,76 | 6,36 | 6,00 | 31,00 |
| | – ResourceUse | 108 | 11,74 | 3,83 | 3,00 | 18,00 | | – ResourceUse | 21 | 8,33 | 3,26 | 4,00 | 14,00 |
| | – Emissions | 108 | 8,90 | 3,23 | 2,00 | 15,00 | | – Emissions | 21 | 9,33 | 3,64 | 2,00 | 15,00 |
| | – EnvInnov | 108 | 4,94 | 2,56 | 0,00 | 10,00 | | – EnvInnov | 21 | 2,10 | 1,22 | 0,00 | 5,00 |
| | BoInd | 108 | 77,42 | 13,39 | 40,00 | 100,00 | | BoInd | 21 | 36,32 | 19,48 | 0,00 | 71,43 |
| | BoGenDiv | 108 | 19,47 | 9,28 | 0,00 | 41,67 | | BoGenDiv | 21 | 23,32 | 16,17 | 0,00 | 62,50 |
| | CSRSustComm | 108 | 0,89 | 0,32 | 0,00 | 1,00 | | CSRSustComm | 21 | 0,76 | 0,44 | 0,00 | 1,00 |
| | GRI | 108 | 0,94 | 0,23 | 0,00 | 1,00 | | GRI | 21 | 1,00 | 0,00 | 1,00 | 1,00 |
| | Ass | 108 | 0,71 | 0,45 | 0,00 | 1,00 | | Ass | 21 | 0,81 | 0,40 | 0,00 | 1,00 |
| Italy | EnvDisc | 290 | 22,17 | 7,50 | 4,00 | 40,00 | Portugal | EnvDisc | 73 | 23,56 | 4,93 | 4,00 | 35,00 |
| | – ResourceUse | 290 | 10,59 | 3,05 | 3,00 | 17,00 | | – ResourceUse | 73 | 10,93 | 2,62 | 2,00 | 17,00 |
| | –Emissions | 290 | 8,83 | 3,95 | 0,00 | 16,00 | | – Emissions | 73 | 9,74 | 2,81 | 2,00 | 15,00 |
| | – EnvInnov | 290 | 2,75 | 2,09 | 0,00 | 9,00 | | – EnvInnov | 73 | 2,89 | 1,36 | 0,00 | 7,00 |
| | BoInd | 290 | 54,97 | 16,87 | 14,29 | 95,00 | | BoInd | 73 | 34,64 | 21,04 | 0,00 | 77,78 |
| | BoGenDiv | 290 | 27,24 | 15,06 | 0,00 | 57,14 | | BoGenDiv | 73 | 16,20 | 11,32 | 0,00 | 44,44 |
| | CSRSustComm | 290 | 0,86 | 0,35 | 0,00 | 1,00 | | CSRSustComm | 73 | 0,84 | 0,37 | 0,00 | 1,00 |
| | GRI | 290 | 0,99 | 0,10 | 0,00 | 1,00 | | GRI | 73 | 0,96 | 0,20 | 0,00 | 1,00 |
| | Ass | 290 | 0,96 | 0,20 | 0,00 | 1,00 | | Ass | 73 | 0,90 | 0,30 | 0,00 | 1,00 |
| Luxembourg | EnvDisc | 32 | 25,09 | 8,84 | 11,00 | 37,00 | Spain | EnvDisc | 294 | 23,59 | 6,30 | 6,00 | 36,00 |
| | – ResourceUse | 32 | 11,72 | 3,12 | 5,00 | 16,00 | | – ResourceUse | 294 | 10,84 | 2,73 | 3,00 | 17,00 |
| | – Emissions | 32 | 10,63 | 3,90 | 5,00 | 15,00 | | – Emissions | 294 | 9,62 | 3,29 | 2,00 | 17,00 |
| | – EnvInnov | 32 | 2,75 | 2,60 | 0,00 | 7,00 | | – EnvInnov | 294 | 3,13 | 1,88 | 0,00 | 7,00 |
| | BoInd | 32 | 61,82 | 13,72 | 36,36 | 91,67 | | BoInd | 294 | 46,01 | 16,04 | 6,67 | 90,91 |
| | BoGenDiv | 32 | 23,01 | 9,58 | 0,00 | 33,33 | | BoGenDiv | 294 | 17,24 | 11,07 | 0,00 | 46,15 |
| | CSRSustComm | 32 | 0,88 | 0,34 | 0,00 | 1,00 | | CSRSustComm | 294 | 0,82 | 0,38 | 0,00 | 1,00 |
| | GRI | 32 | 0,91 | 0,30 | 0,00 | 1,00 | | GRI | 294 | 0,99 | 0,12 | 0,00 | 1,00 |
| | Ass | 32 | 0,88 | 0,34 | 0,00 | 1,00 | | Ass | 294 | 0,95 | 0,23 | 0,00 | 1,00 |

(*Continued*)

**TABLE 6.7** Continued

| *Country* | *Variable* | *Obs* | *Mean* | *Std. Dev.* | *Min* | *Max* | *Country* | *Variable* | *Obs* | *Mean* | *Std. Dev.* | *Min* | *Max* |
|---|---|---|---|---|---|---|---|---|---|---|---|---|---|
| Malta | EnvDisc | 4 | 6,00 | 1,41 | 4,00 | 7,00 | Sweden | EnvDisc | 480 | 20,51 | 7,57 | 1,00 | 35,00 |
| | – ResourceUse | 4 | 4,00 | 1,41 | 2,00 | 5,00 | | – ResourceUse | 480 | 10,41 | 3,80 | 0,00 | 17,00 |
| | – Emissions | 4 | 2,00 | 0,00 | 2,00 | 2,00 | | – Emissions | 480 | 6,46 | 3,01 | 0,00 | 15,00 |
| | – EnvInnov | 4 | 0,00 | 0,00 | 0,00 | 0,00 | | – EnvInnov | 480 | 3,65 | 2,26 | 0,00 | 10,00 |
| | BoInd | 4 | 78,17 | 5,85 | 71,43 | 85,71 | | BoInd | 480 | 61,37 | 17,95 | 0,00 | 100,00 |
| | BoGenDiv | 4 | 22,86 | 7,00 | 14,29 | 28,57 | | BoGenDiv | 480 | 32,81 | 11,80 | 0,00 | 75,00 |
| | CSRSustComm | 4 | 1,00 | 0,00 | 1,00 | 1,00 | | CSRSustComm | 480 | 0,79 | 0,41 | 0,00 | 1,00 |
| | GRI | 4 | 1,00 | 0,00 | 1,00 | 1,00 | | GRI | 480 | 0,98 | 0,15 | 0,00 | 1,00 |
| | Ass | 4 | 0,25 | 0,50 | 0,00 | 1,00 | | Ass | 480 | 0,73 | 0,44 | 0,00 | 1,00 |
| Netherlands | EnvDisc | 239 | 21,82 | 8,95 | 1,00 | 40,00 | | | | | | | |
| | – ResourceUse | 239 | 10,76 | 4,38 | 1,00 | 18,00 | | | | | | | |
| | – Emissions | 239 | 7,46 | 3,14 | 0,00 | 15,00 | | | | | | | |
| | – EnvInnov | 239 | 3,61 | 2,55 | 0,00 | 8,00 | | | | | | | |
| | BoInd | 239 | 85,33 | 20,70 | 0,00 | 100,00 | | | | | | | |
| | BoGenDiv | 239 | 22,15 | 13,91 | 0,00 | 50,00 | | | | | | | |
| | CSRSustComm | 239 | 0,79 | 0,41 | 0,00 | 1,00 | | | | | | | |
| | GRI | 239 | 1,00 | 0,06 | 0,00 | 1,00 | | | | | | | |
| | Ass | 239 | 0,84 | 0,37 | 0,00 | 1,00 | | | | | | | |

**TABLE 6.8** Correlation matrix

| | *VIF* | *EnvDisc* | *BoInd* | *BoGenDiv* | *CSRSustCom* | *GRI* | *Ass* | *BoInd* CSRSustCom* | *BoInd* GRI* | *BoInd* Ass* | *BoGenDiv* CSRSustCom* |
|---|---|---|---|---|---|---|---|---|---|---|---|
| EnvDisc | | 1 | | | | | | | | | |
| BoInd | 1.35 | -0.00 | 1 | | | | | | | | |
| BoGenDiv | 1.09 | 0,03 | 0.12*** | 1 | | | | | | | |
| CSRSustCom | 1.15 | 0.39*** | -0.03 | 0.10*** | 1 | | | | | | |
| GRI | 1.08 | 0.16*** | 0.04* | 0.14*** | 0.12*** | 1 | | | | | |
| Ass | 1.14 | 0.27*** | -0.01 | 0.13*** | 0.22*** | 0.20*** | 1 | | | | |
| BoInd* CSRSustCom | | 0.26*** | 0.64*** | 0.17*** | 0.68*** | 0.10*** | 0.15*** | 1 | | | |
| BoInd*GRI | | 0.05** | 0.93*** | 0.16*** | 0.02 | 0.36*** | 0.05** | 0.63*** | 1 | | |
| BoInd*Ass | | 0.20*** | 0.66*** | 0.17*** | 0.13*** | 0.14*** | 0.68*** | 0.56*** | 0.66*** | 1 | |
| BoGenDiv* CSRSustCom | | 0.22*** | 0.09*** | 0.77*** | 0.61*** | 0.12*** | 0.21*** | 0.50*** | 0.12*** | 0.21*** | 1 |
| BoGenDiv* GRI | | 0.05** | 0.12*** | 0.98*** | 0.11*** | 0.30*** | 0.16*** | 0.17*** | 0.21*** | 0.19*** | 0.76*** |
| BoGenDiv* Ass | | 0.15*** | 0.08*** | 0.79*** | 0.19*** | 0.17*** | 0.61*** | 0.21*** | 0.13*** | 0.49*** | 0.70*** |
| RoleDual | 1.14 | 0.20*** | -0.15*** | 0.03 | 0.09*** | -0.02 | 0.06*** | -0.03* | -0.14*** | -0.08*** | 0.07*** |
| BoSize | 1.87 | 0.38*** | -0.39*** | -0.12*** | 0.20*** | 0.02 | 0.15*** | -0.14*** | -0.35*** | -0.16*** | 0.03 |
| BoMeet | 1.11 | -0.09*** | 0.07*** | 0.04** | 0.06*** | 0.05** | 0.02 | 0.09*** | 0.08*** | 0.06*** | 0.05** |
| BoMemAff | 1.19 | 0.09*** | 0.20*** | -0.05** | -0.08*** | -0.07*** | -0.01 | 0.09*** | 0.16*** | 0.14*** | -0.03 |
| BoTenur | 1.13 | 0.07*** | -0.05** | 0.02 | -0.05** | 0.03 | -0.03 | -0.06*** | -0.04* | -0.06** | -0.00 |
| FirmSize | 1.82 | 0.59*** | 0.02 | -0.10*** | 0.25*** | 0.07*** | 0.23*** | 0.18*** | 0.04* | 0.17*** | 0.09*** |
| Lev | 1.01 | -0.02 | 0.04* | -0.01 | 0.02 | 0.01 | 0.02 | 0.04* | 0.04* | 0.04* | 0.00 |
| ROA | 1.08 | -0.06** | 0.04* | 0.03 | -0.11*** | -0.07*** | -0.10*** | -0.05** | 0.01 | -0.04* | -0.03 |

(*Continued*)

**TABLE 6.8** Continued

| | *BoGenDiv* GRI* | *BoGenDiv* Ass* | *RoleDual* | *BoSize* | *BoMeet* | *BoMemAff* | *BoTenur* | *FirmSize* | *Lev* | *ROA* |
|---|---|---|---|---|---|---|---|---|---|---|
| EnvDisc | | | | | | | | | | |
| BoInd | | | | | | | | | | |
| BoGenDiv | | | | | | | | | | |
| CSRSustCom | | | | | | | | | | |
| GRI | | | | | | | | | | |
| Ass | | | | | | | | | | |
| BoInd* CSRSustCom | | | | | | | | | | |
| BoInd*GRI | | | | | | | | | | |
| BoInd*Ass | | | | | | | | | | |
| BoGenDiv* CSRSustCom | | | | | | | | | | |
| BoGenDiv* GRI | 1 | | | | | | | | | |
| BoGenDiv* Ass | 0.79*** | 1 | | | | | | | | |
| RoleDual | 0.02 | 0.07*** | 1 | | | | | | | |
| BoSize | -0.11*** | 0.00 | 0.20*** | 1 | | | | | | |
| BoMeet | 0.05** | 0.03 | 0.00 | -0.15*** | 1 | | | | | |
| BoMemAff | -0.06*** | -0.02 | 0.07*** | -0.01 | -0.07*** | 1 | | | | |
| BoTenur | 0.02 | -0.00 | 0.22*** | 0.02 | -0.21*** | 0.01 | 1 | | | |
| FirmSize | -0.09*** | 0.06*** | 0.18*** | 0.53*** | -0.08*** | 0.27*** | -0.03* | 1 | | |
| Lev | -0.01 | 0.00 | 0.02 | -0.01 | 0.02 | 0.00 | -0.05** | 0.00 | 1 | |
| ROA | 0.01 | -0.04* | -0.03 | -0.12*** | -0.12*** | 0.04* | 0.14*** | -0.14*** | -0.07*** | 1 |

t statistics in parentheses - *$p<0.05$, **$p<0.01$, ***$p<0.001$

**TABLE 6.9** Regressions for direct effects

| *VARIABLES* | *Model 1 FE with time effects* | *Model 2 OLS* | *Model 3 RE* | *Model 4 FE* |
|---|---|---|---|---|
| BoInd | −0.00665 | 0.00681 | −0.00172 | −0.00323 |
| | (0.00448) | (0.00417) | (0.00448) | (0.00504) |
| BoGenDiv | 0.0309*** | 0.0390*** | 0.0559*** | 0.0629*** |
| | (0.00738) | (0.00686) | (0.00591) | (0.00636) |
| CSRSustComm | 2.049*** | 4.943*** | 4.416*** | 4.307*** |
| | (0.218) | (0.270) | (0.218) | (0.229) |
| Ass | 1.159*** | 1.975*** | 2.033*** | 2.205*** |
| | (0.224) | (0.270) | (0.232) | (0.246) |
| GRI | 1.692*** | 3.149*** | 2.338*** | 2.128*** |
| | (0.388) | (0.578) | (0.414) | (0.428) |
| RoleDual | 0.0749 | 1.223*** | 0.358 | 0.0761 |
| | (0.216) | (0.212) | (0.228) | (0.246) |
| BoSize | −0.0422 | 0.116*** | 0.0161 | -0.0783* |
| | (0.0378) | (0.0296) | (0.0363) | (0.0425) |
| BoMeet | −0.0126 | −0.0352* | 0.0127 | 0.0337* |
| | (0.0183) | (0.0195) | (0.0180) | (0.0202) |
| BoMemAff | −0.139 | −0.306** | −1.071*** | −1.225*** |
| | (0.114) | (0.120) | (0.0988) | (0.102) |
| BoTenur | 0.202*** | 0.123*** | 0.223*** | 0.206*** |
| | (0.0393) | (0.0360) | (0.0394) | (0.0444) |
| FirmSize | 1.302*** | 2.385*** | 2.550*** | 2.011*** |
| | (0.199) | (0.0841) | (0.131) | (0.217) |
| Lev | 0.00627 | -0.0574 | 0.0204 | 0.0117 |
| | (0.0299) | (0.0547) | (0.0341) | (0.0340) |
| ROA | 0.560 | 5.132*** | −1.680 | −2.909** |
| | (1.205) | (1.573) | (1.276) | (1.338) |
| EnvSensSect | – | 4.889*** | 5.017*** | – |
| | – | (0.196) | (0.423) | – |
| Constant | −20.06*** | −46.87*** | −49.37*** | −31.10*** |
| | (4.815) | (1.758) | (2.630) | (4.848) |
| Year dummy | yes | no | no | no |
| Observations | 3,392 | 3,392 | 3,392 | 3,392 |
| R-squared | 0.541 | 0.535 | | 0.400 |
| Number of Idnumber | 592 | | 592 | 592 |

Standard errors in parentheses - ***p<0.01, **p<0.05, *p<0.1

discovered a positive correlation between the level of environmental disclosure and external assurance (Braam et al., 2016; Moroney et al., 2012), confirming that firms implement environmental audits to respond to external pressure or comply with new regulations and standards. Indeed, the company's choice of external audit for environmental disclosure responds to public pressure about the scarce reliability and accuracy of environmental information (Baalouch et al.,

**TABLE 6.10** Regressions for interaction effects

| *VARIABLES* | *Model 1*<br>*FE with time effects* | *Model 2*<br>*FE with time effects* | *Model 3*<br>*FE with time effects* | *Model 4*<br>*FE with time effects* | *Model 5*<br>*FE with time effects* | *Model 6*<br>*FE with time effects* |
|---|---|---|---|---|---|---|
| BoInd | 0.00154 | -0.0120* | 0.00539 | -0.00589 | -0.00671 | -0.00665 |
| | (0.00720) | (0.00727) | (0.0144) | (0.00448) | (0.00446) | (0.00448) |
| BoGenDiv | 0.0314*** | 0.0312*** | 0.0307*** | 0.0597*** | 0.0810*** | 0.0267 |
| | (0.00739) | (0.00739) | (0.00738) | (0.0133) | (0.0132) | (0.0276) |
| CSRSustComm | 2.660*** | 2.054*** | 2.038*** | 2.780*** | 1.983*** | 2.051*** |
| | (0.474) | (0.218) | (0.219) | (0.357) | (0.218) | (0.218) |
| GRI | 1.678*** | 1.711*** | 2.384*** | 1.649*** | 1.625*** | 1.615*** |
| | (0.388) | (0.388) | (0.877) | (0.388) | (0.387) | (0.617) |
| Ass | 1.158*** | 0.773* | 1.147*** | 1.130*** | 2.362*** | 1.160*** |
| | (0.224) | (0.466) | (0.224) | (0.224) | (0.344) | (0.224) |
| BoInd*CSRSustCom | −0.00992 | | | | | |
| | (0.00683) | | | | | |
| BoInd*Ass | | 0.00662 | | | | |
| | | (0.00702) | | | | |
| BoInd*GRI | | | −0.0125 | | | |
| | | | (0.0142) | | | |
| BoGenDiv*CSRSustCom | | | | −0.0334*** | | |
| | | | | (0.0129) | | |
| BoGenDiv*Ass | | | | | −0.0607*** | |
| | | | | | (0.0132) | |
| BoGenDiv*GRI | | | | | | 0.00440 |
| | | | | | | (0.0275) |

| | | | | | | |
|---|---|---|---|---|---|---|
| RoleDual | 0.0812 | 0.0824 | 0.0778 | 0.0627 | 0.0357 | 0.0754 |
| | (0.216) | (0.216) | (0.216) | (0.216) | (0.216) | (0.216) |
| BoSize | −0.0415 | −0.0421 | −0.0422 | −0.0420 | −0.0438 | −0.0424 |
| | (0.0378) | (0.0378) | (0.0378) | (0.0378) | (0.0377) | (0.0378) |
| BoMeet | −0.0108 | −0.0136 | −0.0120 | −0.0120 | −0.00973 | −0.0126 |
| | (0.0184) | (0.0184) | (0.0184) | (0.0183) | (0.0183) | (0.0183) |
| BoMemAff | −0.135 | −0.144 | −0.136 | −0.141 | −0.139 | −0.140 |
| | (0.114) | (0.114) | (0.114) | (0.113) | (0.113) | (0.114) |
| BoTenur | 0.203*** | 0.203*** | 0.202*** | 0.202*** | 0.203*** | 0.202*** |
| | (0.0393) | (0.0394) | (0.0393) | (0.0393) | (0.0392) | (0.0394) |
| FirmSize | 1.292*** | 1.309*** | 1.312*** | 1.307*** | 1.300*** | 1.302*** |
| | (0.199) | (0.199) | (0.199) | (0.199) | (0.198) | (0.199) |
| Lev | 0.00682 | 0.00595 | 0.00674 | 0.00535 | 0.00534 | 0.00625 |
| | (0.0299) | (0.0299) | (0.0299) | (0.0299) | (0.0298) | (0.0299) |
| ROA | 0.556 | 0.565 | 0.568 | 0.685 | 0.457 | 0.567 |
| | (1.205) | (1.205) | (1.205) | (1.205) | (1.201) | (1.206) |
| Constant | −20.51*** | −19.75*** | −21.25*** | −20.50*** | −20.51*** | −20.02*** |
| | (4.824) | (4.827) | (5.001) | (4.813) | (4.799) | (4.825) |
| EnvSensSect | – | – | – | – | – | – |
| Year dummy | yes | yes | yes | yes | yes | yes |
| Observations | 3,392 | 3,392 | 3,392 | 3,392 | 3,392 | 3,392 |
| R-squared | 0.541 | 0.541 | 0.541 | 0.542 | 0.545 | 0.541 |
| Number of Idnumber | 592 | 592 | 592 | 592 | 592 | 592 |

Standard errors in parentheses - ***p<0.01, **p<0.05, *p<0.1

2019; Braam et al. 2016). In other words, companies ensure and signal the credibility of environmental reports to stakeholders and increase their recognition, trust, and reputation.

Regarding the adoption of the GRI, our findings show a significant positive association between environmental disclosure and GRI adoption, confirming $H_5$. They suggest that companies that implement GRI guidelines disclose a higher level of environmental information in their annual reports. This result is consistent with those of previous studies. Galani et al. (2012), for example, highlighted a positive association between the two variables for the largest Greek companies. Similarly, Leal et al. (2019) underlined that companies that adopted the GRI standard tended to present higher levels of greenhouse gases emissions information disclosure. Similarly, Bhattacharyya and Yang (2019) showed that the adoption of GRI G4 guidelines is associated with higher levels of firm biodiversity disclosure for Australian listed companies. García-Sánchez et al. (2019b) discovered that voluntary adoption of the GRI-IFC disclosure strategy will foster the provision of CSR information that is more useful to analysts.

Only the *BoTenur* and *FirmSize* coefficients for the control variables are statistically significant. They exhibit a positive association with *EnvDisc*, indicating that larger businesses and those with boards comprising directors with more expertise are more likely to be interested in or inclined to disclose environmental information.

As discussed above, we used panel regression with a time fixed-effects model to test our hypotheses; thus, the Model 1 regression includes year dummies. The time dummy results suggest that *EnvDisc* decreased from 2002 to 2007 and then increased over time until 2021. The model regression does not include *EnvSensSect* which is a time-invariant dummy variable, and thus cannot be used with fixed-effects models.[2]

Models 2, 3, and 4, shown in Table 6.9, were developed exclusively to compare each of them to the main regression model. However, their results, which are substantially similar to those obtained with the time fixed-effects model, can be considered as a confirmation of the goodness of the results of our analysis, showing its robustness.

Hypothesis $H_1$, which was not confirmed with the main model, was likewise not confirmed with the other models used. The other hypotheses, which were confirmed with the main model, were also confirmed with all other models used.

#### *6.3.2.2 Interaction effects*

Models 1 to 6 in Table 6.10 test hypotheses $H_6$ to $H_{11}$, that is, the joint effects on environmental disclosure of both board independence and board gender diversity with the presence of a CSR sustainability committee, the use of the GRI standard, and the presence of an external auditor of the CSR Sustainability Report. In other words, these models reflect the results of equations (2)–(7) and identify the effects of the interactions between the different mechanisms of corporate governance.

When we include the different interactions in the regression models, the main evidence is that different corporate governance mechanisms work in isolation to affect the level of *EnvDisc*. In fact, the results shown in Table 6.10 highlight that the coefficients of the interaction terms used to test the hypotheses are not significant, with the sole exception of *BoGenDivCSRSustComm* and *BoGenDivAss,* which are significant but have a negative sign contrary to our hypotheses.

Having assumed only positive moderations, this means that none of the hypotheses relating to the interaction effects, from $H_6$ to $H_{11}$, are confirmed. However, Models 4 and 5, which specifically test for $H_9$ and $H_{10}$ show significant interaction coefficients, albeit negative. Hence, Model 4 highlights a negative moderating effect of the CSR Sustainability Committee on the relationship between *BoGenDiv* and *EnvDisc*, whereas Model 5 highlights a negative moderating effect of assurance on the relationship between *BoGenDiv* and *EnvDisc.*

The significant interaction between *BoGenDiv* and *CSRSustComm* shows that these mechanisms operate as substitute governance mechanisms ($\beta = -0.0334$, $p < 0.01$). Accounting for the coefficients, the results support the idea that the positive relationship between board gender diversity and the level of environmental disclosure weakens if the company has a CSR committee. This result can also be interpreted as indicating that the positive relationship between the existence of a CSR committee on the board and the level of environmental disclosure weakens as the percentage of female directors increases.

Similarly, the interaction of *BoGenDiv* and *Ass* shows that the two mechanisms are substitutes for each other ($\beta = -0.0607$, $p<0.01$), supporting the idea that the positive relationship between board gender diversity and level of environmental disclosure weakens if the company has an external auditor in the CSR Sustainability Report. These significant interactions are shown in the following graphs (Figure 6.9):

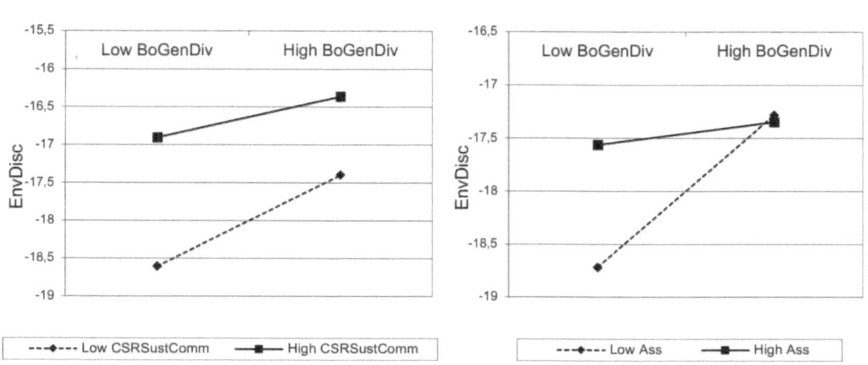


**FIGURE 6.9** Significant interactions

## 6.4 Discussion and concluding remarks

Environmental disclosure has become a useful tool for companies to reduce information asymmetries between agents and principals, respond to institutional pressures, and enhance stakeholder confidence and company reputation. When companies disclose environmental information, they seek to show all parties that they are concerned about social and environmental issues.

This research claims that certain board traits and other corporate governance mechanisms are essential for encouraging environmental disclosure. In keeping with this research, the goal of our study was to examine the effects of various corporate governance mechanisms and the primary board characteristics of international corporations on environmental reporting. The disclosure of environmental information is examined in relation to the direct and combined effects of board independence, board gender diversity, CSR board committee, GRI standards implementation, and assurance services.

Our findings show that all these mechanisms are directly and positively associated with green reporting, except for board independence which has a non-significant impact on environmental disclosure.

Moreover, our findings reveal that each mechanism operates independently of the others in affecting the level of *EnvDisc*. In fact, the analysis of possible complementary or substitution effects between the different corporate governance mechanisms investigated does not show significant interactions, with the sole exception of board gender diversity, which operates as a substitute for both CSR committee implementation and assurance service adoption in stimulating environmental disclosure.

The findings of our study can be interpreted in light of the idea that environmental disclosure itself can be viewed as a governance mechanism that companies use to control their management, manage relationships with stakeholders, reduce information asymmetries between different market players, and legitimise their existence in society.

We refer to the governance function of accounting information, which has been extensively studied, both theoretically and empirically (Bushman and Smith, 2001). Research on the relationship between corporate governance and CSR disclosure has highlighted how this disclosure interacts with other governance mechanisms, mitigating or exacerbating agency issues between ownership and management, between majority and minority shareholders, or, once more, between shareholders and creditors (Lepore et al., 2022). Environmental disclosure can be used by companies as a governance mechanism to realise the aforementioned aims in a complementary or alternative way to other mechanisms.

The significant direct effects that confirm our hypotheses $H_2$ to $H_5$ show that environmental disclosure is used by companies together with gender diversity, sustainability committee, GRI standards adoption, and external assurance services for sustainability reports.

Failure to confirm hypotheses $H_6$ to $H_{11}$ relating to the effects of complementarity between the investigated governance mechanisms prevents us from confirming the existence of positive interactions between, on the one hand, board independence and GRI standards adoption and, on the other hand, assurance of sustainability reports and CSR committee implementation. However, the identification of two significant negative interactions *(BoGenDivCSRSustComm* and *BoGenDivAss)* suggests that board gender diversity operates as a substitute for both CSR committee and assurance services in stimulating environmental disclosures.

These negative interactions can be read in light of legitimacy theory, which argues that companies should comply with society's expectations to achieve legitimation (Guthrie and Parker, 1989; Dowling and Pfeffer, 1975). Society accords legitimacy to a corporation when its acts are deemed desirable, proper, or appropriate within a set of standards and values that have been created by society (Suchman, 1995). Thus, a legitimacy gap develops if companies do not behave in a way that meets society's expectations (Lindblom, 1993). This imbalance makes it more difficult to obtain resources – both human and financial – and has a detrimental impact on the success of the company.

Today, incorporating CSR issues into companies' activities and using different disclosure strategies is essential for survival. In light of legitimacy theory, companies use disclosure to achieve visibility and influence the way external stakeholders view the company (Deegan, 2002). Therefore, companies that are more visible to society tend to release greater disclosure (Cormier et al., 2004) to communicate that their activities are coherent with social values. For example, companies that are well known to have poor environmental performance, need to provide more information to legitimise their actions. Similarly, organisations that lack legitimacy may embrace governance practices that the general public views as necessary to gain support from their customers, shareholders, stock market participants, and other stakeholders. The ability of such governance mechanisms to boost a firm's performance is not a factor in its adoption. Instead, it is driven purely by opportunistic factors.

As highlighted by Mayer and Rowan (1977), stakeholders assign externally defined values to governance bodies and procedures regardless of whether these units contribute to the firm's performance. It is assumed a priori that the board disciplines managers, that gender diversity improves the relationship with stakeholders, that the adoption of GRI standards improves environmental disclosure, and so on. Adopting tools such as board independence, CSR committee, or GRI standards provides legitimacy to the company in the market it works in, increasing its chances to secure funding, forging business linkages with the finest partners, and occasionally even increasing profits. In doing so, a type of ceremonial mechanism creates an illusion regarding the effectiveness of governance mechanisms, even though their actual role is only to create a positive reputation. In this way, a company merely needs to formally meet the high standards of governance institutions to obtain legitimation and enjoy the confidence of market participants, although, in reality, the firm's financial condition may be poor.

The functioning of gender diversity as an alternative mechanism of CSR committee and assurance, highlighted by the results of Models 4 and 5 in Table 6.10, can be read in light of these considerations. That is, companies may opportunistically implement only some of the governance standards considered necessary by society for legitimacy reasons. For example, companies could equip themselves with a CSR committee or alternatively include women on their boards to an extent conventionally deemed sufficient by society or acquire an external assurance service only to gain legitimacy in the eyes of stakeholders. This may explain the results of our regressions, according to which some mechanisms of corporate governance act as alternative mechanisms.

In this scenario, the implementation of some governance mechanisms, as well as the disclosure of environmental information, in response to external pressure could be viewed as opportunistic behaviour by the company to gain legitimacy.

Our research findings have various theoretical and managerial implications.

Regarding managerial implications, our results imply that board composition is a crucial factor affecting companies' actions regarding environmental reporting. Companies should create boards with a significant percentage of female directors and a sustainability committee to disclose more environmental information and demonstrate their commitment to environmental issues to all stakeholders and society. For the same reason, they should implement GRI standards and acquire assurance services for their environmental reports.

Instead, board independence does not seem to play an important role in environmental reporting. Considering the non-convergent role played by independent directors in CSR reporting (Pucheta-Martínez and Gallego-Álvarez, 2019), much research is needed to clarify their role.

Second, our research shows that GRI standards implementation works in isolation in affecting the level of *EnvDisc*, while board gender diversity seems to operate as a substitute for both CSR committee and assurance services in stimulating environmental disclosures. These findings appear to highlight a behavioural pattern among companies primarily motivated by concerns about their legitimacy. Companies may choose to adopt one governance mechanism over another, such as gender diversity over GRI standards or gender diversity over the assurance of a CSR report, solely to gain social acceptance without taking into account how effective they are at raising the level of environmental disclosure.

This interpretation of the findings, one of the many that might be made, would advise companies to act more logically and consciously employ governance systems to encourage environmental disclosure. This is even more true today than it was in the past not only because environmental disclosure is becoming required in an increasing number of nations, but also because of the urgent and unavoidable need to understand how corporate activities affect the environment and the likelihood that future generations will have access to sufficient stocks of biological resources.

Regarding theoretical implications, this study adds to the literature on the factors that influence environmental disclosure. It contributes by urging urgent further study to better understand the potential interactions between various governance mechanisms. This type of research will also aid in the systematisation of the conflicting empirical findings noted by scholars about the direct impact of governance tools, such as board independence, on CSR disclosure (Dalton and Dalton, 2011).

However, this study has some limitations, and further research is necessary. First, given that the sample includes companies from different countries, introducing country-specific control variables could be useful. This study also investigated the quantity of disclosed environmental information. Future research could investigate the characteristics of that disclosure, including its temporal orientation (forward-looking, present, or past) and nature (quantitative or qualitative), to assess the quality of the given environmental information.

## Notes

1 Refinitiv offers one of the most comprehensive ESG databases, covering over 80% of global market cap, across more than 450 different ESG metrics. The ESG ratings for close to 9,000 companies globally are available, with time series data going back to 2002. They are simple-to-understand percentile rank scores (available in both percentages and letter grades from D- to A+).

2 The portion of variation that is given by the distance between each observation and its respective mean is explained by the fixed effect model. We cannot include time-invariant dummies (*EnvSensSect*) in the model since each individual distance between a constant and its mean is obviously equal to zero.

## References

Aguinis, H., Joo, H., & Gottfredson, R. K. (2011). Why we hate performance management—And why we should love it. *Business Horizons*, 54(6), 503–507.

Ali, W., Frynas, J. G., & Mahmood, Z. (2017). Determinants of corporate social responsibility (CSR) disclosure in developed and developing countries: A literature review. *Corporate Social Responsibility and Environmental Management*, 24(4), 273–294.

Amran, A., Lee, S. P., & Devi, S. S. (2014). The influence of governance structure and strategic corporate social responsibility toward sustainability reporting quality. *Business Strategy and the Environment*, 23(4), 217–235.

Armstrong, C. S., Guay, W. R., & Weber, J. P. (2010). The role of information and financial reporting in corporate governance and debt contracting. *Journal of Accounting and Economics*, 50(2–3), 179–234.

Ashforth, B. E., & Gibbs, B. W. (1990). The double-edge of organizational legitimation. *Organization Science*, 1(2), 177–194.

Baalouch, F., Ayadi, S. D., & Hussainey, K. (2019). A study of the determinants of environmental disclosure quality: Evidence from French listed companies. *Journal of Management and Governance*, 23(4), 939–971.

Ballesteros, B. C., Rubio, R. G., & Ferrero, J. M. (2015). Efecto de la composición del consejo de administración en las prácticas de responsabilidad social corporativa. *Revista de contabilidad*, 18(1), 20–31.

Baraibar-Diez, E., & D. Odriozola, M. (2019). CSR committees and their effect on ESG performance in UK, France, Germany, and Spain. *Sustainability*, 11(18), 5077.

Barako, D. G., Hancock, P., & Izan, H. Y. (2006). Factors influencing voluntary corporate disclosure by Kenyan companies. *Corporate Governance: An International Review*, 14(2), 107–125.

Barako, D., & Brown, A. (2008). Corporate social reporting and board representation: Evidence from the Kenyan banking sector. *Journal of Management and Governance*, 12, 309–324.

Bhattacharyya, A., & Yang, H. (2019). Biodiversity disclosure in Australia: Effect of GRI and institutional factors. *Australasian Journal of Environmental Management*, 26(4), 347–369.

Birindelli, G., Dell'Atti, S., Iannuzzi, A. P., & Savioli, M. (2018). Composition and activity of the board of directors: Impact on ESG performance in the banking system. *Sustainability*, 10(12), 4699.

Boiral, O. (2015). Accounting for the unaccountable: Biodiversity reporting and impression management. *Journal of Business Ethics*, 135, 1–18.

Boulouta, I. (2013). Hidden connections: The link between gender board diversity and corporate social performance. *Journal Business Ethics*, 113(2), 185–197.

Braam, G., Uit de Weerd, L., Harck, M., & Huijbregts, M. (2016). Determinants of corporate environmental reporting: The importance of environmental performance and assurance. *Journal of Cleaner Production*, 129, 724–734.

Bueno, G., Marcon, R., Pruner-da-Silva, A. L., & Ribeirete, F. (2018). The role of the board in voluntary disclosure. *Corporate Governance: The International Journal of Business in Society*, 18(5), 809–883.

Bushman, R. M., & Smith, A. J. (2001). Financial accounting information and corporate governance. *Journal of Accounting and Economics*, 32(1–3), 237–333.

Campbell, J. L. (2007). Why would corporations behave in socially responsible ways? An institutional theory of corporate social responsibility. *Academy of Management Review*, 32(3), 946–967.

Carroll, A. B. (1979). A three-dimensional conceptual model of corporate performance. *Academy of Management Review*, 4(4), 497–505.

Cerbioni, F., & Parbonetti, A. (2007). Exploring the effects of corporate governance on intellectual capital disclosure: An analysis of European biotechnology companies. *European Accounting Review*, 16(4), 791–826.

Chau, G., & Gray, S. (2010). Family ownership, board independence and voluntary disclosure: Evidence from Hong Kong. *Journal of International Accounting, Auditing and Taxation*, 19(2), 93–109.

Chen, S., & Bouvain, P. (2009). Is corporate responsibility converging? A comparison of corporate responsibility reporting in the USA, UK, Australia, and Germany. *Journal of Business Ethics*, 87(1), 299–317.

Cheng, E. C., & Courtenay, S. M. (2006). Board composition, regulatory regime and voluntary disclosure. *The International Journal of Accounting*, 41(3), 262–289.

Cucari, N., Esposito de Falco, S., & Orlando, B. (2018). Diversity of board of directors and environmental social governance: Evidence from Italian listed companies. *Corporate Social Responsibility and Environmental Management*, 25(3), 250–266.

de Celis, I. L. R., de Bobadilla-Güémez, S. F., del Mar Alonso-Almeida, M., & Velasco-Balmaseda, E. (2017). Women's occupational health and safety management: An issue for corporate social responsibility. *Safety Science*, 91, 61–70.

Dalton, D. R., & Dalton, C. M. (2011). Integration of micro and macro studies in governance research: CEO duality, board composition, and financial performance. *Journal of Management*, 37(2), 404–411.

Deegan, C. (2002). Introduction: The legitimising effect of social and environmental disclosures–A theoretical foundation. *Accounting, Auditing & Accountability Journal*.

DiMaggio, P., & Powell, W.W. (1983). The iron cage revisited: Collective rationality and institutional isomorphism in organisational fields. *American Sociological Review*, 48(2), 147–160.

Donnelly, R., & Mulcahy, M. (2008). Board structure, ownership, and voluntary disclosure in Ireland. *Corporate Governance: An International Review*, 16(5), 416–429.

Dowling, J., & Pfeffer, J. (1975). Organizational legitimacy: Social values and organizational behavior. *Pacific Sociological Review*, 18(1), 122–136.

Du, S., Bhattacharya, C. B., & Sen, S. (2010). Maximizing business returns to corporate social responsibility (CSR): The role of CSR communication. *International Journal of Management Reviews*, 12(1), 8–19.

Ellwood, S., & Garcia-Lacalle, J. (2015). The influence of presence and position of women on the boards of directors: The case of NHS foundation trusts. *Journal Business Ethics*, 130, 69–84.

Eng, L. L., & Mak, Y. T. (2003). Corporate governance and voluntary disclosure. *Journal of Accounting and Public Policy*, 22(4), 325–345.

Fama, E. F., & Jensen, M. C. (1983). Agency problems and residual claims. *The Journal of Law and Economics*, 26(2), 327–349.

Fernandez-Feijoo, B., Romero, S., & Ruiz, S. (2012). Does board gender composition affect corporate social responsibility reporting? *International Journal of Business and Social Science*, 3, 31–38.

Fernandez-Feijoo, B., Romero, S., & Ruiz-Blanco, S. (2014). Women on boards: Do they affect sustainability reporting? *Corporate Social Responsibility and Environmental Management*, 21(6), 351–364.

Fernández-Gago, R., Cabeza-García, L., & Nieto, M. (2018). Independent directors' background and CSR disclosure. *Corporate Social Responsibility and Environmental Management*, 25(5), 991–1001.

Fich, E. M., & Shivdasani, A. (2007). Financial fraud, director reputation, and shareholder wealth. *Journal of Financial Economics*, 86(2), 306–336.

Forker, J. J. (1992). Corporate governance and disclosure quality. *Accounting and Business research*, 22(86), 111–124.

Frankforter, S. A., Berman, S. L., & Jones, T. M. (2000). Boards of directors and shark repellents: Assessing the value of an agency theory perspective. *Journal of Management Studies*, 37(3), 321–348.

Friaz-Aceituno, J.V., Rodriguez-Ariza, L., & Garcia-Sanchez, M.I. (2013). The role of the board in the dissemination of integrated corporate social reporting. *Corporate Social Responsibility and Environmental Management*, 20(4), 219–233.

Fuente, J. A., Garcia-Sanchez, I. M., & Lozano, M. B. (2017). The role of the board of directors in the adoption of GRI guidelines for the disclosure of CSR information. *Journal of Cleaner Production*, 141, 737–750.

Galani, D., Gravas, E., & Stavropoulos, A. (2012). Company characteristics and environmental policy. *Business Strategy and the Environment*, 21(4), 236–247.

Gallego-Álvarez, I., & Ortas, E. (2017). Corporate environmental sustainability reporting in the context of national cultures: A quantile regression approach. *International Business Review*, 26(2), 337–353.

Garcia-Sanchez, I. M., Cuadrado-Ballesteros, B., & Sepulveda, C. (2014). Does media pressure moderate CSR disclosures by external directors? *Management Decision*, 52(6), 1014–1045.

García-Sánchez, I. M., Gómez-Miranda, M. E., David, F., & Rodríguez-Ariza, L. (2019a). Board independence and GRI-IFC performance standards: The mediating effect of the CSR committee. *Journal of Cleaner Production*, 225, 554–562.

García-Sánchez, I. M., Gómez-Miranda, M. E., David, F., & Rodríguez-Ariza, L. (2019b). Analyst coverage and forecast accuracy when CSR reports improve stakeholder engagement: The Global Reporting Initiative-International Finance Corporation disclosure strategy. *Corporate Social Responsibility and Environmental Management*, 26(6), 1392–1406.

Giannarakis, G., Konteos, G., & Sariannidis, N. (2014). Financial, governance and environmental determinants of corporate social responsible disclosure. *Management Decision*, 52, 1928–1951.

Gul, F. A., & Leung, S. (2004). Board leadership, outside directors' expertise and voluntary corporate disclosures. *Journal of Accounting and Public Policy*, 23(5), 351–379.

Guthrie, J., & Parker, L. D. (1989). Corporate social reporting: A rebuttal of legitimacy theory. *Accounting and Business Research*, 19(76), 343–352.

Hahn, R., & Lülfs, R. (2014). Legitimizing negative aspects in GRI-oriented sustainability reporting: A qualitative analysis of corporate disclosure strategies. *Journal of Business Ethics*, 123(3), 401–420.

Hair, J., Anderson, R., Tatham, R. & Black, W. (1998) *Multivariate data analysis*. 5th Edition, Upper Saddle River, NJ: Prentice Hall.

Haniffa, R. M., & Cooke, T. E. (2002). Culture, corporate governance and disclosure in Malaysian corporations. *Abacus*, 38(3), 317–349.

Harjoto, M., Laksmana, I., & Lee, R. (2015). Board diversity social and corporate responsibility. *Journal Business Ethics*, 132(4), 641–660.

Hawn, O., & Ioannou, I. (2016). Mind the gap: The interplay between external and internal actions in the case of corporate social responsibility. *Strategic Management Journal*, 37(13), 2569–2588.

Hawley, A. (1968). Human ecology. In David L. Sills (Ed.), *International encyclopedia of the social sciences* (pp. 328–337). New York: Macmillan.

Hillman, A. J., & Dalziel, T. (2003). Boards of directors and firm performance: Integrating agency and resource dependence perspectives. *Academy of Management Review*, 28(3), 383–396.

Ho, S. S., & Wong, K. S. (2001). A study of the relationship between corporate governance structures and the extent of voluntary disclosure. *Journal of International Accounting, Auditing and Taxation*, 10(2), 139–156.

Hussain, N., Rigoni, U., & Orij, R. P. (2018). Corporate governance and sustainability performance: Analysis of triple bottom line performance. *Journal of Business Ethics*, 149(2), 411–432.

Ibrahim, N. A., & Angelidis, J. P. (1994). Effect of board members gender on corporate social responsiveness orientation. *Journal of Applied Business Research (JABR)*, 10(1), 35–40.

Ibrahim, N.A., & Angelidis, J.P. (1995). The corporate social responsiveness orientation of board members: Are there differences between inside and outside directors? *Journal of Business Ethics*, 14(5), 405–410.

Jaffee, S., & Hyde, S. J. (2000). Gender differences in moral orientation: The metanalysis. *Psychological Bulletin*, 126(5), 703–726.

Jaggi, B., Allini, A., Macchioni, R., & Zagaria, C. (2018). The factors motivating voluntary disclosure of carbon information: Evidence based on Italian listed companies. *Organization & Environment*, 31(2), 178–202.

Jain, T., & Jamali, D. (2016). Looking inside the black box: The effect of corporate governance on corporate social responsibility. *Corporate Governance: An International Review*, 24(3), 253–273.

Khan, M. H. U. Z. (2010). The effect of corporate governance elements on corporate social responsibility (CSR) reporting: Empirical evidence from private commercial banks of Bangladesh. *International Journal of Law and Management*, 52, 82–109.

Kim, H. (2013). Glass fence thicker than glass ceiling: The puzzling gaps of women's leadership in Korea. In J. Rajasekar (Ed.), *Culture and gender in leadership: Perspectives from the Middle East and Asia* (pp. 253–274). Hampshire, England: Palgrave Macmillan.

Kolk, A., & Pinkse, J. (2010). The integration of corporate governance in corporate social responsibility disclosures. *Corporate Social Responsibility and Environmental Management*, 17(1), 15–26.

Leal, P. H., Rodrigues, R. N., de Freitas, M. A. L., & Lagioia, U. C. T. (2019). Determinants of greenhouse gases emissions disclosure according to GRI guidelines in Brazilian companies. *Independent Journal of Management & Production*, 10(3), 966–988.

Lee, Y. K., Kim, Y. S., Lee, K. H., & Li, D. (2012). The impact of CSR on relationship quality and relationship outcomes: A perspective of service employees. *International Journal of Hospitality Management*, 31,745–756.

Lepore, L., Landriani, L., Pisano, S., D'Amore, G., & Pozzoli, S. (2022). Corporate governance in the digital age: The role of social media and board independence in CSR disclosure. Evidence from Italian listed companies. *Journal of Management and Governance*, 1–37.

Levi, M., Li, K., & Zhang, F. (2014). Director gender and mergers and acquisitions. *Journal of Corporate Finance*, 28, 185–200.

Liao, L., Luo, L., & Tang, Q. (2015). Gender diversity, board independence, environmental committee and greenhouse gas disclosure. *The British Accounting Review*, 47(4), 409–424.

Lim, S., Matolcsy, Z., & Chow, D. (2007). The association between board composition and different types of voluntary disclosure. *European Accounting Review*, 16(3), 555–583.

Lim, J. S., & Greenwood, C. A. (2017). Communicating corporate social responsibility (CSR): Stakeholder responsiveness and engagement strategy to achieve CSR goals. *Public Relations Review*, 43(4), 768–776.

Lindblom, C. K. (1993). The implications of organisational legitimacy for corporate social performance and disclosure. *Critical Perspectives on Accounting Conference*, New York.

Leung, S., & Horwitz, B. (2004). Director ownership and voluntary segment disclosure: Hong Kong evidence. *Journal of International Financial Management & Accounting*, 15(3), 235–260.

Lone, E. J., Ali, A., & Khan, I. (2016). Corporate governance and corporate social responsibility disclosure: Evidence from Pakistan. *Corporate Governance: The International Journal of Business in Society*, 16(5), 785–797.

Lorsch, J.W., & Maclver, E. (1989) *Pawns or potentates: The reality of America's corporate boards*. Boston: Harvard Business School Press.

Mahmood, Z., Kouser, R., Ali, W., Ahmad, Z., & Salman, T. (2018). Does corporate governance affect sustainability disclosure? A mixed methods study. *Sustainability*, 10(-1), 207.

Meyer, J. W., & Rowan, B. (1977). Institutionalized organizations: Formal structure as myth and ceremony. *American Journal of Sociology*, 83(2), 340–363.

Mallin, C. A., Michelon, G., & Raggi, D. (2013). Monitoring intensity and stakeholders' orientation: How does governance affect social and environmental disclosure? *Journal of Business Ethics*, 114, 29–43.

Man, C.K., & Wong, B. (2013). Corporate governance and earnings management: A survey of literature. *The Journal of Applied Business Research*, 29(2), 391–418.

Marano, V., Tashman, P., & Kostova, T. (2017). Escaping the iron cage: Liabilities of origin and CSR reporting of emerging market multinational enterprises. *Journal of International Business Studies*, 48(3), 386–408.

Martinez-Ferrero, J., Ruiz-Cano, D., & Garcia-Sanchez, I. M. (2016). The causal link between sustainable disclosure and information asymmetry: The moderating role of the stakeholder protection context. *Corporate Social Responsibility and Environmental Management*, 23(5), 319–332.

Matsa, D. A., & Miller, A. R. (2013). A female style in corporate leadership? Evidence from quotas. *American Economic Journal: Applied Economics*, 5(3), 136–69.

Michelon, G., & Parbonetti, A. (2012). The effect of corporate governance on sustainability disclosure. *Journal of Management & Governance*, 16(3), 477–509.

Michelon, G., Pilonato, S., & Ricceri, F. (2015). CSR reporting practices and the quality of disclosure: An empirical analysis. *Critical Perspectives on Accounting*, 33, 59–78.

Mio, E. (2009). Corporate social reporting in Italian multi-utility companies: An empirical analysis. *Corporate Social Responsibility and Environmental Management*, 17(5), 247–271.

Miras-Rodríguez, M. D. M., Bravo-Urquiza, F., & Escobar-Pérez, B. (2020). Does corporate social responsibility reporting actually destroy firm reputation? *Corporate Social Responsibility and Environmental Management*, 27(4), 1947–1957.

Moroney, R., Windsor, C., & Aw, Y. T. (2012). Evidence of assurance enhancing the quality of voluntary environmental disclosures: An empirical analysis. *Accounting and Finance*, 52, 903–939.

Nielsen, S., & Huse, M. (2010). The contribution of women on boards of directors: Going beyond the surface. *Corporate Governance: An International Review*, 18(2), 136–148.

Ntim, C. G., & Soobaroyen, T. (2013). Corporate governance and performance in socially responsible corporations: New empirical insights from a neo-institutional framework. *Corporate Governance: An International Review*, 21, 468–494.

Odriozola, M. D., & Baraibar-Diez, E. (2017). Is corporate reputation associated with quality of CSR reporting? Evidence from Spain. *Corporate Social Responsibility and Environmental Management*, 24(2), 121–132.

Pavlopoulos, A., Magnis, C., & Iatridis, G. E. (2017). Integrated reporting: Is it the last piece of the accounting disclosure puzzle? *Journal of Multinational Financial Management*, 41, 23–46.

Petersen, M. A. (2009). Estimating standard errors in finance panel data sets: Comparing approaches. *The Review of Financial Studies*, 22(1), 435–480.

Pfeffer, J., & Salancik, G. R. (1978). *The External Control of Organizations.* New York: Harper & Row.

Post, C., Rahman, N., & Rubow, E. (2011). Green governance: Boards of directors' composition and environmental corporate social responsibility. *Business Society*, 50(1), 189–223.

Prado-Lorenzo, J. M., García-Sánchez, I. M., & Gallego-Alvarez, I. (2009). Características del consejo de administración e información en materia de responsabilidad social corporativa. *Revista Española de Financiación y Contabilidad*, 141, 107–135.

Prado-Lorenzo, J. M., & Garcia-Sanchez, I. M. (2010). The role of the board of directors in disseminating relevant information on greenhouse gases. *Journal of Business Ethics*, 97(3), 391–424.

Pucheta-Martinez, M. C., Bel-Oms, I., & Rodrigues, L. L. (2020). Does stakeholder engagement encourage environmental reporting? The mediating role of firm performance. *Business Strategy and the Environment*, 29(8), 3025–37.

Pucheta-Martínez, M. C., & Gallego-Álvarez, I. (2019). An international approach of the relationship between board attributes and the disclosure of corporate social responsibility issues. *Corporate Social Responsibility and Environmental Management*, 26(3), 612–627.

Rao, K., Tilt, C.A., & Lester, L.H. (2012). Corporate governance and environmental reporting: An Australian study. *Corporate Governance*, 12(2), 143–163.

Roe, M.J. (1991). A political theory of American corporate finance. *Columbia Law Review*, 91(1), 10–67.

Rogelberg, S. G., & Rumery, S. M. (1996). Gender diversity, team decision quality, time on task, and interpersonal cohesion. *Small Group Research*, 27(1), 79–90.

Rupp, D. E., & Mallory, D. B. (2015). Corporate social responsibility: Psychological, person-centric, and progressing. *Annual Review of Organizational Psychology and Organizational Behavior*, 2(1), 211–236.

Salvioni, D. M., & Gennari F. (2019). Stakeholder perspective of corporate governance and CSR Committees, Symphonya. *Emerging Issues in Management* (symphonya. unicusano. it), 1, 28–39.

Savitz, A., & Weber, W. (2006). *The triple bottom line: How today's best-run companies are achieving economic, social and environmental success*. San Francisco, CA: Jossey-Bass.

Schultz, E., Tian, G. Y., & Twite, G. (2013). Corporate governance and the CEO pay–performance link: Australian evidence. *International Review of Finance*, 13(4), 447–472.

Suchman, M. C. (1995). Managing legitimacy: Strategic and institutional approaches. *Academy of Management Review*, 20(3), 571–610.

Tamini, N., & Sebastianelli, R. (2017). Transparency among SandP 500 companies: An analysis of ESG disclosure scores. *Management Decision*, 55(8), 1660–1680.

Tejedo-Romero, F., Rodrigues, L. L., & Craig, R. (2017). Women directors and disclosure of intellectual capital information. *European Research on Management and Business Economics*, 23(3), 123–131.

Wan-Hussin, W. N. (2009). The impact of family-firm structure and board composition on corporate transparency: Evidence based on segment disclosures in Malaysia. *The International Journal of Accounting*, 44(4), 313–333.

Yunus, S., Elijido-Ten, E. O., & Abhayawansa, S. (2020). Impact of stakeholder pressure on the adoption of carbon management strategies: Evidence from Australia. *Sustainability Accounting, Management and Policy Journal*, 11(7), 1189–1212.

Zahra, S. A., & Stanton, W. W. (1988). The implications of board of directors composition for corporate strategy and performance. *International Journal of Management*, 5(2), 229–236.

Zattoni, A., & Cuomo, F. (2010). How independent, competent and incentivized should non-executive directors be? An empirical investigation of good governance codes. *British Journal of Management*, 21(1), 63–79.

# CONCLUSIONS

Worldwide, increasing attention towards environmental issues leads companies to incorporate sustainability matters within their business models and release environmental information to external stakeholders. Corporate environmental disclosure has gained increasing importance since the 1980s as a mechanism that facilitates interrelations between the parties involved in companies' businesses and enables synergies that increase firm value.

For many years, companies have disclosed environmental information on a voluntary basis, referring to different guidance. Among these, the Global Reporting Initiative (GRI) is the most widely used international standard. However, in the last decade, policymakers worldwide have increasingly issued rules related to sustainability information, shifting the disclosure of environmental information from voluntary to mandatory. In EU member states, the Modernisation Directive 2003/51/EC represents the first attempt to introduce a mandatory requirement for the provision of environmental information. However, the generic requirement to discuss environmental information within the management report when considered useful for understanding the company's development and performance gave companies substantial discretion in defining whether and what type of information to release. To overcome this flexibility, the EU legislator issued the Non-Financial Reporting Directive 2014/95/EU, which represents the key passage in the introduction of mandatory environmental disclosure. Directive 2014/95/EU introduces a requirement for larger companies to release environmental information pertaining to the business model adopted, the policies pursued, the outcome of those policies, the principal risks, and non-financial key performance indicators in a specific document termed a non-financial statement.

Although the Non-Financial Reporting Directive introduces clearer and more stringent disclosure requirements compared to the Modernisation Directive,

DOI: 10.4324/9781003245933-8

such as by identifying specific environmental reporting areas to discuss in the non-financial statement, it continues to give companies substantial discretion. Companies can define the specific information to release for all reporting areas, the format for the presentation of such information, and the standard to refer to in disclosing environmental information.

With respect to this last point, Directive 2014/95/EU gives companies the option to refer to national, European, or international standards in preparing their non-financial statements, such as the GRI, the Eco-Management and Audit Scheme (EMAS), the UN Global Compact, and ISO 26000.

Owing to the issuance of Directive 2014/95/EU, the number of companies preparing sustainability reports and releasing environmental information has increased. However, the flexibility in identifying the specific items of information to release as well as the possibility of referring to different standards in defining environmental disclosure, results in incomparable information. Although most companies have chosen to prepare their non-financial statements referring to the GRI standards, the option in Directive 2014/95/EU does not exclude the possibility that different companies may adopt different guidance, thereby making the quantity and quality of the information released incomparable.

The decision regarding the quantity and quality of environmental information to be released depends on several factors. Over the years, scholars have widely investigated the determinants of environmental information by referring to various theoretical frameworks. The most widely used theories to justify the release of environmental information are stakeholder and legitimacy theories, followed by institutional, agency, and signalling theories. Scholars have used previous theories to deepen understanding of the factors that can explain a company's decision to release environmental disclosures. The factors affecting environmental disclosure can be categorised into two groups: (1) internal or firm-specific and (2) external or institutional. Internal factors typically investigated in the literature include company characteristics and corporate governance features. External or institutional factors that are typically investigated include the level of media exposure and other country-level determinants (i.e. normative, mimetic, and coercive factors).

The increasing legal requirements aimed at introducing mandatory environmental disclosure as well as the low level of comparability of the information released made our study of the evolution of sustainability reporting practices in EU member states over the past two decades and our investigation of the factors that influence a company's decision regarding environmental disclosure interesting. More specifically, this study first investigated the environmental disclosure released by a sample of 5,588 non-financial listed European companies (111,760 firm-year observations) for the 2002–2021 period to clarify the evolution of sustainability reporting during the transition from voluntary to mandatory environmental disclosure. To deepen understanding of the influence of different factors on environmental disclosure, this study investigated the relationship between both firm-specific and institutional factors and environmental disclosure.

Referring to different theoretical frameworks to develop the hypotheses, this study first investigated the direct relationship between both board characteristics (i.e. board independence, gender diversity, and the presence of a CSR committee) and institutional factors (i.e. external assurance and the adoption of GRI standards) and environmental information. As a result, the study deepened understanding of the moderating role of institutional factors on the association between board characteristics and environmental disclosure. In this sense, the empirical analysis conducted in this study overcomes the conflicting results found by scholars when investigating the direct relationship between the characteristics of board of directors and environmental disclosure. From an empirical standpoint, the reporting of inconsistent findings by researchers implies that various corporate governance mechanisms may interact in different ways. In these situations, the use of a multilevel approach encourages the comprehension of the interconnectedness among various corporate governance mechanisms. Thus, to make sense of the emphasised results and provide more significant managerial and policymaking implications, independent of the historical period's circumstances and the setting under study, empirical research must consider moderating variables in the examined connection. By examining if and how the existence of a CSR committee, the adoption of GRI standards, and the assurance of a CSR report moderate the links between both board independence and gender diversity and environmental disclosure, this study advances the field of research in this area.

The findings revealed a continuous increase in environmental disclosure by EU companies since the issue of Directive 2003/51/EC. The level of environmental disclosure was significantly enhanced in 2017–2018 in correspondence with the entry into force of Directive 2014/95/EU. These results highlight the effectiveness of EU laws in boosting the increase in companies' environmental disclosure. Regarding influencing factors, the findings showed that several mechanisms are directly and positively associated with environmental disclosure. Gender diversity, the presence of a CSR committee, the adoption of GRI standards, and the assurance of sustainability reports have significant direct effects on environmental disclosure. However, board independence has a non-significant impact. Moreover, the findings revealed that each mechanism operates in isolation, independent of other mechanisms, in affecting the level of environmental disclosure. The analysis of possible complementary or substitution effects among the different corporate governance mechanisms investigated did not show significant interactions, with the sole exception of board gender diversity, which operates as a substitute for both the presence of a CSR committee and the adoption of external assurance in stimulating environmental disclosure. These results can be interpreted using the legitimacy theory framework, according to which companies opportunistically adopt all of the mechanisms considered necessary by society to gain legitimacy.

Although the shift from voluntary to mandatory environmental disclosure due to the issue of different EU directives enhanced the environmental disclosure released, the European Commission detected that a large number of companies did not prepare a non-financial statement because they are not within the scope of Directive 2014/95/EU. In addition, when the information is released, it is often incomparable, unreliable, and difficult for users to find. To overcome these critical issues, the European Commission issued a proposal for a Corporate Social Responsibility Directive, the objectives of which are to extend the requirement to report environmental information to other companies and to boost the comparability, reliability, and ease of access for stakeholders of the sustainability information released. To encourage greater comparability of the information disclosed, the proposal requires companies to release sustainability information in accordance with mandatory EU sustainability reporting standards that need to be developed. To achieve this aim, the European Commission asked EFRAG to develop draft sustainability reporting standards that are to be used by all companies as required in the proposal.

Today, in preparing their non-financial statements, companies can rely on one of the numerous national, international, or EU-based reporting standards regarding sustainability issues. In some countries such as Italy and Poland, companies can also decide to refer to a mixed reporting methodology based on more standards. Simultaneously, standard setters continue to build competing frameworks contending for the global leadership position. Therefore, the flexibility afforded to companies provides them with a wide range of sustainability report formats. In this context, the aim of the EU legislature is to encourage the standardisation of the information released, requiring companies to rely exclusively on one standard. Therefore, the EU legislature's goal is to boost adoption of the same principles and language across companies in regard to releasing environmental information. Only this form of convergence can develop comparability between company reports, which is fundamental to the European market and the EU as a whole.

However, despite the European Commission's decision to request that EFRAG develop draft sustainability reporting standards to be used by all companies in releasing sustainability information, it is important to highlight that in 2021, the IFRS Foundation founded the International Sustainability Standards Board, the aim of which is to develop sustainability-related disclosure standards. Therefore, although the EU legislature's intention is to require companies to rely exclusively on one standard in preparing non-financial statements, to date, both the EFRAG and the International Sustainability Standards Board are developing sustainability reporting standards. In addition, some claim that it could be better to refer to existing standards, such as the GRI, rather than developing new standards.

In conclusion, the comparability of information remains an open question. In this context, academic research could play a crucial role in promoting the enhancement of both environmental disclosure and the comparability of sustainability information. The benefits and drawbacks of diverse reporting frameworks could be a subject of research aimed at linking theory and practice in sustainability reporting and performance. Thus, academics can help to improve future policies and practices. Using prior studies on reporting frameworks and guidelines as a baseline, future research could, for instance, attempt to comprehend the reasons that drive the adoption of a particular reporting framework over others. For instance, researchers could determine that a certain accounting practice or a particular business culture may lead a company to use the GRI standard rather than the IR framework. Thus, this research could address the crucial subject of why and how existing frameworks and recommendations are or are not utilised.

In addition, academic research could contribute to the investigation of the function of new media, especially websites and social media, in transmitting sustainability information. In a broader sense, scholars could contribute to the investigation of the opportunities that modern technology provides for the dissemination of sustainability disclosure. In recent years, the publication of sustainability information via websites and social media has attracted the attention of a significant number of scholars. However, despite the consensus that social media is the superior method for sharing information and engaging stakeholders, many unexplored subjects remain, such as the role of digital media in stakeholder engagement.

# INDEX

Note: **Bold** page numbers refer to tables; *italic* page numbers refer to figures and page numbers followed by "n" denote endnotes.